THE CHAMBER PLAYS
THE GREAT HIGHWAY

Strindberg

THE PLAYS: VOLUME TWO

THE CHAMBER PLAYS

STORM
THE BURNED SITE
THE GHOST SONATA
THE PELICAN
THE BLACK GLOVE

THE GREAT HIGHWAY

translated by

Gregory Motton

OBERON BOOKS
LONDON

First published in these translations
in 2004 by Oberon Books Ltd
(incorporating Absolute Classics)
521 Caledonian Road, London N7 9RH
Tel: 020 7607 3637 / Fax: 020 7607 3629
e-mail: oberon.books@btinternet.com
www.oberonbooks.com

A catalogue record for this book is available from the British
Library.

ISBN: 1 84002 086 5

Cover illustration by Andrzej Klimowski

Cover typography by Jeff Willis

Printed in Great Britain by Antony Rowe Ltd, Chippenham.

Contents

Translator's Introduction, 7

The Chamber Plays

Opus 1, STORM, 37

Opus 2, THE BURNED SITE, 79

Opus 3, THE GHOST SONATA, 123

Opus 4, THE PELICAN, 163

Opus 5, THE BLACK GLOVE, 201

THE GREAT HIGHWAY, 243

Translator's Introduction

Gregory Motton

The fashion at the moment is for versions, or neo-translations, where the aim is to make the text sound as contemporary, and as English, as possible. It is no accident perhaps that this comes at a time of particular homogeneity in contemporary writing itself. We don't perhaps want to hear anything different from what we are used to, and we are used to a narrowing field of variety. How we interpret something seems to be of more interest to us than the thing itself actually is. There have probably never been so many different versions of foreign plays going around. It would be a peculiar coincidence however if all the plays ever written from Aeschylus onwards were written in the style of a second-rate British writer from the early twenty-first century. If we ever want to hear anything but our own chatter we shall have to go back to proper translation.

While I do not want to contribute to what I fear is a strong modern tendency to deconstruct even the possibility of accuracy in translation of plays, I would like to make the usual disclaimers of my own translations, emphasising the necessary imperfections of such work and offering it with the appropriate modesty and apologies for any errors, which of course I do.

I should also warn that this is of course only Strindberg rendered into English one hundred years after it was written, and can only hope to give the audience a flavour of the original. Also that the language I use is a hybrid: modern English written in a style intended where possible to resemble the language of another era and another country. I have not used Edwardian English for example, since that in itself would never have reflected very well turn-of-the-century Swedish. Indeed I have

Note   The first part of this introduction can also be found in *Strindberg: The Plays Volume One.*

tried to avoid idiomatic English altogether, by which I mean ready-made phrases, where possible. This is because I think it gives the wrong feel. (There may be those who think this would necessarily result in a colourless kind of language; readers can judge for themselves. Even when writing my own plays there is a certain kind of idiomatic language that I avoid for its blandness.) Instead I have tried to favour aspects of our English that already are similar to Swedish, using vocabulary of Germanic or Viking origin, instead of Latin or French origin words. Translators into English have the good fortune to be able to choose between three rather distinct layers. It is quite remarkable how often it is possible to use almost exactly the same formulations and vocabulary as the Swedish. The result is a rendition of the directness and simplicity of that language, even when there is a formality in the tone. The Germanic layers of English have the same qualities of expression. It is very convenient.

Where there are idioms in the original I generally try to keep them; that is, I avoid replacing them with a corresponding English idiom if I can, unless it is very similar. This is because idioms contain cultural messages and character, and it would be rather contrary to the intention, to give a particularly English feel to a phrase just at the very point where it has a particularly Swedish feel in the original.

I think it is the job of the translator to give the audience access to the text, not to put himself and his own interpretation there as an obstacle. As a reader I always feel irritated when a translator has presumed me incapable of being interested in or understanding anything that isn't familiar or even banal; when he can't restrict himself to translating the language, but is compelled to explain the text, or even make it palatable. This same attitude is taken by theatre managements when they look for translations. The National Theatre isn't embarrassed to serve the audience second-rate popularisations of foreign classics in which the original is entirely lost – indeed where there is no intention to keep it. Perhaps the public gets what it deserves. It is the kind of narrow-minded insular Philistinism into which we are descending at present and which would shame us, if we only had sufficient self-consciousness to notice the pitying eyes of our neighbours upon us.

The customary praise words for translations are 'vigorous', 'startling', 'radical', etc or even simply 'new'. None of these are necessarily qualities one should look for in a translation. In the current climate the real shocker would be 'accurate'. This would be shocking because it would sound like 'dull' (the worst crime), but in reality 'dull' would of course depend on whether the original were dull. It is perhaps indicative of the age that the idea of rendering the voice of the author is not at all exciting to theatre managements. While the marketing departments of theatres are apparently aware of the concept of 'a distinctive voice', this has not led them to expect that any great writer might have a 'distinctive voice'. Instead, theatres and critics talk as if there is a kind of modern stage-speak which, if achieved by a translator, will produce a vital, lively dialogue, and the opposite of 'dull', and that any text rendered into this stage-speak will benefit from its exciting qualities. Well, they are right, in that there is a ubiquitous kind of dialogue and it is a great favourite with second-rate writers and translators alike. Among the latter it is the (new) academic style, in that it is used because approved, and applied as a standard in accordance with distinct rules. Unfortunately, what people think of generally when they hear the word academic in connection with a translation (always used disparagingly) is a too strict adherence to the original, literal accuracy at the expense of spirit. In fact this style of translation hardly exists. Those who might have committed these errors in the past now adopt the current translatorese; a jollied up, chatty, rather loose rendition of the text into (often ill-chosen) idioms.

It is a fitting irony that these are the same types who despise or fear 'datedness', and who always talk of the importance of renewing translations every five years, little realising that it is exactly their favoured style of translation, that is, 'up to date', which dates so quickly. They make it specific to a time (the wrong time) and specific to a place (the wrong place, England).

The generally accepted notion that translations need constant renewing is to some extent absurd, considering that a piece is written at one particular time and is not renewed. So the original will 'date' in that it belongs to some extent to a particular place and time. We may say that anything may 'date' more or less, but just how much and in what way will depend on its quality. Shakespeare doesn't really date very much although its language is old-fashioned. John Buchan however can be said to date. Anything, a work or a translation, will date in direct ratio to its tendency to express itself in terms which lack genuine expressive power but which are instead current and familiar. This is why fashionable things date quicker than unfashionable ones. The datedness of a translation depends partly on the datedness of the original, that is, the way it is interesting or expressive only at the time of its making. A good translation of a poor work will date at the same rate as the original. A bad translation of a good work will date quicker than the original.

Another reason for the 'dating' phenomenon is the idea that a translation should help a work to seem 'relevant'. This is supposed to be achieved by sweeping away traces in the language of attitudes that are out of keeping with our own, and by emphasising that which is familiar. In short, a good translation is supposed to be one which makes it seem as if the play were written in England, today. But this gives a distortion not a translation. Some are willing to have the distortion instead. But they should beware because what is universal and true can be quite at odds with what is contemporary and fashionable.

It is perhaps a measure of the narrow-mindedness of a culture that feels itself incapable of understanding something from an alien time or place, and instead converts everything into recognisable terms. The result is of course to reinforce its own values and to learn nothing. We fall deeper into our folly, and brook no contradiction. We still perhaps feel uncomfortable with the way Hollywood remakes European films, distorting them beyond recognition to make them palatable to the isolated Midwest rednecks. But unfortunately our theatre is of a similar stamp, to the degree at which we think we are making *Titus Andronicus* more interesting by claiming that it resembles Tarantino. Watching European classics in Britain is often like reading the Victorians' moralised versions of Aesop's fables.

In recent years theatres have developed the habit of commissioning 'versions' of great foreign plays. We cannot understand anything unless it is native or has the appearance of being so. We can hear Strindberg if he sounds like John Osborne, or if we can place him in a category and make him a good friend to us and all we stand for. Theatres are preoccupied with being 'relevant' and we have a ludicrously narrow view of what this is, and in fact it is now beginning to mean nothing more than *familiar.* We think we are iconoclasts but really we seek constant confirmations of our current values.

In short we are Philistines, blind and bigoted. We are not only insular geographically but temporally. Today is more significant to us than yesterday, like children we presume the present is the best of all possible times, and we see the future as the product of our temporary present and are quite inexplicably pleased with that. Theatres regularly announce their 'new version' of this or that classic foreign play, on the presumption that, having been executed today, it is better and more 'relevant' than an already existing translation. The question of merit doesn't come into it. It is hard to see this kind of fetish with renewal as anything but the result of consumerism's brainwashing.

The ubiquitous chatter and babble that is contemporary stage-speak is the real dullness in theatre, and the addiction to it is an impediment to good translation. For if there is a preconceived idea of what good dialogue should sound like, this will prevent anything else from being heard. Contemporary writers will either imitate it or be excluded, and audiences will find all foreign writers, old and new, rendered into it. Increasingly actors will find it impossible to speak other kinds of dialogue. 'I can't say that, it's not natural,' they say (or the director says it for them to justify liberties being taken with a text, by a room full of self-styled experts). But, as Beckett replied, 'You say it every day.' What they all mean of course is that no one says it on TV / the stage etc. But when an actor forces himself to stick to the apparently awkward line of a good writer, the sense of it will reveal itself to him, and will be rewarding.

Naturally with a translation the actor faced with difficult dialogue has to wonder if the source of it is the original text or some quirk or inexpertise on the part of the translator. It is largely a matter of trust, unless he cares to check with the original (not in itself a bad idea, and I recommend it). What I do advise is that actors, and directors, should avoid having their expectations lowered by the general idea of 'naturalness' in dialogue, and remember that it is a passing prejudice, promoted by those with a vested interest in mediocrity, and to bear in mind that a great writer is likely to have a distinctive voice. Otherwise how would it be that we can recognise a page of Wycherly, Wilde, O'Neill or Ayckbourn at first sight. No one would say Pinter's dialogue was unnatural. Good writing, like good music, can sometimes be difficult to perform but no one would insist that symphonies should sound like muzak. I have always found that the more experienced or talented an actor is, the more he will doggedly bend himself to the line until its logic reveals itself to him, rather than trying to bend the line.

Other translations

The late Michael Meyer translated nearly all of Strindberg's and Ibsen's plays, and it is through these that most of us, myself included, first encountered these playwrights, and we should be grateful that his translations are generally of a good standard of accuracy, that he is good at finding the right word and doesn't make many mistakes. His weakness is the tone. Meyer shares the generalised notion of what dialogue should sound like, and so translates Strindberg into Translatorese. It is the same language he uses for Ibsen, a very different writer. The style is a bit too much that of the English drawing-room piece, and as such it carries some of the English class system along with it, which is not of course the same as the Swedish one. The voice is one of easy-going fluency rather than Strindberg's rather less comfortable form of loquacity, stilted and passionate at the same time.

Meyer uses English idioms liberally. He makes little attempt to retain the Nordic flavour of the language and uses French origin words where he might use Germanic words. He sometimes uses metaphors where the original is plain, and he extends lines to 'explain' them when he feels they are obscure or difficult. He also has the unfortunate habit of intervening just when Strindberg is most characteristic. When a character in *Creditors* 'looks at a woman underneath her eyelids to see what she's like behind them', he gives us 'squinting at her to see what you're like behind that pretty face'. The last three words of that sentence being impossibly glib for Strindberg, and having a very English feel to them. When you translate it back into Swedish, it sounds, in a Swedish context, as if the character is insane, or at least horribly inane. Meyer uses the expression because he judged that eyelids was a synecdoche for beauty, and so wanted to indicate this. His mistake, in my opinion is, that he ends up explaining the line unnecessarily, and inadvertently alters the whole tone of it in doing so. Leaving eyelids there, as I have done, retains the rather horrible and also comic aspect of scrutiny, whilst also conveying, through the image of the half-closed female eyelid, the personal beauty aspect of the line, but in a way that is not a ready-made phrase that would sit typically in the mouth of an English bore, but one that suits this rather dry character in *Creditors*. It is also the phrase Strindberg used, presumably for the same reason.

Also, Meyer inexplicably replaces Scandinavian cultural references with French ones. Karin Månesdotter becomes Joan of Arc, and 'it was shit as they say in Denmark' becomes 'it was what the French call merde', and so on. This happens often enough for one to get the impression that Strindberg was either French or English.

Meyer seems to believe that Strindberg would have liked to conform to the norms of British theatre and so he helps him by removing his idiosyncrasies, and gives him a style more easily digestible to a British audience. But Strindberg has never been easily digestible, even to a Swedish audience, he has never been a decent chap, and had very little distance from his writing. For me, Meyer removes Strindberg's personality and in doing so makes it ultimately harder to understand some of the strange things contained in these plays.

It is fashionable to consider that Meyer's translations are dated, and any theatre that can afford it likes to commission a new one. This has spawned a frightening selection of frankly Philistine, substandard 'versions' or poor translations. It is worth noting that Meyer is only dated insofar as he tried to update or anglicise Strindberg, and impose a generic 'good dialogue' style upon him. But in this Meyer is the least of all offenders.

The late Kenneth McLeish opts for a wild paraphrasing and completely alters Strindberg's style. His rule of thumb is to use as few words as possible, and he sacrifices everything to brevity and briskness, which gives a peculiar sensation of inexplicable haste to each speech, as well as an admixture of crudeness, even clumsiness, altogether alien to Strindberg. These translations clearly aim to satisfy the modern presumptions of what dialogue should be, rather than being any attempt to render Strindberg into English. Strindberg was generally direct, but he took his time to say what he wanted to say. He savoured his phrases and didn't have the lesser writer's fear of prolixity. Here he finds himself at odds with modern translatorese, and the confusion of vulgarity or briskness with effectiveness.

Peter Watts' translations from the 1930s are not at all bad but far less accurate than Michael Meyer's, which in general are a vast improvement in style also. Watts does have his moments however and makes a useful comparison, but he sometimes makes obvious mistakes.

These are the translators; the version writers are many. Essentially they work from literal translations, or crib from

Meyer perhaps, and then take their own particular shot in the dark, not caring about the target in any case, creating, as they do, something after their own mind.

Most of Strindberg's plays are not written in anything that could be called a naturalistic style, although the dialogue is psychologically consistent with the characters which are usually convincingly drawn. Even in plays where he is most controlled by his misogynist demon, Strindberg manages surprisingly well to get inside the female characters, even while he manipulates them wildly to confirm his thesis.

It is a shame that audiences are not very well acquainted with the strange atmosphere in much of Strindberg's writing as this is perhaps what is most attractive about it. Theatres tend to see him as a revolutionary hero, a role made problematic by his misogyny, and as a reformer of dramatic writing, although it is mostly his reform in the direction of naturalism which gets attention in this country. The rest of his contribution, in the other direction, can be seen here in these, the Chamber Plays. At any rate some translators try to give him the brisk style a revolutionary should have.

Strindberg's idiosyncrasies are of a far different nature. For a start he tended to write quickly and hated revising or even reading over what he had written. One can feel with him that indeed once he began to correct his excesses the whole thing would unravel. So he leaves it. Sometimes, as with *The Father,* he was surprised and horrified himself when he saw it on the stage. We might as well accept it warts and all. There are errors or repetitions and inconsistencies. Some translators have removed these (perhaps feeling they may get the blame). He writes confidently and fluently, inventing some words, taking liberties with grammar, using, in short the language as it suits him. He has a wide and sometimes quaint vocabulary which can be surprising and funny. He doesn't write the kind of dialogue we have learnt from the TV and we shouldn't try to make it fit our expectations

It may be worth noting that his style is very different from Ibsen's, whose actual speeches tend to be plainer and simpler, and to have a more everyday feel. Ibsen is essentially poetical in his technique, and the beauty of his plays is how the splitting of doom reverberates through his characters' words and actions, a lyrical *deus ex machina*. In Strindberg the characters themselves take a very active role in presenting the concerns of the play; they argue, accuse, and describe their experience and interpretations of life. This gives the dialogue an almost constant dialectical, rather anguished tone. The language itself has a consequent hard formality. The anger is of the kind that needs to prove its point and that aggravates itself whilst doing so, bewildered by the success of its self-justification. At its most vigorous it verges on pomposity which sometimes manifests itself in rather stiff formulations. Translators shy away from this – it seems ungracious and doesn't resemble the smooth flowing modern dialogue we have learned to expect. But it is nevertheless part of the way Strindberg writes.

A little detour: Translating and writing in an era of director-controlled theatres

Sometimes when I am translating Strindberg I am aware that certain turns of phrase Strindberg used are not going to be very popular with directors; and as I translate as best I can what Strindberg has written I know that most likely directors will chose another phrase (possibly from another translation), one which rolls off the tongue more easily, one which isn't awkward or perplexing or odd-sounding. I have come to accept this as inevitable, given the current way of thinking, and I can only hope that in the future more people may find use once again, for another kind of translation. But I would say this to our current masters, that they ask themselves if they are willing to allow the writer, even a dead one, to choose his style or not; I suspect at the moment that the answer may often be not. Not content with being the self-appointed autocracy that chooses the plays which get done (rather than writers and actors choosing amongst themselves, an idea the power-holders have convinced everyone is impossible, as impossible as democracy seemed in the nineteenth century), theatre producers and directors are trying to influence what gets written as well. Witness the plethora of 'help' groups for writers, and theatres' doctrine of developing young writers (ones they can discover and control). Believe it or not, this goes so far as to include developing sets of 'rules' by which play writing ought to be governed. If this sounds like something from a long-forgotten past let me tell you I have seen these rules written on a whiteboard at the Young Writers group at the prominent London theatre that dubs itself 'The Writers' Theatre' (run by directors of course). It is the same theatre that sends staff around the world from India to Brazil and Siberia, teaching the said rules, and I have met the writers from five continents that have been taught these rules. If you want to know what the rules are just imagine Stanislavsky's guidelines to actors turned into rules for writing. For example each character must have an 'intention' for each line, each scene (albeit a scene is a random division of time not known to the character), and he must also have a life-intention. What single-minded, goal-motivated characters must populate our stages, no wonder they all speak in that mannered way, which we now take for granted, and stand with their legs apart, hands on hips. In other words young writers are encouraged only to write scenes or even plays where the characters know what they want. (All this comes from is the common sense practice in directing of always trying to establish why a character is doing something.) This would be like hospitals refusing to admit patients unless they suffer from easily curable illnesses. It's easy to see which group this suits – plays must be very easy to direct if they are written according to the rules of directing. And it is giving us theatre with a view of the world that conveniently flatters the dominant way of thinking and living, where each life is a project, each person and country a PLC, and fortune serves those who know what they want – and take it. If theatre managements, by definition a powerful group of people, are not willing to let a writer's style develop randomly, or more rightly, according to what he needs to express, but try to impose their own notion of what it ought to be, then we must expect writing styles that fail to serve what is being expressed.

At any rate, given that managements are not generally willing to allow contemporary writers or young writers to develop their own styles, then it isn't perhaps surprising that they also try to impose their notions of style, and through it, their world view, upon translations, largely because it is seen as fair game; it's a soft target since no one, they might argue, can say what a foreign writer's style really is, far less render it into English. It is indeed the fashion these days to emphasise the difficulties (impossibilities) of translation to deconstruct any remaining notion of faithful rendering of a text by pointing out that each epoch has its own view of a text which will always determine the translation, like it or not. The truth in this argument is used to try to justify a free-for-all. As if the difficulties involved in catching thieves should mean that we should all just take what we want. And like other deconstructions of texts, it leaves a convenient power vacuum, in the absence of the departed text, to be filled by the nearest professional, the academic, the teacher, the theatre director, etc. In the theatre it gives us productions of texts from other times and places which are distorted into serving as confirmations of all our favourite errors and biases (we don't have beliefs anymore, but we have preserved our blind presumptions). Literature throughout the ages becomes nothing but a jolly pageant (in modern dress or a kind of temporal cross-dressing orgy) of familiar faces looking just like our own, speaking just like us, waving encouragement to us because all they ever wanted, those folk from olden times, was that everything would turn out exactly as it has turned out. Our so-called 'takes' on this or that grow into a mile-high pile that silences the past. And these 'takes' grow more conservative and self-congratulatory, in that they confirm the status quo, rather than contradict or criticise; this kind of conservatism, is especially easy to get away with when the more you 'modernise' something in this way, the more 'radical' you are perceived as being.

In the light of this, I must say that one of the consolations of translating Strindberg who is rather uneven in terms of quality, who is sometimes crude, far-fetched, slapdash and paranoid, and who often lacks the artistic grace of Ibsen's best work, is that at least I know how heartily he would despise the current age, more even than he did his own; if you see a production of one of his plays that seems to suggest otherwise, my personal advice is to treat it with suspicion.

The Great Highway

This is Strindberg's last play. Like Ibsen with his last play *When We Dead Waken*, Strindberg barely troubles to conceal that he is writing about himself looking back upon life. That isn't to say that he doesn't invent an imaginative environment for the play. Some of the settings are rather inspiring and certainly well-chosen, albeit in an oddly obvious way: the Alps, the cemetery; and they give a nice picture of a man looking back on his life and staring death in its vulgar, ugly face. I rather enjoy imagining a quite literal, or let me rather say painterly, approach to the scenery; for me a wobbly piece of board with a nice Alp painted on it efficiently conveys the metaphor as well as a sense of place, where a more abstract approach may fail in both. I rarely see the point in making the pictorial part of a metaphor abstract, since that's two abstracts and I think they cancel each other out. I humbly suggest that Strindberg may have rather liked the idea of the play being set in the Alps. I don't think that to substitute them for 'high', 'cold', 'lonely' or 'white' is a sufficiently thrilling crystallization of an idea to warrant the loss of the concrete and the particular. 'Intellectual' directors should try to let the audience, and the writers, have a bit of fun. Personally I'd give anything to see a production where they wear those funny alpine hats and stout brown shoes…

Essentially the story is about a man on a walking holiday, but we later learn that he is in fact revisiting places he once lived in. Here there is a similarity to *The Burned Site;* he meets old acquaintances, or old enemies. Strindberg has a habit of talking (more or less generally) about issues of betrayal without always going to the lengths of creating fictions (other than by report) within the play to hang them upon. This is a very rare step for a writer and it is at these points that we may get the impression of the writer hurriedly putting down what he wants to say about his own experiences. But while this trait, which we may as well call a weakness, undermines the convincingness of the play in one way, it does bring another ingredient; this overflow, or spillage of real life into the play, despite paradoxically making the play unconvincing, charges the atmosphere with something hard to evaluate. While Strindberg often falls down in terms of artistic unity, it is often in the details of his writing that his originality and inventiveness appear; this sits uneasily with the tendency of directors to try to find a unity with their productions. I venture to say that a less tidy approach may be more fruitful. This is not to say that Strindberg wasn't interested in artistic unity; he was. I wouldn't doubt that he fantasised about the total play, like Wagner; but his way of constructing it was through a multiplicity of details, unlike Ibsen whose details manifested a strong central idea which ran through each play like the name in a stick of rock.

Examples of bits that are not fully integrated into the fiction of the play are many. In fact whenever Strindberg introduces a story within a story, if a character tells something within his experience, one tends to get the feeling that it is not properly justified, not a part of the play because not wholly a part of the character; or again the tale may be too far fetched simply because the writer wants to make a certain point which is not necessary to the play itself; bad writing in other words. Strindberg often lapses, or indulges himself in 'bad writing', far more than any other writer of his stature that I can think of. When the hunter talks of having been a lawyer we feel it is only because Strindberg wants to talk about himself having taken up certain causes, public issues; and, because he later became disenchanted with some of these, he speaks of having been taken in by false arguments put up by criminals, as well as exhibiting his habit of blaming them for his own mistakes. It's a very tenuous parallel which has a false ring to it, reading it one wonders why Strindberg went to the trouble of inventing anything here at all, he may as well have written about it plainly. At another point he speaks of the man having been an architect (a device also used by Ibsen to allow him to write from his own standpoint of writer). Strindberg's architect even built a theatre. He also says he didn't always build well, but that he was often most severely criticised for his best work. It is hard here to remember that this is the character talking about buildings, rather than Strindberg reviewing his own career. This is the kind of writing that, after having allowed oneself to write it, one blushes so hotly on re-reading it that putting it into the bin is a pleasure.

When the hunter and the wanderer look at the girl through the window and conjecture upon starting a relationship with her, Strindberg's alter-ego immediately lists the kind of personal betrayal to be expected in a relationship; again it's hard not to hear Strindberg's own misogynist paranoia at this point. But just when you think he has reached a nadir of smugness and self-justification he undercuts it all; the character claims to have guessed everything about the girl and goes on to describe it all in great detail while she listens, apparently impressed. Seconds later she tells him it was all wrong and gives him a good seeing-off.

How are writers to write about themselves? And why should they want to? They occupy a sometimes unique and sometimes interesting place in relation to society, and how can they write about that position without writing about a writer? We can be builders, with Ibsen, bishops, painters, lesser writers, greater writers, kings, inventors of new things, great scientists with world-changing knowledge, doctors with a cure, perhaps the wittiest is Gogol's dissolute 'government inspector', an impostor after all. It's not such a terrible problem, as things go, but there are aspects of being a writer that can be quite telling, not about the writer but about the society and how it feels about itself, and how it responds to criticism, and to an outsider.

And it often seems, to a writer, as if the most efficient way of writing about these aspects of the society he finds himself in, and that are revealed to him through being a writer, is simply by writing about a writer, even though it seems such bad form, and poor taste. Put another way, insofar as a writer experiences the world from the point of view of a writer (as well as primarily that of a man or woman), that is, one whose job it is to observe and criticise, how can he write about the society's responses to observations and criticisms without there being a character who observes and criticises, publicly? There are solutions: giving the character a job that shares some of the characteristics of being a writer. But parallels are often an imperfect solution, strained and forced and rather constricting – it's hard to be writing things in disguise. It is similar to a different but related problem writers have had since the advent of parliamentary democracy: the king is no longer a character whose mind and body is a common metaphor for the nation – or for the self, itself an analogy interchangeable with the nation. Shakespeare certainly had a big advantage in this respect. Which maybe accounts for royal histories remaining popular with writers long after their political relevance had expired. Both Ibsen and Strindberg wrote their share of them. The demise of such figures as kings has robbed writers of a quick and ready and rich metaphor for the self and the state, which gave easy embarkation upon great themes. The state, itself a many-headed creature, we now know as the embodiment of the will of the people, an impossibly many-headed character to put on a stage (although it offers rich rewards for that writer who can find a way to write good 'mob' scenes).

To write about great themes now the writer is forced to write about instances and manifestations of them. This has the clear disadvantage of all examples in argument of inviting quibbles about the particulars of the case. Writing itself has more or less surrendered to writing solely about these particulars…this style is known as realism. In the past if you wanted to write about ambition or foolishness in an ageing parent, the neutral character of A Man was A King. How does a writer find a neutral man now? He will always be an ambitious bishop or a foolish businessman, and in this issue-hungry little world of the theatre the writer finds he has written an exposé of clerical envy, or about how money turns your head. A state at war against itself does better represent a fractured self than does the world of take-overs and mergers which resembles nothing so much as itself and the temporary conditions of our political economy. The final descent into a narrowed scope comes when our brightest sparks go the whole way in the wrong direction by attempting to make a great play about the human heart into a metaphor for something temporary and local, by literally squeezing great drama into tightly fitting uniforms. One metaphor that's clear enough I think!

The reason I mention this is that I think it may partly explain why writers so often *want* to write about themselves: it isn't only vanity; in the absence of the king as metaphor to represent the state or the self, the nearest ready metaphor is the writer himself, especially in our present epoch, when the Self stands somewhat to the side of the society it is in, rather than being merged into it in a symbiosis. And who better to express this position than the writer himself who is especially much in that position? (You will see that I am trying to suggest that the reason is not vanity and narrow-mindedness of writers, the which explanation I would not however like to deny entirely to the reader since it seems just as likely as my own.) One reason for the resemblance is that the writer, like the old kings of fiction at least, has no *other* function (unless you include entertaining audiences which we can forget about here). Like the king character who is the state, the writer is the critical conscience of the state (though not the only one and here is a difference); and like the king character whose only role is to be himself, and that selfhood will determine events so that we can write about the self by writing about the events it produces, the writer equally requires a healthy self or bad consequences will follow. The job requires little more, and therefore in the absence of any better, the writer himself is a useful metaphor for the self.

In brief therefore, my defence of writers such as Strindberg who seem to be writing about themselves, is that they often believe that, by doing so, they are writing about either the self or society.

Whether or not this is true, you might say that it *ought* to be true, if what a writer writes is to be of more than biographical interest. It is perhaps also worth adding that this is not the situation for writers who do not write about the self or the state. Chekhov, who wrote about neither, but who wrote comedies where destiny was the main character and history played the part of the Temporarily Absent Master, was easily able to put himself on stage as a doctor and as a writer, for he was both, and give no special significance to either character.

The Pelican

I've met quite a few people who like *The Pelican* and I'm always surprised. To me the play seems narrow and mean and to have only one thing to say, and this is said after just a few minutes. The play seems to have come into being merely because its central metaphor or conceit appealed to the writer so greatly (indeed he used it again later). What strikes me as odd is that the metaphor, apparently taken from nature, doesn't remain in the background behind a story with a fuller meaning: a story where a mother greedily consumes all opportunity for happiness rather than cede these to her children; the opposite of a self-sacrificing mother; she may take wealth, health, love or happiness, at her children's cost; this would seem to be the interesting application of the supposed phenomenon of the animal world. But what Strindberg gives us is not that but a mother who literally starves and freezes her children to death, *as well as* taking their wealth, health and happiness. It is maybe part of the attraction of Strindberg that he makes metaphors concrete, but here it is as if we have a human story turned into a metaphor for the animal kingdom, which would be fine if Strindberg was writing for an audience of pelicans; they would no doubt be shifting awkwardly in their seats. Perhaps it doesn't matter but it strikes me that the play is bursting at the seams of its too-narrow conceit, so that once it is apparent that we are really being asked to believe this, it doesn't seem to be worth the strenuous suspension of disbelief required. As the play humourlessly labours the point, there is a growing need to giggle – and the spell is broken.

This, I should say, is not a question of style, so much as a narrowness of thought which makes the play so fragile. I cannot see the point of being asked to believe an exaggeration just for the sake of it. It is then as if the playwright is saying: 'Some parents are terribly selfish, it puts me in mind of the habits of the pelican, let me show you how nearly like (or unlike, depending on your view of the myth about pelicans) a pelican I can depict a selfish parent.' The point being how nearly like the supposed habits of the animal it can be, rather than being particularly enlightening about selfish parents.

For all its awkwardness, though, there is some originality in the atmosphere and circumstances of the play, as well as a high degree of psychological accuracy in the depiction of characters – especially the son and daughter – and pretty lively dialogue throughout.

The Ghost Sonata

The Ghost Sonata is for me at the other end of Strindberg's range of achievement. The first scene is highly successful and original and, like the whole play, it has a truly liberated structure, without being in the least lacking in form. Strindberg's demands upon the theatrical form have here come a long way from *Miss Julie*. In the foreword to that play, he reminds the actors that it is alright to turn their backs to the audience and instructs Kristin to employ real time in the silent action before the dialogue commences. The stage directions in *The Ghost Sonata* go further: the old man eavesdrops a conversation that he hears but we do not. The play opens with a scene featuring a character who does not exist. The absurd or dreamlike atmosphere relies on having mastered a natural stage language first. When the young lady drops her bracelet and thanks the young man stiffly for picking it up we are far from the conventions of Elizabethan or French classical drama whence the gesture originates. The success of that moment requires a quite new naturalism for its execution, and in this and other stage directions Strindberg may as well be directing a film.

Quite which film is another question, for film has largely disappeared up the black hole of so-called naturalism and arrived in that unimaginative and strangely dull land called fantasy. There is for me though a similarity between the first scene in *The Ghost Sonata* in the street, and the atmosphere of *Wild Strawberries (Smultron Stället)* by Bergman, especially in the dream sequence. Both scenes by the way are set in the quiet streets of Stockholm on a warm summer afternoon. If you go there you may find the atmosphere for yourself.

Of course the achievement doesn't put Strindberg ahead of the Russians whose sense of the absurd was no doubt helped by the complexities of the Russian character, brought on by living in a vast country with dreadful weather and the Tsar's secret police force, as well as the salvationist hope of their wildly pious and spiritual religion with its other tendency to be superstitious and irreligious.

Without these helps Strindberg had only his personal paranoia to push him that extra mile along the stylistic road. At least that's one explanation, but one which serves best only to account for his lesser achievements. When he's writing well this explanation is not sufficient. It is perhaps worth looking at what benefits the style brings in Strindberg's case. The chief advantage is the rapid juxtaposition of objects and ideas that in the normal run of things seems unlikely, but which nevertheless shows a telling connection. This accounts for the fact that, most often, absurd or dreamlike elements in a writer's style are more or less accidentally so, and arise merely from connections which seem apparent perhaps only to the writer, at first. It may well be possible to trace the life of such a trait in a piece of writing, from the day of its introduction when it seems too absurd, through a period when it is liked and enjoyed for being absurd, thence to when it seems no longer absurd at all, as people get used to looking at life in the light of what that work and others like it have revealed. Then, later, when the subject matter has been quite forgotten as the world changes, the writing doesn't seem absurd at all, but merely outlandish or 'out of date'. Kafka is beginning to seem like naturalism. Ionesco wouldn't have bothered with all those chairs if he hadn't felt he was writing about conditions pertaining in the actual world, or if he had we wouldn't have bothered with him. Presumably we don't like 'absurdism' because we admire the style.

One thing this style facilitates is directness and economy, something Strindberg already usually has, insofar as if he feels like saying something he pretty much goes ahead and says it, without too much preamble.

A characteristic of much of Strindberg's writing is the proximity of each character's personal destiny, as it were along-side them. This is not the same as Ibsen's Destiny, which is a spiritual bond between the soul of the individual and the force which controls him, but it is rather the result of the alchemy of the individual's nature and the typical kind of raw deal life gives us all, essentially a more concrete notion, albeit a product of a sort of mystic marriage.

This gives us the tea party scene where a selection of people sit stewing in their own juices, or karma let us call it, for Strindberg might have – a kind of *huis clos* situation, although unlike the atheist Sartre who has to take us to a rather Jesuitical afterlife to find it. Strindberg rather typically gives us hell here on earth, which for all its absurd little touches is pretty plainly rooted in the everyday morality of reaping what you sow, and has an atmosphere of empiricism, like the butterfly collector's garret in *The Black Glove*.

Strindberg gives Hummel the familiar role of self-righteous avenging angel, a mechanism which although unavoidably built into the structure of the play, gives the scene a clumsiness it could do without: 'Don't call him or I'll have him arrested and whoever stays I'll have arrested,' have to be two of the worst lines Strindberg ever wrote. But once again it is just as a character or the writing seems at its most complacent that Strindberg turns the tables, and Hummel gets his comeuppance for his smugness. I can't help feeling, as in the similar situation in *The Great Highway* that it is not just the character that is being punished but the writer too. Strindberg tends to identify not with the play as a whole, but with each moment of it separately. The result is that he both is and isn't an imposing presence, and it gives the writing a mercurial quality; just when you may be getting bored there is a chance that Strindberg is too, and will change tack.

But Strindberg is in good form in the first act: and if you wanted to find an example of the best characteristics of his writing it may as well be the following:

> HUMMEL: See that old woman in the window...she was my fiancée once. Sixty years ago... Don't be afraid she doesn't recognise me. We see each other every day without it making the least impression upon me, even though we once swore to be eternally faithful to one another; eternally!

Although as usual we may feel that Strindberg is being rather self-consciously miserable about things, here the sheer scope of Time and Truth and Life encompassed in those lines transcend his personal bitterness and produce great writing. For what it depicts here is not just disillusionment but the sheer weight and effect of the passing of time, the awful effect of simply being alive the allotted time. It is sad and beautiful because it makes you want to prove that it need not be so. Strindberg follows it up with another cracker, when the student replies: 'How imprudent you were in those days. We don't talk about things like that to our girls these days!', which whilst being a funny exposé of the shallowness and mean pretentious-ness typical of youth, seems also to redeem, by implication, the notion of romantic love which the previous line had stomped upon so brutally and finally; and this resuscitation is confirmed by the irony of Hummel's next line: 'Forgive us my boy, we didn't know any better.'

The last act is almost entirely static and depends for its argument upon flowers and their symbolism. Not at all the ingredients for an exciting finish but the gracefulness of structure it gives the play must have been irresistible to Strindberg, who was anyway very keen on both topics, and clearly intent upon handing the play over to youth, albeit morbid youth doomed to death. It is a curious scene. First it ought to be known that hyacinths are the funeral flower in Sweden. Perhaps as translator, I should have changed them to orchids or lilies or whatever our equivalent is to make it clear to British audiences, but I didn't fancy being greeted with a curse when I meet Strindberg in Swedenborg's Heaven, so I kept the hyacinths: the detailed descriptions would have been nonsense otherwise. I trust to hope that British audiences will find the room full of flowers sufficiently funereal to match the morbidity of the two youngsters.

The cook makes an entrance and the two paragraphs about her antics in the kitchen are so packed with meaning that they ought to have obviated the need for *The Pelican*. It works far better here and also this is a great and unusual moment, along with the other in the first act, when there is a hiatus in the dialogue: the cook overhears about herself and interjects, 'No, that wasn't why,' and shows her teeth. But we never hear what the real reason was. Ordered to go, she stays: 'When it suits me. (*Pause.*) It suits me now.' Oddly trivial and realistic, like the German governess in Chekhov. Immensely effective in creating the play's atmosphere, but also for broadening the scope when she suddenly explains: 'You suck the nourishment out of us and we from you.' This rumbling of hatred and resentment from below stairs is sudden and pretty isolated. It comes just after a long and curious list of complaints about life's little discomforts and annoyances, for which the poor conduct of the servants is blamed. This, while being mawkish and petty, shows the young girl and the student as vulgar and trivial people, which is quite surprising until you consider that there's no reason to suppose them otherwise. It does however sit awkwardly in the scene, if the scene is intended to have a redemptive aspect at all, rather than being intended to make one tired and impatient for these dismal and narrow folk to be swept away. Does Strindberg intend to show that there is something so corrupt and lifeless in that house that even new generations have not escaped its influence, and are likely to be the same? Are we all doomed by the sins of our fathers? Maybe Strindberg couldn't find it in himself to end the play on a note of unalloyed hope. In an earlier draft, apparently, the girl had cancer of the womb. Or maybe an early death is the best one can hope for. At least then one can die with one's naivety intact. The only difference between these two young people and the others is that they have not yet been subject to the rotten tricks time plays.

The Burned Site

For some reason this play is very rarely performed. To me it seems at least as good as other more popular plays of Strindberg's. It has the benefit of a few comic characters, of the kind one might find in Strindberg's *Hemsöboarna,* short stories of life in Stockholm's archipelago (the islands off the eastern coast of Sweden where Strindberg's father's steamboats used to go), or from the short stories of Albert Engström. Directors, I think, prefer the melodrama of his intenser plays. It's easier to make an impression with those. This is about a man, called here The Stranger, who returns to his childhood home after being in America, to find that the house has just burnt down. Like *The Ghost Sonata* and *Storm* and *The Black Glove*, it is set around a building, or rather this time in the ashes of one, and concerns the inhabitants and the neighbours. It involves stirring up the ashes and looking at the denuded undone remains of the paraphernalia of a family's life and the deceptions therein contained. The walls are all broken, the cupboards too have spilled their contents onto the ground. People stand around talking about it. There is a stone cutter, a hearse driver, a policeman, a bricklayer, a sign painter, and the landlady of The Last Nail, an inn on the edge of town where the hearse drivers stop for a drink on their way out to the graveyard. It's an effective conceit and Strindberg handles it with a lightness of touch that sometimes otherwise eludes him. The student too is present once again, and is in fact this time accused of starting the fire. (In *The Ghost Sonata* he appears just after having rescued people from a fire.) I say 'he' because there is no great difference between the two characters. In *The Ghost Sonata* the student is Hummel's friend's son; here he turns out to be the Stranger's son. The Stranger adopts an aloof position throughout, and there is something of the tone of the exile returning to claim his birthright from the usurping villains (the Stranger's brother in this case). The tone is one we find in Hummel in *The Ghost Sonata*, and the situation is similar to that in *The Great Highway*. Strindberg had been in various forms of exile and knew what it was to come home (on one occasion when he returned to Sweden to face charges of blasphemy, crowds thronged the train platform to greet him). In *The Burned Site* the returning brother finds nothing worth reclaiming, and when he has finished pointing out to his old friends and relations their falsehoods and their failings, he sets off out into the world once again, a wanderer. It is worth noting that some of those he meets have complaints against him which he dismisses rather easily. It invites one to think that here the writer is giving his alter ego too easy a passage, except that we may wonder why he allows us to have the very clear impression that the character of the Stranger is a man who cannot take criticism. The flaw in his character is never addressed and the play ends.

Storm

An old man divorced from his wife much younger than himself, separated from his child, living alone, savouring the peace and quiet of old age, but dwelling too on what has passed, on the dishonour brought to him by his wife, on the possible fate of his daughter, and actually not so sure he really wants to sink quietly into old age. The storm is one which passes, without really breaking. The flat above his own has new occupants who turn out to be his ex-wife and her new gambling husband, and they run a disreputable establishment, like a kind of night-club. Finally the gambler runs off with the teenage daughter of an honest neighbour (a working class, jam-making version of the man himself). His wife comes to him for help in the crisis, she sees he is not as old as he had led her to believe (when he divorced her because he could no longer satisfy her sexually). She is offended by this since it means he rejected her rather than the other way around. There is an element of this play which is merely an old divorcee's letter of consolation to himself. There is though a degree of imagination and invention in the depiction that makes the play an intriguing one. The stage device of having upstairs windows visibly inhabited but by parties unknown, whose comings and goings are nefarious as well as nocturnal, has an effect upon the atmosphere beyond its theatricality. As in some of the other chamber plays there is a dreamlike quality, even though here nothing unusual happens. Perhaps it is simply because the layout of the stage in some way, and by chance perhaps, resembles the mind, if we allow upstairs here to be the unconscious: the incomprehensible goings on in the apartment behind the curtained windows eventually burst in upon the precarious peace and serenity of the man's own well-ordered apartment, where he preserves the treasured memories of his wife and child. Much of the action of the play takes place behind windowed glass; we see it as if with our mind's eye.

The man has a brother, as does the Stranger in *The Burned Site*: this brother is a good companion, although they keep their feelings from one another, and as characters they are barely distinct from one another. Indeed it turns out that the man feels that his brother has betrayed him by being too understanding with his wife. One of the few events in the play is the two men going for a walk in the warm evening air, but no sooner have they set off than one returns without the other. The man has a problem with light and lights. The long light midsummer evenings are to him unnatural in a town and he cannot be at ease, he says, until the street lights are lit (the effect of which, paradoxically, is to make the dark darker). The last speeches of the play concern Louise turning off the lights in the now empty upstairs apartment, and then the lighting of the first street lamps:

> (*The LAMPLIGHTER comes in, lights the lamp.*)

•

MAN: The first lamp! Now it is autumn! It's our time of year boys! It's growing dark, but then comes wisdom to guide us, with a lantern so he won't go astray.
(LOUISE is seen upstairs through the window; a moment later it goes dark.)
(To LOUISE.) Close the windows, and then pull down the blinds, let the memories lie down to sleep, in peace! The peace of old age! And in the autumn I will move away from this silent house.

The Black Glove

The Black Glove takes the form of a Christmas morality story in which a young bourgeoise mother has her child taken away from her as a punishment for being mean and selfish and not realising how lucky he is. She has accused a servant girl of stealing a ring she has lost. It is a creature called the *Jultomte* who is the *deus ex machina.* He looks like a gnome and busies himself with stopping the lift from working and messing up the papers of an elderly scientist up in the garret. This old gentleman has written the riddle of creation down on a scrap of paper, the conclusion of a lifetime's work, the futile fruits of long labour. He sets out to find it but his papers have been muddled up by the *Jultomte;* the old man is overcome with exhaustion, looking for it in vain. He dies, contented and reconciled we are told: Strindberg doesn't shrink from giving the old fellow the *coup de grâce.* The little child is found again however, and youth is given a second chance. The play is like a black version of Hollywood's *It's a Wonderful Life.* It benefits and suffers from a characteristic in Strindberg's writing, that is, a certain randomness; none of the elements seem essential to the play. The benefit of this is that we can find in it details and fragments we don't otherwise see. Strindberg allows himself on occasion to go into more detail than other playwrights, who would be afraid of a slackening pace, and it is through the details that he gets his point across. In this play he adopts a leisurely pace, giving us a series of brief portraits held together by the concierge, who sits at the bottom of the building operating the levers and buttons that keep the modern building working; Strindberg usually lets us see a telegraph or a telephone; here we are introduced to the electricity at the heart of the building, there is even a heart-shaped electric light flashing on and off by the concierge's lair, where he sits like a troll. Strindberg presents himself to the public in his autobiography *En Tjänsterkvinnas Son* as the son of a servant woman, and it was always grist to his mill to show a glimpse of the domestics or the working people who kept the wheels turning. We see the house from the viewpoint of the basement; from the working-class or troll viewpoint. In this play, instead of the cook popping in to say her critical word at the gentry's goings-on, the tables are turned and an elderly gentlewoman turns up and catches sight of the concierge's well-stocked Christmas table declaring that it seems rather lavish:

> You are not as poor as you seem, and I am not as rich as I seem.

Once you turn the tables there's no need to stop them turning. The difficulty with this play for us is that we don't believe in gnomes or house fairies any more. In Sweden however the one who comes with the presents at Christmas is called *Jultomten* and is related to all the other *tomtar* who live in your garden or on your plot of land, as well as inside the house, and who bring either good or ill fortune depending on how you treat them. *Jul* (or *yule)-tomten* was the Swedish adaptation to the new Christian lore, in all his essentials he is the same as the pagan *tomtar*. Although we still speak of fairies at the bottom of the garden, fairy wouldn't be the right translation. The creature we are dealing with here is a little man looking more like a troll, a heavy-limbed fellow with a red hood, white hair and beard. The nearest thing we have to it is the garden gnome who looks similar and previously had the same function. At Christmas in the red and white cottages scattered about the Swedish landscape it was customary to set out a bowl of porridge for *Jultomten* much in the same way as we (used to?) put out sherry and a mince pie for Father Christmas. For Swedish children it is *jultomten* who brings presents to any well-behaved children he may find.

Gnomes in England are supposed to be the original inhabitants of the Earth guarding its treasure. In other countries they are aboriginal peoples (Paracelsus made the word mean pygmies), and aboriginals in Romania are equated with gypsies. In Sweden the aboriginals are the Lapps to whom *tomtar* bear an obvious resemblance, with their short stubby physique and in their traditional clothing of leather boots with up-turned toes and their pointed hoods. In other words the Swedes were aware in their folk memory of the original inhabitants pressing their noses up against the windows of their own implanted civilization. Perhaps this awareness included the advisability of keeping on the right side of them. City planners of Iceland still work around the spirits of the land. Gnome was the word given by Cabbalists and Rosicrucians (who share Strindberg's interest in alchemy) to the English version of these diminutive aboriginals.

I say all this not only to justify my choice of the word gnome to translate *tomte* but also to remind readers what gnomes are, since we are so used to seeing them fishing in the imaginary ponds of Suburbia, that we may have forgotten that they were here before we were. Early miners in England attributed the knocking sound heard in mines to gnomes and believed them to be guarding the Earth's underground treasures. The idea of a creature guarding all that is good against our own poor stewardship is precisely the idea in this play, in that Strindberg's gnome is somewhat more of an active investigating judge than the usually more aloof *tomte*.

Here he takes an unusual interest in the psychology of his clients and the healthiness or otherwise of their attitude to life. This makes him less like a common-or-garden gnome and a little more like, not our Father Christmas so much, but God himself. To be sure it wasn't a long leap from gnomes to God. All Strindberg did was to extend the areas of *tomtes'* kind offices from the land we are on to our inner landscapes and at once the gnome is a God. Perhaps it is interesting that our conception of God (whose Paradise we usurped) is so like our idea of the gnomes who, remember, are the aborigines whose land we have stolen. Maybe that is why Americans are so religious, and why it is the crucified Christ that appeals to them, who knows. It is rather a theme too of Strindberg's – that of a character coming to reclaim what was his and was stolen from him. In *The Ghost Sonata* and *The Burned Site* Hummel and The Stranger both return from exile in a stolen land (America), to, in some sense, rout the impostors. It happens in *The Great Highway* and in *The Storm* that a man surveys what was once his and is now despoiled. Even in *Creditors* the God-like Gustav has come to reclaim his stolen wife. Strindberg seems to identify strongly with this feeling. He certainly gives the upper hand to the returning exile.

At first I could not see any such figure returning to reclaim his rights in *The Black Glove,* until I realised what gnomes or *tomtar*, or even Gods, were. However I am sure that any resemblance between Strindberg and God, or gnomes for that matter, is entirely unintentional.

GM
London, 2003

Opus 1

STORM

Oväder

(1907)

Characters

MAN
a retired civil servant

BROTHER
consul

HERR STARK
baker

AGNES
his daughter

LOUISE
the Man's relative

GERDA
the Man's ex-wife

FISCHER
Gerda's new husband, non-speaking

ICEMAN

POSTMAN

LAMPLIGHTER

Scenery

Act One: the outside of the house

Act Two: the interior

Act Three: the outside of the house

ACT ONE

Exterior of a modern building[1] with a semi-basement of granite, the other floors of brick, with yellow plaster; the windows are ornamented with sandstone; in the centre of the semi-basement is a door to the courtyard and entrance to the bakery; the façade of the house ends at the corner on the right where there is a small square with rose trees and other flowers; at the corner is a letterbox; above the basement floor is the ground floor with large windows which are open; four of these belong to a dining room, elegantly furnished; above the ground floor we can see the apartment on the first floor, whose four central windows have red blinds drawn down, illuminated from inside.

In front of the building is a pavement with an avenue of trees; in the foreground is a green bench and a gas street lamp.

The BAKER comes out with a chair and sits on it on the pavement.

A MAN is visible at the table in the dining room. Behind him a glazed earthenware tile-stove, green, with a shelf, upon which stands a large photograph between two candlesticks and flower vases; a young girl in light-coloured clothes serves him the last course.

BROTHER: (*Outside. Coming in from the left, knocking with his stick upon the window pane.*) Will you be finished soon?

MAN: Just coming.

BROTHER: (*Greets the BAKER.*) Good evening, Herr Stark, it's still warm... (*Sits on the bench.*)

BAKER: Good evening Consul, it's the hot, rotten time of August and we've been making jam all day...

BROTHER: Oh yes?... Fruit any good?

BAKER: Decent enough; the spring was cold, but the summer was unbearably hot; we townsfolk felt it well enough...

BROTHER: I came in from the country yesterday, and when the evenings draw in, you begin to want to go in...

BAKER: Neither me or the wife have been beyond the turnpikes. There doesn't seem to be much happening in

1 Meaning a large apartment building of the kind to be found in most cities in Europe, except in Britain.

41

the shop, but you have to be at your post and prepare
for winter; first there's the strawberries and wild
strawberries, after that there's the cherries, then we've
got the raspberries and the gooseberries, melons and the
whole autumn harvest...

BROTHER: Tell me something Herr Stark, is this house
being sold?

BAKER: No, not so's I've heard!

BROTHER: Are there many people living here?

BAKER: I think there are ten households, if you count the
rear side of the building, but they don't know each other,
that is to say there's unusually little gossip in this
building, it's more like people hide themselves away. Ten
years I've lived here, and for the first two years my
neighbours were unknown gentlefolk, who kept quiet all
day, but set in motion at night, when carts used to come,
collecting something. Not until the end of the second
year did I find out that it was a hospice, and what they
were collecting was corpses.

BROTHER: Nasty!

BAKER: And they call it the silent house!

BROTHER: Yes, there's not much talking done here.

BAKER: There's dramas enough here though...

BROTHER: Tell me, Herr Stark, who lives here, on the first
floor, above my brother?

BAKER: Well up there, where you see the red curtains,
that's where the tenant died this summer, and it was
empty for a month, then eight days ago some gentlefolks
moved in that I've never seen...don't know what they're
called; I don't think they even go out. Why do you ask,
Consul?

BROTHER: Well now... I don't know! Those four red blinds
look like theatre drapes, behind them they're rehearsing
bloody dramas...that's what I imagine to myself; There's a
phoenix palm standing there throwing a shadow on a
curtain... Now if we could see some shapes.

BAKER: I've seen a few, but not until later, at night!

BROTHER: Were they ladies or gentlemen?

BAKER: Both I think...but I'm going back to my
saucepans... (*Goes in through the main door.*)
(*The MAN inside the room has left the table and now lights
a cigar; at the window now, he talks to the BROTHER.*)

MAN: I'm nearly ready. – Louise is just going to sew a
button onto my glove.

BROTHER: Are you going into town then?

MAN: I thought we might go down for a little while... Who
was that you were talking to?

BROTHER: Just the baker...

MAN: I see, yes he's a decent chap; my only company here
this summer, for that matter...

BROTHER: Have you really stayed in every evening,
never gone out?

MAN: Never! These light evenings make me nervous, they
may be pretty in the countryside, but in town it seems to
be against the laws of nature, almost terrible; once they
light the first lamp I feel calm again and can go for my
evening walk. I become tired and I get a better night's
sleep...
(*LOUISE hands him the glove.*)
Thank you, my child...you can leave the windows open,
there aren't any mosquitoes here... Right, I'm coming!
(*After a moment we see the MAN come out from the courtyard
and put a letter in the postbox at the front of the stage, then
sit on the bench, next to the BROTHER.*)

BROTHER: Tell me then; why do you stay in town, when
you could be in the country?

MAN: I don't know! I've become immovable, I am bound
to this appartment by the memories...only in there do
I have peace and security. In there! It is interesting to see
one's home from the outside; I imagine it is someone
else wandering about in there...just think! I have
wandered to and fro in there for ten years...

BROTHER: Is it ten now?

MAN: Yes, time passes quickly, once it's gone, but while
it's passing it is slow... The house was new in those days;
I watched them put down the parquet flooring in the

43

rooms, paint the wall panels and doors, and she chose the wall paper, which is still there... Yes, that was that! The baker and I are the eldest on this side of the house, and he's had his troubles too, he is...one of those people who never succeed, always some difficulty or other; it is as if I have lived his life and carried his burden in parallel with my own.

BROTHER: Does he drink then?

MAN: Oh no! He's not a shirker, but he has no forward motion... All the same, he and I know this building's history: we've watched them draw in the wedding carriages and drag out the hearses, and that postbox on the corner, well that's certainly received some confidences...

BROTHER: You had some deaths didn't you, in the summer?

MAN: Yes, we had a case of typhus, it was a bank clerk; and then the flat stood empty for a month; the coffin came out first, then the widow and children, and last came the furniture...

BROTHER: That was on the first floor?

MAN: Up there, where the lamp is lit, where the new arrivals live, whom I don't know yet.

BROTHER: Haven't you seen them either?

MAN: I never ask about the tenants; those who offer of themselves I receive, without abusing it or getting involved, because I'm careful to protect the peace and quiet of my old age...

BROTHER: Yes, old age! I think it is pleasant to become old, because then you don't have so much left on the record.

MAN: Yes, quite right, it is pleasant; I am closing the book on life and people, and have already started packing for the journey; solitude is as it is, but when no-one has any claims upon you, freedom has been won. The freedom to come and go, to think and act, eat and sleep as you please. (*The roll blinds are pulled up in the upper floor apartment but only a bit, so we can see a woman's dress, then the blind is hastily lowered again.*)

BROTHER: Someone's moving up there. Do you see?

MAN: Yes, they're very secretive, but it's worst of all at night; sometimes there's music, but of a poor type; sometimes I think they are playing cards, and then late, after midnight carriages come to collect... I never complain about the tenants, because then they only take revenge, and no one ever improves. It is best to know nothing...!

(*A man, bareheaded and in a dinner jacket, comes out from the courtyard and puts a large number of letters in the box; then he disappears.*)

BROTHER: He had a lot of post, that one!

MAN: It looked like circulars!

BROTHER: But who was the man?

MAN: It can't have been anyone else than the tenant on the first floor...

BROTHER: That was him? What type was he, do you think?

MAN: I don't know! Musician, conductor, a bit of operetta, bordering on variety, cardplayer, Adonis, a little of everything...

BROTHER: His white skin ought to have been accompanied by black hair, but it was brown, therefore dyed or a wig; a dinner jacket at home implies a careful wardrobe, and the movements of his hands as he posted the envelopes suggested shuffling, to pick up and to deal... (*We can hear very faintly a waltz being played on the first floor.*) Always waltzes, perhaps they have a dance school up there, but it's nearly always the same waltz; what is that one called?

MAN: Now I think you'll find...it is 'Pluie d'Or'... I know it by heart.

BROTHER: Have you had it at home?

MAN: Yes! I have had that and 'Alcazar'...

(*LOUISE can be seen inside the drawing room bustling about with dried glasses on the dresser.*)

BROTHER: Are you still happy with Louise?

MAN: Very!

BROTHER: Isn't she going to get married?

MAN: Not that I know of!

BROTHER: Is there no fiancé?

MAN: Why do you ask that?

BROTHER: Perhaps you are considering it?

MAN: Me? No thanks! When I married last time I wasn't too old, since we got children straight away; but I am now, and now I want to age in peace... Do you think I want a master in MY house to deprive me of life, honour and chattels?

BROTHER: You kept your life and chattels...

MAN: Was there any stain upon my honour then?

BROTHER: Don't you know?

MAN: What do you mean?

BROTHER: She murdered your honour, when she left...

MAN: Then I have walked around for five years, a murdered man, without realising it?

BROTHER: Haven't you known?

MAN: No, but now I shall tell you in two words the real facts of the matter... When I was fifty years old and I remarried to a relatively young girl, whose heart I had won, and who without fear or coercion gave me her hand, I promised her that when my age became burdensome to her youth I would leave and give her back her freedom. Then when the child came in due time, and neither party wished for any more such additions, and after my daughter grew apart from me, and I felt myself to be superfluous, I left, that is to say; I took a boat, since we lived on an island, and with that the tale ended. I had kept my promise, and saved my honour, what more of it?

BROTHER: Yes, but she felt her own honour to be slighted because she had wanted to go herself, and therefore she murdered you, with silent accusations, which you never knew of.

MAN: Did she accuse herself too?

BROTHER: No, she had no grounds.

MAN: Well, that's alright then.

BROTHER: Do you know anything of the fate of her and the child after that?

MAN: I have no wish to know! When I had gone through all the horrors of separation, I realised that the affair was buried, and since only beautiful memories remained in the flat, I remained here. Meanwhile, thank you for your valuable enlightenment.

BROTHER: Which?

MAN: That she had nothing to accuse herself of, for that would have been an accusation against me...

BROTHER: I think you are living under a great delusion...

MAN: Let me live under it brother; a clear conscience, relatively clean, has always been to me a diving suit with which I have gone down into the depths without suffocating. (*Stands.*) Just think! I have escaped from it all with my life! And now it is passed! Shall we take a short walk along the avenue?

BROTHER: Yes, let's. We can watch them light the first lamp.

MAN: But there will be moonlight tonight, August moonshine?

BROTHER: I think there is even going to be a full moon...

MAN: (*At the window, talking.*) Louise, would you be so kind as to give me my walking stick! The light summer stick, just to hold in my hand.

LOUISE: (*Passes out a cane.*) Here you are, Sir!

MAN: Thank you, my child! Put out the lamp in the room if you've nothing left to do there...we'll be away a while, can't say how long...

(*The MAN and the BROTHER go out to the left.*
LOUISE is at the window. The BAKER comes out through the door.)

BAKER: Good evening, Miss, it's a bit on the warm side... has your master gone out?

LOUISE: Yes, they've gone out along the avenue...the first evening the master's gone out this summer.

BAKER: We old folk love the twilight, it hides so many shortcomings in ourselves and others...do you know Miss, my old woman is going blind, but won't have the operation! There's nothing to look at, she says, and she wishes she was deaf as well.

47

LOUISE: You can wish you were – sometimes!

BAKER: You lead a lovely peaceful life in there, prosperous and without worries; I never hear a raised voice or a door slammed, perhaps a little too quiet for a young lady like yourself?

LOUISE: No, God preserve us, I love the calm and the dignified, graceful, decline, when you don't have to say everything and where you consider yourself obliged to overlook the less pleasant things of daily life...

BAKER: You never have guests either?

LOUISE: No, there's only the Consul that comes, and such a brotherly love I never have seen.

BAKER: Which of those two is the oldest?

LOUISE: I couldn't say... If there's one year between them or two, or if they're twins, I don't know, because they treat each other with mutual respect, as if they both were the elder brother.

(*AGNES comes out, tries to sneak past the BAKER.*)

BAKER: Where are you off to my girl?

AGNES: I'm just going out for a stroll!

BAKER: Good idea, but don't be long!

(*AGNES goes.*)

Do you think the master is still grieving the loss of his loved ones?

LOUISE: He's not grieving, doesn't miss them either because he doesn't wish they would come back, but he lives with them in his memory, where there is only the good things...

BAKER: But the fate of his daughter worries him sometimes...

LOUISE: Yes, he must be afraid that the mother will remarry, and then it would depend on who became the stepfather...

BAKER: But he told me that his wife at the beginning declined any kind of support from him. But after five years had passed she sent a solicitor with a long list of charges worth several thousand...

LOUISE: (*Dismissive.*) I don't know anything about that...

BAKER: While at the same time I think his wife is at her most beautiful in his memory…

●

POTMAN: (*Comes in with a crate of wine.*) Excuse me, does Herr Fischer live here?

LOUISE: Herr Fischer? Not that I know of.

BAKER: Maybe he's called Fischer on the first floor? Ring the bell on the first floor, on the corner.

POTMAN: (*Goes towards courtyard.*) First floor, thanks very much.

●

LOUISE: There's another sleepless night in store then if they're carrying up bottles.

BAKER: What kind of people are they? Why do we never see them?

LOUISE: They go out the back way, don't they; I've never seen them. But I hear them!

BAKER: I've heard doors banging and corks popping too, maybe other loud bangs too…

LOUISE: They never open their windows, and in this heat! They must be southerners… Look, lightning! One, two, three… It's just heat lightning! You can't hear any thunder!

VOICE: (*From below in the basement.*) Herr Stark, come and help me in the sugar store, pet!

BAKER: Just coming my dear! – We're making jam you see… I'm coming, I'm coming… (*Goes down into his basement.*)
(*LOUISE remains standing by the window.*)

●

BROTHER: (*Comes in slowly from the right.*) Hasn't my brother come back?

LOUISE: No Herr Consul.

BROTHER: He went inside to telephone, I was to go on ahead. Well, he'll be back soon… What's this? (*He bends*

down to pick up a postcard.) What does it say? – 'Boston
Club, after midnight... The Fischers' – Who are the
Fischers?, do you know Louise?

LOUISE: There was a man here just now with a crate of
wine, looking for a Fischer on the first floor.

BROTHER: On the first floor, Fischer! The red blinds that
shine like a tobacconists at night; I think we've got
ourselves some bad company in this house!

LOUISE: What's The Boston Club?

BROTHER: It could be something quite innocent, though
in this case I don't know... How did that card go again?
It was that fellow dropped it just now; I'll just put it in
the postbox... Fischer? I've heard that name before, in
connection with something which I have forgotten...
Louise, may I ask you something. Does my brother
never talk about...the past?

LOUISE: Never to me.

BROTHER: Louise...may I ask you...

LOUISE: I'm sorry, here comes the evening milk, I have to
go and take the delivery.
(*She withdraws, the MILK GIRL is seen from the right, and
goes in through the courtyard.*)

●

BAKER: (*Comes out again, breathing heavily, takes off his white
cap.*) In and out like a badger from his hole...it's terrible
in there beside the ovens...and no evening breeze at
all...

BROTHER: There's going to be rain, there's lightning...
It's not very nice in town, but up here it's peaceful;
you've got no wagons rumbling along, even fewer trams,
its just like the countryside!

BAKER: It may well be peaceful but for the shops it's too
peaceful; I know my job but I'm a bad salesman, always
have been, and I can't learn, or maybe it's something
else... I haven't got the right attitude; if a customer
treats me like a swindler I just go timid at first, and then
I get as angry as I can get, I can't manage to get really

angry these days; it's wearing out, everything's wearing out.

BROTHER: Why don't you get a job somewhere?

BAKER: No-one would want me!

BROTHER: But have you asked?

BAKER: What would be the point?

BROTHER: Yes... Well?

(*A long drawn out 'Ooh' from the floor above.*)

BAKER: What in heaven's name are they up to up there? Are they killing each other?

BROTHER: I don't like these new unknowns that have come here. They are like a red thunder cloud hanging over one; what kind of people are they? Where do they come from? What do they want here?

BAKER: It's so dangerous to dig into other people's concerns, you only get involved...

BROTHER: Do you know anything about them?

BAKER: No, I don't know anything...

BROTHER: They're screaming again now, in the staircase...

BAKER: (*Cautiously withdraws.*) I don't want anything to do with this...

●

(*Fru GERDA, the MAN's divorced wife, comes out into the courtyard, bareheaded with dishevelled hair, upset; the BROTHER goes towards her, they recognise each other, she recoils.*)

BROTHER: So it was you, my former sister-in-law?

GERDA: It is me!

BROTHER: What are you doing in this house and why don't you let my brother in peace?

GERDA: (*Enraged.*) He gave the wrong name, I thought he had moved, I'm not responsible for it...

BROTHER: Don't be afraid of me, you mustn't be afraid of me, Gerda...can I help you, what's happening up there?

GERDA: He hit me!

BROTHER: Is your little girl there?

GERDA: Yes!

BROTHER: Then I understand she has a stepfather?

GERDA: Yes!

BROTHER: Put up your hair, and calm yourself, then we
can try to sort this out, but spare my brother...

GERDA: He hates me I suppose?

BROTHER: No, don't you see how he tends your flowers in
your flowerbeds here, he carries earth here himself, do
you remember, in a basket, do you recognize your blue
gentian and mignonette, your roses, Malmaison and
Merveille de Lyon that he has grafted himself; do you
understand how he has cared for your memory and your
daughter's?

GERDA: Where is he now?

BROTHER: He is walking in the avenue, he'll be here soon
with the evening paper, and when he comes in from the
left here, he'll go in the courtyard entrance, sits down in
the dining room to read; stand still and he won't notice
you! – But you must go back up to your apartment...

GERDA: I can't, I cannot go back to that man...

BROTHER: Who and what is he?

GERDA: He...used to be a singer!

BROTHER: Used to be, and now he is? An adventurer!

GERDA: Yes!

BROTHER: Keeps a gaming house?

GERDA: Yes!

BROTHER: And the child? The bait!

GERDA: Don't say so!

BROTHER: It's horrible.

GERDA: You're being too harsh.

BROTHER: Should one handle filth gently? But a righteous
thing must be smeared with filth! Why did you violate
his honour, and why did you fool me into being your
accomplice? I suppose I was childish enough to believe
your word, and I defended your unjust case against his!

GERDA: You forget that he was too old.

BROTHER: No, he was not then, you had the child
straightaway; and when he proposed, he asked you if you
wanted to have a child with him; and in view of that he
promised to return to you your freedom when he had

fulfilled his undertaking, and when old age began to be burdensome.

GERDA: He abandoned me, and that was an affront.

BROTHER: Not for you! Your youth protected you from shame...

GERDA: He should have let me leave!

BROTHER: Why? Why did you want to disgrace him?

GERDA: It's inevitable.

BROTHER: How strangely you think! Meanwhile you have murdered him and fooled me into doing the same; how shall we restore him?

GERDA: If he is restored, then it will be at my cost!

BROTHER: I cannot follow your reasoning, it feeds only on hate; but if we left aside restoring him, and thought about saving his daughter, what should we do?

GERDA: She is my daughter, the law has awarded her to me, and my husband is her father...

BROTHER: You are being too harsh! And you have become wild and crude... Quiet, here he comes!

(*The MAN comes in from the left with a newspaper in his hand and walks thoughtfully in through the courtyard entrance, during which the BROTHER and GERDA stand motionless, hidden by the corner of the building by the courtyard. The BROTHER and GERDA come out upon the stage. Moments later we see the MAN take a seat inside the room and read the paper.*)

GERDA: That was him!

BROTHER: Come here and look at your home! How he has kept everything the way it was ordered according to your taste? – Don't be afraid, he can't see us in the dark – the light dazzles him, you see.

GERDA: Just think how he has lied to me...

BROTHER: In what respect?

GERDA: He hasn't aged! He had grown tired of me, that was all. Look at his collar and that cravat, in the latest fashion; I'm sure he has a mistress!

BROTHER: You can see her portrait upon the tile-stove there, between the candlesticks.

GERDA: It's me and the child! Does he still love me?

53

BROTHER: Your memory!

GERDA: That's so strange!

(*The MAN stops reading and stares out of the window.*)
He's looking at us!

BROTHER: Stand still!

GERDA: He's looking straight into my eyes.

BROTHER: Stand still! He can't see you!

GERDA: He looks like a dead man...

BROTHER: He *has* been murdered!

GERDA: Why do you say such a thing!

(*The BROTHER and GERDA are illuminated by a big
flash of lightning.*
The MAN in the room shudders, stands up.
GERDA flees behind the corner of the courtyard.)

MAN: Karl Fredrik! (*By the window.*) Are you alone? –
I thought... Are you really alone?

BROTHER: As you see!

MAN: It's so stuffy, and the flowers give me a headache...
I shall just finish my newspaper. (*Goes back to his seat.*)

BROTHER: (*At GERDA's side.*) Now to your concerns! Shall
I come up with you?

GERDA: Perhaps! But there will be such trouble!

BROTHER: But the child must be saved! And I'm a legal
man!

GERDA: Very well, for the child's sake! Come with me!
(*They go.*)

●

MAN: (*From inside.*) Karl Fredrik! Come and play chess! –
Karl Fredrik!

End of Act One.

ACT TWO

Inside the room. Upstage the tile-stove; to the left of this a door opening to the pantry; to the right the door to the hall. Stage left a sideboard with a telephone; stage right a piano and dining room clock. Doors in the left- and right-hand walls.

LOUISE enters.

MAN: Where did my brother go?

LOUISE: (*Worried.*) He was outside just now, he can't be far away.

MAN: There's a terrible racket going on up there; it's as if they're trampling on my head; they're pulling out all the drawers now as if they were off on a journey, perhaps to run away... If only you knew how to play chess, Louise!

LOUISE: I do know a little...

MAN: Well, so long as you know how to move the pieces I suppose it will be alright... Sit down my child! (*He sets up the pieces.*) They are making such a racket up there the chandelier is shaking, and underneath we've got the baker lighting his stoves... I think I'll move soon.

LOUISE: I think you ought to anyway Sir, I've long thought so.

MAN: Anyway?

LOUISE: It's no good to sit with the same old memories for too long.

MAN: Why not? With the passing of time all memories are good ones.

LOUISE: But you might live another twenty years Sir, and that's too long to be sitting with your memories, which fade anyway and perhaps, one fine day, change colour.

MAN: You know such a lot my little child! – Start now, move a pawn! But not the queen's pawn because then it will be check-mate in two moves.

LOUISE: Then I'll start with the knight...

MAN: That's just as bad my dear...

LOUISE: But I think I'll start with the knight anyway!

55

MAN: Good! Now I move my bishop's pawn...
(*The BAKER appears with a tray in the hall.*)

LOUISE: It's Herr Stark with the cakes. He walks so quietly, like a little rat! (*She stands and goes out into the hall, takes the tray and goes into the pantry.*)

MAN: Well, Herr Stark, how is the wife?

BAKER: Alright, thank you, there's her eyes as usual...

MAN: Have you seen my brother at all?

BAKER: He's strolling about outside isn't he?

MAN: Has he company?

BAKER: No, no! I don't think so.

MAN: It wasn't yesterday Herr Stark you saw this apartment.

BAKER: No, it was ten years ago...

MAN: When you came with the wedding cake... Does it seem the same?

BAKER: Quite the same... The palms have grown of course; yes it's the same...

MAN: And will be until you come with the cakes for the funeral. After a certain age nothing changes, everything stops, moving forwards only like a sledge on the slope...

BAKER: Yes, that's how it is!

MAN: And in that way it is peaceful... No love, no friends, just a little company in the isolation; and so people become people, with no claims upon one's feeling and sympathies; then you work loose like an old tooth, and fall out without pain or sense of loss. Louise for example, a young beautiful woman, the sight of whom affords me the pleasure, like that you receive from a work of art you don't require to own; nothing disturbs our relationship! My brother and I keep company like two old gentlemen, who never come too close to each other or intrude upon one another's intimacies. By maintaining neutrality with people, one achieves a certain distance, and from a distance it is easier to extricate oneself. In a word, I am pleased with old age and its peace and quiet – (*Calls in.*) Louise!

LOUISE: (*At the door left, friendly as always.*) I've brought home the washing, and I have to count it...

MAN: Well, Herr Stark, don't you want to sit down for a chat, perhaps you play chess?

BAKER: I can't be away from my saucepans, and at eleven the baking oven has to be lit... Thanks all the same for the kind offer.

MAN: If you do see my brother, ask him to come in and keep me company...

BAKER: I will... I most certainly will! (*Goes.*)

●

MAN: (*Alone; moves the chess pieces for a few seconds, then stands and wanders about.*) Yes, the peace and quiet of old age! (*Sits down by the piano and plays a couple of chords, gets up and wanders about again.*) Louise! Can't you do whatever it is with the washing later?

LOUISE: (*In the left hand doorway.*) No I can't, the washer woman is in a hurry, and she's got a husband and children waiting for her...

MAN: Oh well. (*He sits down at the table and drums with his fingers; tries to read the paper, but tires of it; lights matches and blows them out; looks at the clock. A noise in the hallway.*) Is that you Karl Fredrik?

●

POSTMAN: (*Comes in view.*) It's the postman! Excuse me for coming in, but the door was open!

MAN: Is there a letter for me?

POSTMAN: Just a postcard! (*Leaves it and goes.*)

●

MAN: (*Reads the card.*) Herr Fischer again! Boston Club! It's him up there! Him with the white gloves and dinner jacket! Writing to me! How rude! I must move! – Fischer! (*Tears up the card. Noise in the hall.*) Is that Karl Fredrik?

●

ICEMAN: It's the iceman!

MAN: Well, that's nice, to have ice in this hot weather! But mind the bottles in the box! Put the thing on its side, so I can hear when it melts and the drops fall – it's my water clock, that measures out the hours, the long hours... Listen, where do you get that ice from? – Has he gone? – They all go home, to hear their voices and have some company...

(*Pause.*) Is that you Karl Fredrik?

(*From above we can hear Chopin's* Fantasie Impromptu, *Opus 66, being played on the piano; but only the first parts.*)

(*Listens, wakes up, looks up to the ceiling.*) Who is that playing? My impromptu? (*He lays his hand across his eyes and listens.*)

●

(*The BROTHER comes in from the hall.*)

MAN: Is that you Karl Fredrik?

(*The music stops.*)

BROTHER: It's me!

MAN: Where have you been all this time?

BROTHER: I had some business to sort out; have you been on your own?

MAN: Of course! Come and play chess now!

BROTHER: I'd rather talk! Maybe you need to hear your own voice too.

MAN: Quite true, but we so easily end up talking about the past...

BROTHER: That way we forget the present...

MAN: There is no present, what we have now is the empty nothingness; before us and behind us – preferably before us, for there lies hope!

BROTHER: (*At the table.*) Hope, for what?

MAN: A change!

BROTHER: Well! Do you mean you have had enough of the peace and quiet of old age?

MAN: Perhaps!

BROTHER: Definitely you mean! And if you now could choose between loneliness and the past...

MAN: No ghosts though!

BROTHER: Your memories then?

MAN: They don't haunt; they are my poems upon certain... realities; but if the dead could walk again, that would be ghosts!

BROTHER: At any rate, in your memory then, which of the two give the most beautiful illusion, the woman or the child?

MAN: Both! I cannot separate them, and therefore I never tried to keep the child.

BROTHER: But was that the right thing to do? Didn't you think of the possibility of a stepfather?

MAN: I didn't think that far then, but later I have of course – reflected – upon – that aspect.

BROTHER: A stepfather who could mistreat, perhaps degrade your daughter!

MAN: Quiet!

BROTHER: What can you hear?

MAN: I thought I heard 'those tiny footsteps', her tiny tripping footsteps in the hallway, when she would come looking for me. – It *was* probably the child that was the best. To that intrepid little creature, who feared nothing, had no idea of the treachery of life, who had no secrets. I remember her first experience of people's wickedness. She saw a beautiful-looking child in the park, and she went with open arms towards this stranger in order to kiss her; the beautiful child answered her friendliness by biting her on the cheek and then sticking out her tongue. You should have seen my little Anne-Charlotte!; she stood there petrified, not by the pain, but by the horror of seeing the abyss open up before her of what we call the human heart. I have seen it once, when behind the most beautiful eyes suddenly appeared the foreign look of an evil animal; I became quite literally so afraid, that I looked to see if there was anyone there behind her face, which looked then like a mask. But why are we sitting here talking about this? Is it the heat or the thunderstorm or what?

BROTHER: Loneliness brings heavy thoughts, and you
   need company; this summer in town seems to have
   crushed you!

MAN: It's just these last few weeks; that case of illness and
   the corpse lying up there overwhelmed me, as if I had
   gone through it myself; the baker's sorrows and worries
   have also become my own, so that I go around worrying
   about his finances, his wife's eye disease, his future...and
   now recently I dream every night about my little Anne-
   Charlotte... I see her in danger, unknown, undiscovered,
   without a name; and before I fall asleep, when the
   hearing is so extraordinarily sharp, I hear her tiny steps,
   and once I heard her voice...

BROTHER: Where is she then?

MAN: Oh well.

BROTHER: If you were to meet her on the street...

MAN: Then I imagine, that I would lose my mind, or fall to
   the ground... I was once abroad a very long time, during
   the time my sister was growing up...after the passage of
   several years I came back on the steamer, and on the
   keyside found a young girl, who put her arms about me.
   I saw with horror two eyes penetrating into mine, but
   with an alien look, which expressed the most dreadful
   terror at not being recognised. 'It's me,' she repeated
   several times, before I recognised there my sister!
   That, more or less, is how I imagine a reunion with my
   daughter. Five years at that age can make you
   unrecognizable! Imagine, not recognising your child!
   The same, but a stranger! I couldn't survive that! No, in
   that case I would rather keep my little four-year-old on
   the altar at home; I don't want another...
   (*Pause.*)
   Is that Louise rumaging about in the linen cupboard? It
   smells clean, and it reminds me... Yes, the housewife at
   the linen cupboard, the good fairy, who preserves and
   renews; the housewife with the iron that levels out all the
   unevennesses and the wrinkles...yes, the wrinkles...
   I'm – going – in – now, to write a letter; if you'd like to
   stay here I'll be back soon. (*He goes out left.*)

●

(*The BROTHER coughs.*)

GERDA: (*Visible in the hallway door.*) Are you...
(*The clock in the dining-room strikes.*) Oh God! That
ringing... I've carried it in my head for ten years! That
clock, that never kept the right time, but measured out
hours lasting five years, days and nights. (*Looks about her.*)
My piano...my palms...the dining table; he's kept it,
shiny as a shield! My sideboard. With Eve and the
knight, Eve with the apples in her basket... In the right
hand drawer, all the way in, there was a thermometer...
(*Pause.*) I wonder if it's still there... (*Goes to the buffet,
pulls out the right hand drawer.*) Yes, it is!

BROTHER: What's it supposed to mean?

GERDA: Well, it ended up being a symbol! Of
impermanence! – When we set up home, the thermometer
was left, it was meant to be outside the window of
course... I promised I would put it out...forgot; he
promised to put it out, and forgot. So we nagged each
other, and finally, to get rid of it I hid it here in the
drawer... I began to hate it and so did he. Do you know
what it means? – Well, neither of us believed in the
permanence of our relationship, since we immediately
threw off the masks, and showed our antipathies. We lived
during that first time on the run...ready to leave at any
moment. – It was the thermometer...and it's still lying
here! Upside down, always changeable, like the weather.
(*She puts it down and goes to the chess set.*) My chess set!
Which he bought to pass the longs days of waiting,
before the little one came! Who does he play with now?

BROTHER: With me!

GERDA: Where is he?

BROTHER: He is in his room writing a letter!

GERDA: Where?

BROTHER: (*Points left.*) There!

GERDA: (*They stand together.*) And this is where he's been
for five years?

BROTHER: Ten years, five years alone!

GERDA: He loves solitude doesn't he?

BROTHER: I think he's had enough.

GERDA: Will he send me away?

BROTHER: Try! You risk nothing, he's always civil.

GERDA: That runner isn't one I've made…

BROTHER: You mean to say that you risk that he asks after the child.

GERDA: But it is he who is going to help me find her…

BROTHER: Where do you think Fischer has betaken himself, and what is the point of this flight of his?

GERDA: To get away from unpleasant neighbours, firstly; then to make me run after him; he wants the child as a hostage and then to bring her up to the ballet, for which she has shown real aptitude and talent.

BROTHER: Ballet? Her father mustn't get to know of it, for he hates the stage!

GERDA: (*Sits by the chess set and sets out the pieces absentmindedly.*) The stage! I have also been there!

BROTHER: You?

GERDA: I used to do the accompaniment!

BROTHER: Poor Gerda!

GERDA: Why? I loved the life; and when I sat prisoner here, it wasn't the gaoler's fault but the prisoner's, that I didn't like it!

BROTHER: But now you've had enough?

GERDA: Now I love the peace and solitude…my child above all else!

BROTHER: Quiet, he's coming!

GERDA: (*Stands up to run away, but falls back upon the chair again.*) Oh!

BROTHER: I'll leave you now! – Don't think about what you shall say; it will come of itself, like 'the next move' in chess!

GERDA: I fear his first glance most, for in it I can read if I have changed for the better or the worse…if I have become old and ugly…

BROTHER: (*Goes in right.*) If he finds that you have aged, then he will dare to approach you; if he finds you still as

62

young, then he has no hope, and he is less demanding than you think! – Now!

●

(*The MAN is seen walking slowly through the open door to the pantry left; he carries a letter in his hand; he disappears, but becomes visible again in the hall, and then goes out.*)

BROTHER: (*In the doorway right.*) He went out to the letterbox!

GERDA: I can't go through with this! How can I beg him for help in this divorce? I shall run away! It's too shameless!

BROTHER: Stay! You know his unlimited kindness! He will help you, for the child's sake!

GERDA: No, no!

BROTHER: And only he can help!

●

MAN: (*Comes in hurriedly from the hall, nods to GERDA who in his shortsightedness he takes for LOUISE; goes to the telephone on the sideboard, and phones; but in passing he says a word to GERDA.*) Finished already! Set up the pieces, Louise, and we'll start again from the beginning...
(*GERDA is petrified, understands nothing.*)
(*With his back to GERDA, telephones.*) Hello – Good evening, is that you Mother? – Yes thanks, fine! Louise is already sitting with the chess pieces, but she is tired after a little argument she has had. – Yes, it's over now, and everything is settled! Just trivial things! – Is it warm? The storm has passed over our heads, directly over us, but it didn't break! False alarm! (*Blindly.*) – What did you say? Fischers! Yes, but they are just about to go away it seems! – Why? I don't know of anything in particular! – Really? Really? – Yes, it leaves at a quarter past six; through the outer archipelago, and arrives, let me see, at twenty-five past eight! – Well did you have a pleasant time? (*Chuckles.*) Yes, he's a fool, once he starts; what did Maria say to that? – What's the summer been like? Well,

not too bad, Louise and I have kept one another
company; she has such a good even temper. – Oh, she's
so nice, she is! – No thanks, not that!
(*GERDA has begun to understand, stands up in horror.*)
My eyes? Well, I'm becoming shortsighted, but I say
with the baker's wife; there's nothing to look at! Wish
I were deaf as well! Deaf and blind! The neighbours
upstairs make such a dreadful noise at night...it's some
kind of gaming club. There now, they're on the line now
listening! (*Rings again.*)

●

(*LOUISE is visible in the hallway door, unseen by the MAN.
GERDA watches her with admiration and hatred; LOUISE
withdraws through the door on the right.*)

MAN: (*At the phone.*) Are you there? Imagine, they're
interrupting the call with their eavesdropping! So,
tomorrow, six fifteen! – Thank you very much, you too!
– Of course I will! Goodbye Mother! (*Hangs up.*)
(*LOUISE has withdrawn; GERDA stands in the middle of
the room.*)

●

MAN: (*Turns round; catches sight of GERDA and gradually
recognises her; clutches at his heart.*) Oh my God, is it you?
Wasn't Louise there just now?
(*GERDA is silent.*)
(*Flatly.*) Have – you – come here?

GERDA: Forgive me, I was travelling this way, I came past,
and got this longing to see my old home...the windows
were open...
(*Pause.*)

MAN: Is it the same, do you think?

GERDA: It's the same, but different, there is something
different here now...

MAN: (*Reluctantly.*) Are you content – with your life?

GERDA: Oh yes! I have what I wanted.

MAN: And the child?

GERDA: Well, yes, she's growing up and getting along, she's fine.

MAN: Then I shan't ask anymore. (*Pause.*) Do you want anything, of me, can I be of any service to you?

GERDA: Thank you, but... I don't need anything, since I can see you are doing fine too! (*Pause.*) Do you want to see Anne-Charlotte?

(*Pause.*)

MAN: I don't think so, since you tell me she's fine. – It's so difficult to start over again: it's like revision homework, which you already know, even though the teacher doesn't think so. – I'm so far far away from all this – I have been altogether somewhere else – and I can't reconnect with the past – I don't like to be impolite, but I won't ask you to sit down – you are another man's wife – and you are not the same person I separated from.

GERDA: Am I so – changed?

MAN: So unfamiliar! Voice, expression, manner...

GERDA: Have I aged?

MAN: That I don't know! – They say that after three years not one atom of a person's body remains – in five years everything is renewed, and so you who stand there are quite another from the one who sat here and suffered – I can hardly say – you, so wildly unfamiliar do I find you! And I presume I would feel the same towards my daughter!

GERDA: Don't speak like that, I would prefer you were angry.

MAN: Why should I be angry?

GERDA: For all the harm I have done you!

MAN: Have you; I don't feel that way.

GERDA: Didn't you read the affidavit?

MAN: No, I left that to the lawyer. (*Sits.*)

GERDA: The judgement then?

MAN: I haven't read that either. Since I do not intend to remarry, I have no need of such papers!

(*Pause.*

GERDA sits.)

65

What kind of thing did it say in them? That I was too old?
(*GERDA holds silent in confirmation.*)
It was only the truth, you shouldn't be embarrassed!
I wrote exactly the same in my affidavit, and agreed that
the court should give you back your freedom.

GERDA: Did you write that you...

MAN: I wrote, that I, was not but was becoming, too old for
you!

GERDA: (*Stung.*) For me?

MAN: Yes! – I couldn't say that I was too old when we were
married, for then the arrival of the child would be given
an unpleasant interpretation, and she is our child isn't she?

GERDA: You know she is! – But...

MAN: Am I to be ashamed of my age? Of course, if
I started dancing the Boston and playing cards at night,
then I would soon end up in a wheelchair or on the
operation table, and that would be shameful!

GERDA: You don't look that way...

MAN: Did you think I would die after the divorce?
(*GERDA keeps an ambiguous silence.*)
There are some who say you murdered me. Do you
think I look as if I have been murdered?
(*GERDA is embarrassed.*)
Your friends apparently did drawings of me in the
journals, but I never saw them, and they've been waste
paper now for five years! Don't trouble your conscience
on my account.

GERDA: Why did you marry me?

MAN: You know very well why a man marries; and you
know too that I didn't have to beg for your love. And
you ought to remember how we smiled together at all
the wise advisers who tried to warn you. – But why you
attracted me I have never been able to explain... When
after the ceremony you didn't see me, but behaved as if
you were at someone else's wedding, then I thought that
you must have had a bet that you would murder me. All
my subordinates hated me for being the boss, but they
soon became your friends. As soon as I acquired an

enemy, he became your friend! The which gave me reason to say: you shouldn't hate your enemies, true, but you shouldn't love my enemies! – Meanwhile, since I knew where I had you I started packing, but I needed a living witness that you had trafficked with untruth, and for that reason I waited until the little one's birth.

GERDA: To think how false you have been!

MAN: I kept silent, but never lied! – You gradually turned all my friends into detectives, and you led my brother into disloyalty towards me. But worst of all, you stirred doubt about your child's legitimacy with your thoughtless talk!

GERDA: I have taken that back!

MAN: You cannot clip the wings of a word once you've put it to flight. And the worst is, that the false rumour has found its way to the child, who considers her mother to be a...

GERDA: Oh! No!

MAN: Yes, it is true! – You built a tower on a foundation of lies, and now the tower of lies is falling on top of you!

GERDA: It's not true!

MAN: Oh yes, I met Anne-Charlotte recently...

GERDA: You met...?

MAN: We met on the stairs, and she said that I was her uncle; do you know what uncle means? It means an older friend of the family and the mother. And I know that at school I am known as her uncle, too! – It is horrible for the child.

GERDA: You've met?

MAN: Yes! But I didn't have to tell anyone. Haven't I the right to keep silent? And besides the meeting was so disturbing, that I struck it out of my memory, as if it had never happened.

GERDA: What can I do to give you redress?

MAN: You? You cannot give me redress, I can only do that for myself. (*They stare at each other long and hard.*) That is to say, I have already had redress...
(*Pause.*)

GERDA: Can't I put it right, can't I beg you to forgive, forget...

MAN: What do you mean?

GERDA: To restore, repair...

MAN: Do you mean to retie the knot, to start again, to reinstate yourself as mistress over me? No thank you! I don't want you!

GERDA: That I should hear this!

MAN: See how it feels!

(*Pause.*)

GERDA: That's a pretty table runner you have there...

MAN: Yes, it is pretty!

GERDA: Where did you get it?

(*Pause.*)

●

(*LOUISE appears in the door to the pantry with a bill in her hand.*)

MAN: (*Turns round.*) Is that a bill?

(*GERDA stands, pulls on her gloves, popping the fasteners.*)

(*Takes out the money for the bill.*) Eighteen seventy-two! That's right!

LOUISE: May I have a word Sir?

MAN: (*Stands and goes to the door, where LOUISE whispers something to him.*) Oh my G – !

(*LOUISE goes out.*)

●

MAN: Poor Gerda!

GERDA: What do you mean? That I should be jealous of your maid?

MAN: No, I didn't mean that!

GERDA: Yes you did, and you meant that you may be too old for me but not for her. I understand the insult...she is beautiful, that I don't deny, for a maid...

MAN: Poor Gerda!

GERDA: Why do you say that?

MAN: Because you are wretched! Jealous of my servant, that is surely redress...

GERDA: Me, jealous...?

MAN: Why then do you rage against my decent and quiet friend?

GERDA: 'More than just a friend.'

MAN: No, my child, I have given up long ago...and so am content with my solitude. (*The phone rings, the MAN goes over to it.*) Herr Fischer? That's not for here. I see, yes, that's me – Has he run off? – Who has he run off with? – the baker's daughter! Oh, my God! How old is she? – Eighteen! Just a child!

GERDA: That he had run off I already knew. – But with a woman! – Are you happy now?

MAN: No, I am not happy; however much it relieves my mind when I see that there is justice in the world! Life moves quickly, and now you are sitting where I sat!

GERDA: Her eighteen years against my twenty-nine – I am old, too old for him!

MAN: Everything is relative, even age! – But now to another matter! Where is your child?

GERDA: My child! I had forgotten! My child! My God! Help me! He has taken the child with him; he loved Anne-Charlotte as his own daughter...come with me to the police...come!

MAN: Me? Now you are asking too much!

GERDA: Help me!

MAN: (*Goes to the door right.*) Karl Fredrik, would you get a droska and go with Gerda to the police? – Don't you want to?

●

BROTHER: Of course I do! We are only human in Jesus' name!

MAN: Quickly! But don't say anything to Herr Stark; everything can still be repaired. Poor man – and poor Gerda! (*To them both.*) Hurry!

GERDA: (*Looks out the window.*) It's beginning to rain, lend me an umbrella... Eighteen – just eighteen – quickly! (*Goes out with the BROTHER.*)

MAN: (*Alone.*) The peace of old age! – And my child, in the hands of an adventurer! – Louise!

(*LOUISE comes in.*)

Play chess with me!

LOUISE: Has the Consul...?

MAN: He has gone out upon an errand...is it still raining?

LOUISE: No, it's stopping now!

MAN: Then I shall go out to cool down. (*Pause.*) You are a kind girl, and sensible; you knew the baker's daughter?

LOUISE: Yes, just a little!

MAN: Was she beautiful?

LOUISE: Y-yes.

MAN: Did you know the people living upstairs?

LOUISE: I've never seen them!

MAN: Evasive!

LOUISE: I have learned to keep quiet in this house.

MAN: I admit that the assumed deafness can go too far and become life threatening.

Make tea, while I go out and cool down. – Just one thing, my child, you can see what is going on here, but don't ask me anything.

LOUISE: Me? No, Sir, I'm not curious.

MAN: Thank you!

End of Act Two.

ACT THREE

The front of the house as in Act One. A light is shining from the BAKER's; lights are on, on the first floor, the windows are open and the blinds are up.

The BAKER is outside his door.

MAN: (*On the green bench.*) That was a good shower we had.

BAKER: A real blessing; now we'll have raspberries...

MAN: Then I must ask to order a few litres, for we have tired of making jam ourselves – it just sits there and ferments and goes mouldy...

BAKER: Yes, I know what it's like; you have to tend those jam jars like naughty children; there are those who put in salicylic acid, but that's just a new trick, I can't be doing with it...

MAN: Salicylic acid, yes, that's supposed to be antiseptic – and it could be good...

BAKER: Yes, but it leaves an after-taste...and it's a trick...

MAN: Listen, do you have a telephone Herr Stark?

BAKER: No, I've no telephone...

MAN: I see!

BAKER: Why do you ask?

MAN: Well, I was just thinking...one needs a telephone sometimes...orders...important messages...

BAKER: Could be; but sometimes it's best to avoid – messages.

MAN: Admittedly, admittedly! – Yes! My pulse always races when it rings – you never know what you are going to hear...and I want peace...peace above all else!

BAKER: Me too!

MAN: (*Looks at his watch.*) They'll be lighting the lamps soon!

BAKER: Looks like he's forgotten us, the avenue is already lit...

MAN: Then he'll be here soon! It will be really pleasant to have the light again...

(*The telephone rings inside the room; LOUISE is seen inside. The MAN stands, clutches at his heart, and tries to listen, but he doesn't hear the conversation.*

Pause.

LOUISE comes out from the courtyard.)

(*Worried.*) What news?

LOUISE: No change!

MAN: Was that my brother?

LOUISE: No, it was Sir's wife!

MAN: What did she want?

LOUISE: To speak with you Sir!

MAN: I don't want to! Am I to comfort my executioner? I have done it before, but now I am tired of it! – See up there! They have gone away and left the lamps burning – empty rooms that are lit are worse than when they are dark...one sees the ghosts. (*Half whisper.*) And the baker's daughter Agnes, do you think he knows anything?

LOUISE: It's hard to say, he never talks about his sorrows, and no-one else does either in this silent house.

MAN: Should we tell him?

LOUISE: No, for God's sake...

MAN: But it is surely not the first time she has given him trouble?

LOUISE: He never talks about her...

MAN: It's terrible! Shan't we see the end of this soon! (*The telephone rings again in the room.*) It's ringing again! Don't go! I don't want to know! – My child! In that company! An adventurer and a slut! – There's no limit to it! Poor Gerda!

LOUISE: It's better to know for certain – I'll go in – you must do something Sir!

MAN: I cannot move... I can take it, but hit back, no!

LOUISE: But if you try to fend off a danger, it forces itself on you, and if you don't resist, you go down under it!

MAN: But if one doesn't engage, one is untouchable!

LOUISE: Untouchable?

MAN: Everything turns out better if one doesn't complicate things by intervening. How am I supposed to steer, where the winds of so many passions blow! How can I curb their sufferings or alter their course?

LOUISE: But the child?

MAN: I have relinquished my rights...and besides – quite honestly, I am not concerned – not at all now, since she came in and destroyed my memories; she has obliterated all that was beautiful and I had hidden, now nothing is left.

LOUISE: That is what sets you free!

MAN: See how empty it is in there! Like after a removal... and up there, like after a fire!

LOUISE: Who's this coming?

●

(*AGNES comes in, upset, afraid. She composes herself, goes towards the courtyard entrance, where the BAKER is sitting.*)

LOUISE: (*To the MAN.*) It's Agnes! What does it mean?

MAN: Agnes! – Things will soon be alright!

●

BAKER: (*Quite calmly.*) Good evening, my child, where have you been?

AGNES: I've been out for a walk!

BAKER: Mama has asked after you several times.

AGNES: Has she! Well, I'm here now!

BAKER: Go down now and help her light the small stove, please!

AGNES: Is she angry with me then?

BAKER: She can never be angry with you!

AGNES: Yes she can, but she doesn't say anything.

BAKER: That's good then, my darling, that you aren't scolded!

(*AGNES goes in.*)

●

MAN: (*To LOUISE.*) Does he know or doesn't he?

LOUISE: May he live in his ignorance...

73

MAN: But what has happened? Have they broken up? (*To the BAKER.*) Listen here Herr Stark!

BAKER: Hello? Did you want me?

MAN: I was thinking... Did you see anyone come out from here a while ago?

BAKER: I saw the ice-man, and a postman I think.

MAN: I see! (*To LOUISE.*) Perhaps it's a mistake – could have heard wrong – I can't explain it... Perhaps he was fibbing! What did my wife say on the telephone?

LOUISE: She wanted to speak with you Sir.

MAN: How did she sound? Was she upset?

LOUISE: Yes.

MAN: I find it somewhat shameless appealing to me in such a circumstance...

LOUISE: But the child!

MAN: Imagine, I met my daughter on the stairs, and when I asked if she recognised me, she called me uncle, and she informed me that her Papa was upstairs... Of course he is her stepfather and has all rights over her – they've eradicated me, slandered me...

LOUISE: A cab has stopped at the corner!

(*The BAKER retires.*)

MAN: Just don't let them come back again, so I have them on my back – imagine, to hear my child singing her father's praises, the other one – and then the same old story starts off all over again: 'Why did you marry me?' – 'You know very well, but why did you want me?' – 'You know very well' and so on until the end of time.

LOUISE: It's the Consul!

MAN: How does he look?

LOUISE: He's in no hurry.

MAN: He's rehearsing what to say; does he look pleased?

LOUISE: Thoughtful rather...

MAN: I see... It was always like that; as soon as he came anywhere near that woman, he became unfaithful to me... She could charm anyone, except me! To me she was always raw, common, ugly, stupid, and to others she was refined, lovable, beautiful, intelligent! All that hate which my independence awakened around me, gathered itself around her like a limitless sympathy for the one who did me wrong. Through her they tried to control and influence me, wound me, and finally kill me!

LOUISE: I'm going in now to keep watch by the telephone – this storm should pass too!

MAN: People cannot tolerate the independent; they want you to obey them; all my subordinates right down to the caretaker at the works wanted me to obey them; when I didn't want to obey, they called me a despot. The maids in the house wanted me to obey them and eat warmed-up food, but when I didn't want to, then they incited my wife against me, and finally my wife wanted me to take orders from the child, but then I left, and so there was a conspiracy against the tyrant – that's me! – Hurry in now Louise, we can set alight the mine out there!

●

(*The BROTHER comes in left.*)

MAN: The result! – No details!

BROTHER: May we sit down, I'm a little tired...

MAN: It seems to have rained on the bench...

BROTHER: But since you've been sitting there, it can't very well do me any harm!

MAN: As you like! – Where is my child?

BROTHER: May I begin at the beginning?

MAN: Begin!

BROTHER: (*Slowly.*) I came down to the station with Gerda – at the ticket office I saw him and Agnes...

MAN: So Agnes was with him?

BROTHER: Yes, and your daughter! – Gerda stayed outside, and I approached them. In the same moment he gave Agnes the tickets, but when she saw that they were third class, she threw them in his face and went out to a cab.

MAN: Usch!

BROTHER: While I engaged the gentleman in trying to obtain an explanation Gerda rushed up and took the child, then disappeared in the crowd...

MAN: What did the gentleman say?

BROTHER: Well you know, when you get to hear the other side…et cetera!

MAN: I want to hear! – Naturally he wasn't as bad as we have imagined, he had of course his good sides…

BROTHER: Exactly!

MAN: Thought so! But you don't want me to sit here and hear eulogies over my enemy?

BROTHER: No, not eulogies, but mitigating circumstances…

MAN: Did you ever listen to me when I informed you of the true circumstances? Yes, you heard and answered with a disapproving silence, as if I sat and lied. You always stood on the side of wrongdoing, and you believed only lies, and that because – you were enamoured with Gerda. But there was still one more motive…

BROTHER: Don't say any more now, brother! – You see it only from your own point of view!

MAN: How do you expect me to see my case from the point of view of my enemy, I can't very well lift my hand against myself?

BROTHER: I am not your enemy.

MAN: Yes you are, when you befriended the one who has done me wrong! – – – Where is my child?

BROTHER: I don't know!

MAN: How did it end at the station?

BROTHER: The gentleman travelled south alone!

MAN: And the others?

BROTHER: Disappeared!

MAN: Then I may have them living above me once again! (*Pause.*) Did you see if the others went with him?

BROTHER: No, he travelled alone!

MAN: Then that's clear at least! Next – the remainder: the mother and child!

BROTHER: Why are the lamps burning up there on the first floor?

MAN: Because they forgot to extinguish them.

BROTHER: I'll go up...

MAN: No, don't go! – Just don't let them come back!
Repeat, repeat, do your homework all over again!

BROTHER: But the beginning has sorted itself out...

MAN: And the worst remains... Do you think they are
coming back?

BROTHER: Not she, since she had to pay redress to you in
front of Louise.

MAN: I had forgotten that! She really did do me the honour
of being jealous! I think there is justice in the world!

BROTHER: And then she heard that Agnes was younger.

MAN: Poor Gerda! But in such cases as these one shouldn't
say that to people, that there is justice, an avenging
justice...for it is only a lie that they love justice!
And one is expected to handle their filth delicately!
And Nemesis – that is only for other people!...
The telephone is ringing, it sounds like a rattlesnake!

●

(*LOUISE can be seen inside by the telephone.*
Pause.)

MAN: (*To LOUISE.*) Did the snake bite?

LOUISE: (*At the window.*) May I speak with you Sir?

MAN: (*Through the window.*) Speak!

LOUISE: The mistress has gone to her mother in Dalarne
to settle down there with the child.

MAN: (*To the BROTHER.*) Mother and child gone to the
country, to a good home! Now it has come to rights! Oh!

LOUISE: The mistress asked me to go up and put out the
lights in their apartment.

MAN: Do it at once Louise, and pull down the blinds so we
don't have to look at it all!
(*LOUISE goes.*)

●

(*The BAKER comes out again.*)

●

BAKER: (*Looks upwards.*) I think the storm has passed over.

MAN: It certainly seems to have cleared up, so there will be moonlight.

BAKER: It was a blessed rain! Really lovely!

MAN: Look, here comes the lamplighter, at last!
(*The LAMPLIGHTER comes in, lights the lamp.*)

●

MAN: The first lamp! Now it is autumn! It's our time of year boys! It's growing dark, but then comes wisdom to guide us, with a lantern so he won't go astray.
(*LOUISE is seen upstairs through the window; a moment later it goes dark.*)
(*To LOUISE.*) Close the windows, and then pull down the blinds, let the memories lie down to sleep, in peace! The peace of old age! And in the autumn I will move away from this silent house.

The End.

Opus 2

THE BURNED SITE

Brända Tomten

(1907)

Characters

THE DYER
Rudolf Valström[1]

THE STRANGER
his brother Arvid Valström

THE BRICKLAYER
(brother-in-law to the gardener) Andersson[2]

THE OLD WOMAN
his wife

THE GARDENER
Gustavsson[2], the bricklayer's brother-in-law

ALFRED
his son

THE STONECUTTER
(cousin to the hearse driver) Albert Eriksson

MATILDA
his daughter

THE HEARSE DRIVER
(cousin to the stonecutter)

POLICE INSPECTOR

THE PAINTER
Sjöblom[3]

FRU VESTERLUND
Landlady of 'The Last Nail', former nurse in
the dyer's household

THE WIFE
the dyer's wife

THE STUDENT

1 Pronounced Vahl-*Stroem*, as in 'labur*num*'.

2 Ander*sson*, Gustav*sson*, Erik*sson* – as in '*shone*'.

3 Pronounced 'Sher-bloom'.

The left-hand half of the upstage area is taken up by the walls of a burned-out single-storey house; we can see the wallpaper on the walls, and the tilestoves.

Behind this can be seen a blossoming orchard.

In the wings stage right a tavern with a pole with a garland upon it as its sign; outside are tables and benches.

To the left, upstage, salvaged furniture and household items thrown in a pile.

The PAINTER is standing painting the window shutters of the tavern; he listens attentively to all the conversations.

The BRICKLAYER stands digging about in the ruins.

POLICE INSPECTOR: (*Comes in.*) Is it properly out now?

BRICKLAYER: There isn't any smoke anyway.

INSPECTOR: Then I'll put a few questions again. (*Pause.*) Now, you're a bricklayer and you were born in this neighbourhood?

BRICKLAYER: Oh yes! Seventy-five years I've lived on this street; when I wasn't yet born, this house was built, my father laid the bricks...

INSPECTOR: Then you know everyone in the area?

BRICKLAYER: We all know each other, because there's something particular about this street; the ones as come here don't ever leave it, that is to say, the ones as move away come back all the same, sooner or later, till they're carried out to the cemetery, which is down the end of the street.

INSPECTOR: Do you have any particular name for your neighbourhood here?

BRICKLAYER: We call it the swamp; and everyone hates everyone else, is suspicious of everyone else, slanders everyone else, they torture each other...
(*Pause.*)

INSPECTOR: Now listen, the fire broke out at ten thirty in the evening; was the door closed at that time?

BRICKLAYER: Yes, well I don't know about that, see, 'cause I live in the courtyard alongside...

INSPECTOR: Where did the fire start then?

BRICKLAYER: Up in the attic,[4] where the student lives.

INSPECTOR: Was he at home?

BRICKLAYER: Nah, he was at the theatre.

INSPECTOR: Had he left the lamp burning then?

BRICKLAYER: Now, I wouldn't know, see...

(*Pause.*)

INSPECTOR: Is the student related to the owner of the house?

BRICKLAYER: Nah, I don't think so. – Are you with the police?

INSPECTOR: How come the tavern didn't catch fire?

BRICKLAYER: They covered it with fire blankets and sprayed water on it!

INSPECTOR: It's strange that the apple trees weren't destroyed by the heat!

BRICKLAYER: They were in bud and it had rained during the day, but with the heat they went into bloom in the middle of the night, a bit early you might say, since if there's a frost now, then the gardener will be up the spout.

INSPECTOR: What kind of a fellow is the gardener?

BRICKLAYER: He's called Gustavsson...

INSPECTOR: Yes but what kind of fellow is he?

BRICKLAYER: Now listen, I'm seventy-five years old...and so I don't know any ill of Gustavsson, and if I did know, I wouldn't be standing here telling you!

(*Pause.*)

INSPECTOR: And the owner of the house is called Valström, the dyer, about sixty years old, married...

BRICKLAYER: You go on! You're not getting any more out of me.

INSPECTOR: Do people think it's arson?

4 This one-storey house seems to have had an attic.

84

BRICKLAYER: People think all fires are arson.

INSPECTOR: Who do they suspect?

BRICKLAYER: The interested parties are always suspected by the fire insurance company; so that's why I've never had any insurance.

INSPECTOR: Did you find anything when you were digging about?

BRICKLAYER: You normally find all the door keys, since no-one has the time to take them out of the locks, when the flames are at the door, except sometimes, exceptionally, when they do take them out of course...

INSPECTOR: There was no electric lighting in the house?

BRICKLAYER: Not in this old house, and it's just as well, because then they can't go and blame a short circuit.

INSPECTOR: Blame? Just as well! – Now listen...

BRICKLAYER: Trying to catch me out? Don't, because then I'll take it back.

INSPECTOR: Take it back? You can't!

BRICKLAYER: Can't I?

INSPECTOR: Oh no!

BRICKLAYER: Oh yes I can, because there's no witness!

INSPECTOR: Isn't there?

BRICKLAYER: No!

(*The INSPECTOR coughs.*)

●

(*WITNESS comes in from the left.*)

INSPECTOR: Here is *one* witness!

BRICKLAYER: What a fox!

INSPECTOR: One uses one's sense, even when one isn't seventy-five years old! (*To the WITNESS.*) We'll continue now with the gardener.

(*They go left.*)

BRICKLAYER: I'm in for it now! But that's what you get for talking!

●

(*The OLD WOMAN comes in with food tied in a bundle.*)

85

BRICKLAYER: It's just as well you came!

OLD WOMAN: Now we're going to sit nicely and have breakfast, you must be hungry after all that palaver. I wonder how Gustavsson will ever recover after this, he'd started with the hot-bed frames and was just about to do the flower-bed; eat up, Sjöblom's already at the controls, just imagine Mrs Vesterlund just escaped the fire! Good mornin' Sjöholm[5], there's work to do now alright!

(*FRU VESTERLUND comes in from the tavern.*)

Good mornin', good mornin', Mrs Vesterlund, you had a lucky escape, I'll say, and I'll say it again too...

FRU VESTERLUND: I wonder who exactly is going to compensate me for the money I lose today, because they're having a big burial over at the graveyard and it's my busiest time, I had to carry away food and glasses...

OLD WOMAN: What burial is it today, I've seen so many folk going past the turnpike, and then they all want to see the fire too...

FRU VESTERLUND: I don't think it is a burial, but I think they're putting up a memorial on the bishop's grave – but the worst of it is that the stonecutter's daughter was going to have her wedding with the gardener's son. As you know, he works in a shop down in the town, but now the gardener has lost everything he owns; isn't that his furniture over there?

OLD WOMAN: It must be the dyer's too, it all came out at once, topsy-turvy, where's the dyer now?

FRU VESTERLUND: He's down at the police station giving a statement.

OLD WOMAN: Is he now? I see! Look...there's my cousin the hearse driver, he always likes a drink on his way home...

●

5 The Old Woman accidentally calls Sjöblom Sjöholm.

HEARSE DRIVER: Good morning, Malvina, you were lighting fires last night I hear, very nice too, but it would have been better if you'd got a new house...

FRU VESTERLUND: God preserve us! So who've you taken out now?

HEARSE DRIVER: I don't remember what his name was, and there was only one car that followed him, and no wreath on the coffin...

FRU VESTERLUND: Not a long awaited death then, at least... If you want a drink, you'll have to go round to the kitchen, 'cause I haven't got anything ready on this side, and besides Gustavsson's going to come with his wreath, there's some do on at the cemetery today...

HEARSE DRIVER: Yes, they're putting up a monument to the bishop, he wrote books they say, and collected grubs. He was an insect hunter; that's what they told me.

FRU VESTERLUND: What's that?

HEARSE DRIVER: He had bits of cork which he stuck needles into, with flies on them...beyond us...but I'm sure it's very proper...can I come into the kitchen now?

FRU VESTERLUND: Go in the back way, and I'll give you a drop...

HEARSE DRIVER: But I want to talk to the dyer before I go. I've got the horses next door, here with the stone-cutter, my cousin, you know; I don't like him, as you also know, but we do business together, that is, I recommend him to the relatives of the deceased, and that's why I can keep the horses there sometimes in his yard. Tell me when the dyer comes, it's lucky he didn't have his dye-works here... (*He goes behind the tavern.*) (*FRU VESTERLUND goes through the doors.*)

●

(*The BRICKLAYER has finished eating, starts digging about again.*)

OLD WOMAN: Find anything?

BRICKLAYER: Well, nails and hinges; all the keys are hanging there in a bunch on the doorpost...

OLD WOMAN: Were they already hanging there or have you picked them up?

BRICKLAYER: They were hanging there from the start, when I arrived.

OLD WOMAN: That's odd, then someone must have locked all the doors and took out the keys, before the fire started! That's odd!

BRICKLAYER: It's a bit odd, yes, because that way it was harder to put it out and contain it. Aha! Oho!
(*Pause.*)

OLD WOMAN: Now I've been in service at the dyer's house, for forty years I have, and I know those people, both the dyer, and his brother who went to America. Though they say as he's come back; the father was a regular sort, but the boys weren't up to much. – Mrs Vesterlund over there, she took care of that Rudolf, they could never get along those brothers, fighting and quarrelling all the time. – I've seen it all I have; the goings on in this house, such goings on, I thought it was time it was smoked out – tush, what a house! The one came and the other went, but back they came. And here they were born, here they were married and here they separated. – And that brother in America, Arvid, was believed for many years to be dead, at least he never took out his inheritance, but now like I said they say he's come back, though nobody's seen him – folk do talk so much! – Look, here comes the dyer from the police station!

BRICKLAYER: He doesn't look too happy, but you can't expect him to... Well, so who was the student in the room up there? They're as thick as thieves around here.

OLD WOMAN: I wouldn't know about that. He came for his meals, and taught the children!

BRICKLAYER: With the mistress in the house and all?

OLD WOMAN: Nah, they used to play at that there tennis and always argued besides; everyone argues and insults each other around here – – –

BRICKLAYER: Well, when they broke open the student's door, they found a load of hair pins on the floor, so it came to light right enough, but those tracks will have to be burnt over...

OLD WOMAN: I don't think it was the dyer after all, it's Gustavsson...

BRICKLAYER: He's always angry of course, but today it's worse than ever, and now he's going to call in my debt, after he's lost out in the fire...

OLD WOMAN: Hush!

●

GARDENER: (*Comes in with a basket of burial wreathes and so on.*) Am I going to sell anything today so that we have money to eat, after this 'do' here, do you think?

BRICKLAYER: Were you insured then?

GARDENER: Yes, for panes of glass in the glazier's insurance, but this year I had to go and be mean and just have oiled paper. Why did I have to be such an utter fool! – (*Tears at his hair.*) – And I won't be paid for it! Six hundred paper panes I'm going to have to cut out and glue and oil! Well, they always said I was the stupidest of seven brothers and sisters, such an ass, such a cloth head! And then I went and drank yesterday, why the hell did I have to get drunk yesterday of all days, when I need my wits today? It was the stonecutter who paid, we were to marry our two children this evening, but I should have said no! – I didn't want to! But I'm just a poor wretch, who can't say no! And it's like that when they come and borrow money from me too; I can't say no, poor fool that I am! And then I had that policeman on top of me, asking questions and trying to catch me out; I ought to have kept my mouth shut, but I said one thing and then another, and he wrote it all down, and now I'm going to be called as a witness!

BRICKLAYER: What did you say, brother-in-law?

GARDENER: I said that I thought – that it was crazy, and that someone lit the fire!

BRICKLAYER: You said that?

GARDENER: Abuse me, go on, I deserve it, I'm a blockhead!

BRICKLAYER: Who was it lit the fire then? – Don't be shy, Sjöblom here, and my wife aren't ones to gossip.

GARDENER: Who lit the fire? The student of course, it started in his room...

BRICKLAYER: No, *under* his room!

GARDENER: Was it under? Then I've gone and made a mess of things... I'll come to no good, I will; was it *under* his room? What was there underneath then? The kitchen?

BRICKLAYER: No, it was a wardrobe; look yourself! The cook's wardrobe.

GARDENER: Then it was her then!

BRICKLAYER: Well, don't say that when you don't know!

GARDENER: The master was none too pleased with the cook yesterday, he could tell you a thing or two...

OLD WOMAN: Don't go repeating what he says, you can't believe someone who's been inside...

GARDENER: Ach! That was so long ago, and besides, the cook was a dragon, she always haggles over the vegetables...

OLD WOMAN: Here comes the dyer from the police station...quiet now!

●

(*The STRANGER comes in with a morning coat, top hat with mourning bands, stick.*)

OLD WOMAN: No, it's not the dyer, but he looks very like him!

●

STRANGER: What does one of those wreathes cost?

GARDENER: It costs fifty öre.[6]

STRANGER: Then it's not dear.

GARDENER: Well, see I'm such an oaf, that I can't drive a hard bargain.

STRANGER: (*Looks about him.*) Has there...been a fire – here?

6 100 öre = 1 krona.

90

GARDENER: Yes, there was a fire here, yesterday evening.
STRANGER: Oh my God! (*Pause.*) Who owned the house then?
GARDENER: Valström, the works owner.
STRANGER: The dyer?
GARDENER: Yes, he was a dyer.
(*Pause.*)
STRANGER: Where is he?
GARDENER: We're expecting him in a minute.
STRANGER: Then I shall walk about a bit here, and leave the wreath here until I come back. I'm going back out to the cemetery again.
GARDENER: Are you going to the bishop's monument sir?
STRANGER: Which bishop?
GARDENER: Why, Bishop Stecksén[7] from the Academy of course!
STRANGER: Is he dead?
GARDENER: Yes, long ago!
STRANGER: I see! – Well, I'll leave the wreath here for now. (*Goes out left, looking closely at the ruins.*)

●

OLD WOMAN: Was he from the insurance company do you think?
BRICKLAYER: Oh no, not him; then he would have asked in a different way.
OLD WOMAN: But he really was *like* the dyer, anyway.
BRICKLAYER: But he was taller!
GARDENER: I've just remembered something – I'm supposed to get a bridal bouquet for this evening, and I'm to go to my son's wedding, but I haven't got any flowers and my black coat has burnt up. It's completely... Madam Vesterlund was going to provide the myrtle for the crown, her being the bride's godmother. Now this myrtle, she stole the shoot for it[8]

7 Pronounced Steck-Ian – Ian as in the name.

8 Tradition has it that a stolen shoot of myrtle is best for a bride – similar to 'Something old, something new, something borrowed, something blue'.

from the dyer's cook, who got hers from the first wife, her who ran away; but I was supposed to bind it together but I forgot about it – I'm the world's biggest idiot. (*Opens the door to the tavern.*) Fru Vesterlund, can I have the myrtle now, so I can do it! Can I have the myrtle now I said! – Shall there be garlands as well...will there be enough? – No? – Then to hell with the wedding, that's all I can say! – Let them just go to the priest and get married that way but the stonecutter is going to be furious. – What shall I do then? – I can't do that – I haven't slept a wink all night! – It's too much for a man. – Yes, I'm a weakling, I know, go ahead and scold me! – There's the pot, well, thanks very much – and a pair of scissors too please, I haven't got any, and some wire too we need, and garden string, where am I to get that from? – No-one wants to leave their work, do they! – I'm sick of the whole lot, you work for fifty years then the whole lot goes up in flames; I haven't the strength to start again; and it all happens all at once, one thing after another; you know what, I'm quitting everything... (*Goes.*)

●

DYER: (*Comes in, shaken, ill-dressed, dark blue on his hands.*) Is the fire out now, Andersson?

BRICKLAYER: Yes, it's out now!

DYER: Has anything come to light?

BRICKLAYER: Has there ever? What you hide in the snow comes out in the thaw.

DYER: What do you mean, Mr Andersson?

BRICKLAYER: Whoever digs it up, finds it, so they say.

DYER: Have you found anything to explain how the fire started?

BRICKLAYER: Oh no! Nothing like that!

DYER: Then we're still all under suspicion!

BRICKLAYER: Not me though surely?

DYER: Goodness, yes! You were seen in the attic at an unusual time.

BRICKLAYER: I can't very well always go at a usual time to look for my tools which I've left behind, can I? When

I mended the student's tilestove, I left my hammer behind!

DYER: And the stonecutter, and the gardener, and Madam Vesterlund, even the painter there, we're all suspected, the student, the cook and most of all, me. It was lucky though that I had paid the insurance the previous day otherwise I'd be in the ditch. – Imagine, the stonecutter suspected of arson, and he so afraid of doing the slightest thing wrong; *nowadays* he's got such a conscience, that if you ask him the time, he'll tell you, but he won't swear to it because the clock *might* be wrong. We know about his two-year sentence, don't we? He went straight, and now I swear he's the most honest man in the neighbourhood.

BRICKLAYER: But the courts suspect him precisely because he made that mistake... and now he's stripped of his civil rights![9]

DYER: Yes, well there we are, people see things in different ways! – You'd better be off now again, Andersson. You've got a wedding to go to this evening!

BRICKLAYER: Yes, that wedding... There was someone looking for you, guv'nor, just now, and he said he'd be back shortly.

DYER: Who was it?

BRICKLAYER: He didn't say!

DYER: Well, was it a policeman?

BRICKLAYER: No, I don't think so! – Here he is anyway!
(*Goes out with the OLD WOMAN.*)
(*The STRANGER comes in.*)

DYER: (*Observes him with curiosity, then with fear; wants to get away, but cannot.*) Arvid!

STRANGER: Rudolf!

DYER: Is it you?

STRANGER: Yes!
(*Pause.*)

---

9 A kind of probation where the culprit of certain serious crimes, for example arson, would lose some of his rights as a citizen.

DYER: You're not dead, then?

STRANGER: Yes, I am, in a way! – I've come back from America, after thirty years, something drew me back, I had to see my childhood home again – – – and here I find a ruin. (*Pause.*) Was there a fire here last night?

DYER: Yes! You came at just the right time.

(*Pause.*)

STRANGER: (*Slowly.*) So there's the site; imagine, such a small space for so many destinies! – There's the dining room with the painted walls; the palms, cypresses, a temple, under a rose pink sky; that's what I dreamed the world looked like, if you could only manage to leave home! – And the tilestove with the pale flowers growing out of shells – the niche with the tin doors[10] – I remember how as a child when we moved in, there was a name scratched in the tin – and grandmother told us how the man whose name it was had killed himself in that room. – I soon forgot about it; but when later in life I became married to the dead man's niece, I felt that it was my own fate that had been written there on the piece of metal. – No, you don't believe in that kind of thing! – You do know at any rate how my marriage ended?

DYER: Yes, I had heard...

STRANGER: There's the nursery! Yes!

DYER: Don't let's dig in the ruins!

STRANGER: Why not? Now it's burnt, we can read in the ashes, like we read the ashes in the grate as children...

DYER: Sit down here at the table!

STRANGER: What's this tavern here? The Last Nail, where the hearse drivers used to come in, and where in the old days the criminals would be given their last drink before being driven out to the gallows on the hill... Who runs it?

DYER: Madam Vesterlund, my old wet nurse.

STRANGER: Madam Vesterlund! I remember her... It's as if the bench here collapsed beneath me and I sank back through time, sixty years, back into childhood – I can feel the air in the nursery, and the pressure on my chest

10 The doors to the tilestove.

– you older ones crushed me, and you made such a terrible din, that I was always afraid; I hid in the garden in fear; was dragged out and beaten, always beatings, but I could never find out why, and I still don't know! – She was still my mother after all...

DYER: Stop it!

STRANGER: Yes, you were the favourite and always won approval... And then came our stepmother. – Her father was an undertaker, and we had seen him for years driving past here on the hearse... In the end he was so familiar that he used to nod to us, and grimace as if to say, 'I'll be coming to get you one day.' And then one day he did come in to this house, and we called him grandad, when our father remarried to his daughter.

DYER: Nothing remarkable in that!

STRANGER: No, but the way it all wove together, one's own destiny with those of others...

DYER: It's like that everywhere...

STRANGER: Oh quite, everywhere it's the same... When you're young you see the weave being set up: parents, relations, friends, acquaintances, servants are all the warp; later on you see the weft; and now destiny's shuttle goes back and forth with the yarn; it breaks sometimes, but gets knotted back together, and so it continues; the bar shoots across, the yarn is forced into twists and turns, and there it is, the weave! In old age when the eye can see, you discover that all the little twists and turns form a hieroglyph, that can finally be discerned, that is life! The great weaver has woven it!

(*Pause. He gets up.*)

I see in the pile of rubbish over there, the family photograph album. (*He goes over to the pile and picks up an album.*) It's our book of Fate! Grandfather and grandmother, mother and father, brothers and sisters, relations, acquaintances, or those so-called friends, school-friends, maids, god-parents... And the remarkable thing is, that for me who's been in America, Australia, the Congo and Hong Kong, wherever I went, there was a fellow-countryman, at least one, and after we'd rooted around, then this fellow would always know my family or at least a godparent or a maid, a common acquaintance, in other words. On the island of Formosa I even met a relative...

DYER: Where did you get all these ideas?

STRANGER: Through the fact that, however life took shape – I have been rich and poor, high and low, suffered shipwrecks and earthquakes, however life seemed to be, I always found a continuity and repetition. – In each situation I would see the result of the previous one; when I met this person I was reminded of that person, from the past. There are even scenes from my life which have been repeated several times, so that I have often said to myself: I've done this before. And there are events which have seemed to me quite simply unavoidable or predestined.

DYER: What have you been doing all these years?

STRANGER: Everything! I've seen life from all points of the compass, from above and below, but always as if it was being staged for me in particular; and through that I have at last been reconciled with something of the past, and managed to exculpate my own and other's so-called faults. You and I, for example, had a good deal of unfinished business.

(*DYER recoils.*)

No, don't be afraid now!

DYER: I'm never afraid!

STRANGER: You haven't changed.

DYER: What about you!

STRANGER: Haven't I changed? That's interesting! – Yes, you continue in your illusion that you are so brave; and I remember when you got that false fixed idea; you'd landed on your head in a swimming lesson, and our mother said: You see, Rudolf has courage! – That was aimed at me; at me, whom you had all robbed of my courage and self-confidence. But then came the day, you'd been stealing apples, and were cowardly enough not to be able to admit it, but blamed me instead.

DYER: Haven't you forgotten that?

STRANGER: I haven't forgotten, but I have forgiven. – I'm sitting here looking at the very same apple tree, that's why I remember it so well. It's standing over there, it's a White Golden – And if you look, you can see the mark of a large branch that's been sawn off. – Because in fact I didn't get angry with you for the unjust punishment, but took out my anger on the tree, and cursed it. – Two years later that big branch was rotten, and got sawn off. It made me think of the fig tree damned by Our Saviour, but I drew no presumptuous conclusions. – However, to this day I still know all the fruit trees by heart; and when I had the yellow fever one time in Jamaica, I listed them all out! Most of them are still here, I see! There's the *Rosenhager* with its red-striped fruits; and in it a chaffinch builds its nest; there are *Gravensteiner* outside our attic window, where I took my technical exams; there's *Hampus,* there's *Autumn Astrakan*; the cinnamon-pear tree which is like a little pyramid poplar tree; and there's our *Stewing pear,* which never ripened, and which we despised, but which mother praised above the rest; there was a woodpecker in the old tree, twisting its neck around and making such an ugly screech… It's fifty years ago!

DYER: (*Angry.*) What are you getting at?

STRANGER: Just as suspicious and bad tempered as ever! It's interesting. – I have no intention behind what I'm saying, the memories press themselves forwards… I recall the garden was hired out once; but we were allowed to walk in it. It seemed to me then as if we were driven out of paradise – and the tempter stood behind every tree! In the autumn, when the apples lay ripe upon the ground, then I fell for the temptation, it was irresistible…

DYER: You stole too?

STRANGER: Of course! But I didn't blame you for it! – When later, at forty years old, I leased a lemon plantation in the Southern States of America, well then I had thieves every night in the garden; I couldn't sleep, I grew thin and became ill… And then I thought of Gustavsson the poor gardener – here!

97

DYER: He's still alive!

STRANGER: Perhaps he also stole apples in his childhood?

DYER: Quite likely!

STRANGER: Why are your hands black?

DYER: Because I handle dyed articles... Do you mean something else?

STRANGER: What should that be?

DYER: That my hands aren't clean!

STRANGER: Oh!

DYER: Maybe you're thinking of the inheritance!

STRANGER: Still as petty as ever! You're just as you were when you were eight years old!

DYER: And you are just as thoughtless, philosophical and stupid!

STRANGER: It's so strange! – How many times have we sat here, saying the self-same things?

(*Pause.*)

I see here in your album... Our brothers and sisters! Five dead.

DYER: Yes!

STRANGER: And our school friends?

DYER: Some have been taken up, some left behind.

STRANGER: I met one in South Carolina – Axel Eriksson,[11] remember him?

DYER: Of course!

STRANGER: He told me, one long night when we were on a train, that our esteemed family which enjoyed such respect, consisted only of crooks, and that the fortune was accrued by means of smuggling past the toll here, and that this house was built with double walls to hide the goods; can you see there are double walls?

DYER: (*Crushed.*) That's why there are so many wardrobes everywhere!

STRANGER: This fellow Eriksson's father had worked at the toll-gate, knew our father, and told me tales which turned my whole imagined world of illusions upside down.

11 Axe-ell Ee-rick-*sson* (rhymes with *gone*): stress on last syllable.

DYER: Didn't you hit him then?

STRANGER: Why would I hit him? – In the meantime
I went grey overnight. I had to re-examine my whole
life. You know we lived in mutual admiration, that we
considered our family to be of the best, and that our
parents in particular were regarded in almost religious
awe. Now I had to sit and repaint their faces, undress
them, drag them down, and get them out of my mind. It
was terrible! Then they began to haunt me; the pieces of
the broken figures put themselves back together, but
didn't fit, and it became a wax-works of monsters. All
those grey-haired men who frequented our houses, men
we called uncles, who played cards and ate supper, were
smugglers; some of them wore the ball and chain... Did
you know that?

DYER: (*Completely dejected.*) No!

STRANGER: The whole dye-works was just a hiding place
for smugglers' wool, which was dyed to make it
unidentifiable – I remember I always hated that smell
from the dyeing vats, there was something disgustingly
sweet...

DYER: Why did you have to tell me all this?

STRANGER: Why should I keep quiet, and allow you to be
a figure of fun when you go about boasting of your
highly respected family? Have you never noticed them
smirking at you?

DYER: No, I haven't!

(*Pause.*)

STRANGER: Sitting here, I can see in that pile of rubbish
over there our father's book cabinet; you will remember
it was always locked. But one day, when father was out,
I found the key. The books which stood at the front I had
already seen through the glass – they were books of
sermons, the works of great poets, and gardening books,
anthologies concerning customs and excise practises,
confiscations, the law of the land, and a book on foreign
currency, a technological book, which later determined
my course in life; but I discovered that behind these

books was space for other things, and I explored: first there was the cane – these days I know how that bitter plant bears a fruit which produces the red colourant called Dragon's Blood, it's odd, isn't it. – Then next to it stood a jar with the label Calcium Cyanide...

DYER: That was for dyeing...

STRANGER: Perhaps for other things too! – But listen to this: There were bundles of papers, with illustrated covers, which aroused my interest... Yes, without any preconceptions I took this to be the memoirs of a certain renowned knight – I took them out, closed the cabinet. And beneath the great oak tree over there I studied them. We did call it the Tree of Knowledge, after all! And with that I stepped out of the paradise of childhood and was initiated, too early, into the secrets which...well!

DYER: You too?

STRANGER: I see! You too!

(*Pause.*)

Anyway – we should talk about something else, because all that has turned to ashes now. – Were you insured?

DYER: (*Angry.*) Didn't you just ask that?

STRANGER: I don't remember doing so; I so often confuse what I have said with what I meant to say, mainly because I think so intensely, ever since the day I hanged myself in the wardrobe!

DYER: What did you say?

STRANGER: I hanged myself in the wardrobe!

DYER: (*Slowly.*) Was that what had happened that Maundy Thursday, and what we were never told about? When you were taken to the hospital?

STRANGER: (*Slowly.*) Yes! – You see how little one knows about one's closest relatives, one's home, one's own life!

DYER: But why did you do it?

STRANGER: I was twelve years old, and found life insufferable! It was like entering upon a great darkness... I didn't know what I was supposed to be here for...and I thought the world was a madhouse! – I discovered that one day, when the school sent us all out with torches and banners to honour 'Our Nation's Destroyer'.[12] I had just read a book where the worst kings were shown to be the ones who enlarged the kingdom – and these we were now to celebrate with anthems and tributes!

(*Pause.*)

DYER: What happened at the hospital?

STRANGER: I lay for dead in the mortuary, my dear fellow. Whether I was dead or not, I don't know – but when I awoke I had forgotten most of my previous life, and began a new one, but in a way which made the rest of you think I was strange. – Are you remarried?

DYER: I have a wife and child! Somewhere!

STRANGER: When I came round, it seemed to me as if I was inside someone else; I accepted life with a cynical calm; it was meant to be so! And the worse it was, the more interesting it became... I regarded myself by that time as someone else, and I observed and studied this other person and his fate, and this made me insensitive to my own suffering. But I had in death found new accomplishments... I could see right through people, read their thoughts, saw their intentions. When I was in the company of others, I saw them naked... Where did the fire begin?

DYER: No-one knows of course!

STRANGER: But it said in the paper that it started in a wardrobe beneath the student's attic. What student is that?

DYER: (*Afraid.*) Does it say that in the paper? I haven't had time to read it today. What else does it say?

STRANGER: It says everything.

DYER: Everything?

STRANGER: The double walls, the well-respected family of smugglers, the ball and chain, the hair pins...

DYER: What hairpins?

STRANGER: I don't know. But it says in there. Do you know?

---

12 Strindberg's title for Karl XII (1697–1718). See note to the *The Great Highway*, p. 264.

DYER: No!

STRANGER: Everything came to light, and we're expecting crowds to come and gape at the misery revealed.

DYER: For Christ's sake! And this pleases you, to see your family scandalised?

STRANGER: My family? I have never felt myself to be related to you lot, I have never had any feelings for my fellows or for myself, I just think it's interesting to look at them... What kind is your wife?

DYER: Is there something about her in the paper too?

STRANGER: Yes, about her and the student.

DYER: Good! Then I was right! Just you wait and see! – Here comes the stonecutter!

STRANGER: Do you know him?

DYER: And so do you! An old school friend! Albert Eriksson!

STRANGER: Whose father worked at the toll and whose brother I met on the train, the one who was so well informed about our family.

DYER: In that case it's this bastard who has told tales to the papers!

•

(*The STONECUTTER comes in with a pickaxe. Looks at the ruins.*)

STRANGER: What a dreadful thing to do...

DYER: He's been inside too, two years... Do you know what he did? He erased something on a contract I had with a...

STRANGER: And you had him put away; so now he's got his revenge!

DYER: But the strange thing is, that nowadays he is considered to be the most honest bloke in the neighbourhood; he's become a martyr, a near saint, so one daren't go near him.

STRANGER: That's very interesting.

•

INSPECTOR: (*Comes in. To the STONECUTTER.*) Are you going to pull down this wall?

STONECUTTER: The one by the wardrobe?

INSPECTOR: That's the one!

STONECUTTER: That's where the fire started, and I'm sure there's a candle or a lamp there; I know what these people are like all right!

INSPECTOR: Go on then!

STONECUTTER: The wardrobe door burnt up of course, but the false floor collapsed, so we couldn't get to the bottom of it, but now we're going to draw the sting! (*Strikes with the pickaxe.*) There we are! – That's got it! – That's done it! Do you see anything?

INSPECTOR: Not yet!

STONECUTTER: (*As before.*) Now I can see something! – The lamp has exploded, but the base is still there! – Anyone recognise the forfeit! – I thought the guv'nor was there!

INSPECTOR: Yes, there he is! (*Takes the base of the lamp and shows it.*) Do you recognise your lamp, sir?

•

DYER: It's not mine, it belongs to the tutor.

INSPECTOR: The student? Where is he?

DYER: He's in town, but he'll be back soon I expect, since his books are lying here.

INSPECTOR: How did his lamp come to be in the cook's cupboard? Did he have relations with her?

DYER: Probably!

INSPECTOR: So long as he admits the lamp is his, he'll be prosecuted. What do you think about it?

DYER: Me? What is one to think?

INSPECTOR: Well, what motive does he have to start a fire in someone else's house?

DYER: I don't know! Wickedness, destructiveness; people are so unpredictable, aren't they... Maybe he wanted to hide something...

INSPECTOR: A poor method he chose, since all these shady secrets have come to light. – Did he have anything against you?

DYER: Very likely! Because once I helped him when he was in need, and so he hated me, of course!

INSPECTOR: Of course! (*Pause.*) Who is this student, then?

DYER: He's from the workhouse, of unknown parentage.

INSPECTOR: Don't you have a grown-up daughter?

DYER: (*Angry.*) Of course I have!

INSPECTOR: I see!

(*Pause.*)

(*To the STONECUTTER.*) Bring your twelve men now, and rip down these walls, quickly, so we can see what else will come to light. (*Goes.*)

STONECUTTER: It won't take a moment. (*Goes.*)

(*Pause.*)

STRANGER: Have you really paid the insurance?

DYER: Of course!

STRANGER: Yourself?

DYER: No, I sent someone, as usual.

STRANGER: You sent – someone else! That's like you – shall we walk around the garden a bit, look at the apple trees?

DYER: If you like, we can see what happens next.

STRANGER: It's going to be interesting.

DYER: Not so interesting if you're involved.

STRANGER: Me?

DYER: Who knows?

STRANGER: What a web!

DYER: You had one of your children in the house, didn't you?

STRANGER: God bless you...![13] – Let's go into the garden!

●

13 In English in the original.

Same as before, except that the walls have been pulled down so that the garden can be seen with its spring flowers; mezercon, dentsia, daffodils, narcissus, tulips, auricula, etc, and all the fruit trees in bloom.

The STONECUTTER, the MASON with his WIFE, the GARDENER, the HEARSEDRIVER, MADAM VESTERLUND and the PAINTER, all stand in a row looking at the burned site.

STRANGER: (*Comes in.*) There they stand, revelling in the disaster, waiting for the victim, which seems to be the main attraction. That it was arson is taken for a fact, because they want it to be! – And all these villains are my childhood friends, playmates; I'm related to the hearse-driver through my stepmother, whose father carries coffins – – – (*To those close by him.*) Don't stand there, good people, there might be dynamite in the cellar there could be an explosion at any moment.
(*The crowd dissolves and disappears.*)
(*By the pile of rubbish, looking through the books.*) The student's books! – The same rubbish as in my own youth. – Livy: Roman history, lies every word apparently– but here's a book from my brother's collection! – *Columbus, or The Discovery of America*! – It's my book which I got as a present in 1857; the name has been scratched out; so it's been stolen from me, and I accused the maid who was then dismissed! That's nice, perhaps it ruined her! Fifty years ago! – There's the canvas stretcher from a family portrait: my fine grandfather, the smuggler who ended up in chains; very nice! – But what have we here? The headboard of a mahogany bed – the one I was born in! Damn! – Item; the legs of a dining table – handed down through the generations – yes! They said it was ebony, and it was admired as such, and is exposed now, after fifty years, by me, to be dyed maple – everything was dyed in our house, to make it unrecognisable, and our children's clothes were dyed too, so our bodies were always stained

with dye. Humbug! Ebony! – Here's the mantle clock, also smuggled goods, which has measured out the hours for two generations; was wound up each Saturday, when we were given dried cod and beer posset for dinner – it used, as a fully conscient clock, to stop whenever someone died; but when I died it carried on going. – Let me look at you, how you look inside, old friend. (*The clock falls apart at his touch.*) Can't be touched! Nothing can be touched, nothing! Vanity, vanity! – Look, there's the globe which went on top, even though it should have gone underneath. You little Earth: the most compact of all the planets, the heaviest, that's why it weighs so heavily upon you, and makes it so hard to breathe, so heavy to bear; the cross is your symbol, but it could have been the fools cap and bells or a straight-jacket; – the world of delusions, the world of the fool. – O Eternal Father! Has your world lost its way in space? And how come she spins round and makes all her children dizzy and lose their sense, so that they can never see things as they are but only as they seem to be? Amen! There's the student!

●

(*The STUDENT comes in. Searching for someone with his eyes.*)

STRANGER: He's looking for the dyer's wife and reveals everything with his eyes! Happy Youth! – Who are you looking for?

STUDENT: (*Embarrassed.*) I was looking for...

STRANGER: Speak up, young man, or hold your peace! I understand you so well already anyway!

STUDENT: With whom do I have the honour of speaking?

STRANGER: It's no honour to talk to me, you know that, I once ran away to America to escape debt...

STUDENT: That was wrong of you...

STRANGER: Right or wrong, it's a fact. You were looking for the lady of the house, she isn't here, but she'll be here soon, like everyone else, they're drawn to the fire like moths...

STUDENT: ...to the candle!

STRANGER: You say that, but I should rather say – to the lamp, to choose a more poignant expression. – Anyway, conceal your feelings young man, if you can, I can conceal mine! – We were speaking of the lamp! What happened with the lamp?

STUDENT: Which lamp?

STRANGER: There you go! Lying and denying, all of you! – The lamp which stood in the cook's wardrobe, and which set fire to the house.

STUDENT: I know nothing of any such lamp.

STRANGER: Some people blush when they lie, others' noses go white. – This one has invented some new way!

STUDENT: Are you talking to yourself, sir?

STRANGER: Yes, I have that unfortunate habit! – Are your parents still alive?

STUDENT: No, they are not!

STRANGER: He's lying again, though without realising it!

STUDENT: I never lie!

STRANGER: Three times in this short while! I know your father, sir.

STUDENT: I don't believe you!

STRANGER: All the better for me! – Do you see this breast pin? It's beautiful, isn't it? But I can never see it myself, and get no pleasure out of it, while everyone else does. At least it's not egocentric, and there are moments when I would like to see it on someone else's cravat so I can admire it. Would you like it?

STUDENT: I don't understand... Perhaps it's better not to have it, as you say.

STRANGER: Perhaps! – Don't be impatient, she'll be here soon! Is it enviable to be young?

STUDENT: No, I don't find that it is.

STRANGER: You're not your own master, you eat other's bread, never have any money, can never speak in company, are treated like an ass, and when you're not able to get married you have to look at other people's wives, with all the dangerous consequences that brings. Youth! Humbug!

STUDENT: Yes, in truth! When you are a child you want to be grown up, that is to say fifteen years old, to take one's confirmation, get a top hat; then you want to be old, that is to say, twenty-one! So no-one wants to be young!

STRANGER: And when you grow really old, you wish you were dead. There's not much that's desirable remaining!
– Do you know you are going to be charged?

STUDENT: Am I?

STRANGER: Yes, the policeman said so just now!

STUDENT: Me?

STRANGER: Does it surprise you? Don't you realise that in this life you must be prepared for anything?

STUDENT: So what have I done?

STRANGER: You don't need to have done anything to be charged; it's enough to be suspected of doing something!

STUDENT: Then you could charge everyone!

STRANGER: Quite right, yes! You could put a rope around the neck of the whole family, if you wanted to be fair, but one doesn't want to be fair! It's a dreadful family, ugly, sweaty, stinking; dirty linen, filthy stockings with holes, chilblains, corns, ugh! No, an apple tree in bloom is far lovelier; see the lilies on the ground, it's as if they're not at home here, such perfume!

STUDENT: Are you a philosopher?

STRANGER: I'm a great philosopher!

STUDENT: You're just joking with me!

STRANGER: You said that so you can go! Get going then! Hurry along!

STUDENT: I was waiting here for someone!

STRANGER: Yes, I thought so. – But it's probably best to go to meet her!

STUDENT: Did she say that to you?

STRANGER: She didn't need to.

STUDENT: Then I don't want to be at fault...if that is the case... (*Goes.*)

●

STRANGER: Is that my child? Well, I suppose I was young myself once, for that matter; and it was neither

remarkable nor fun. – And I'm his... What more?
Besides...who knows? – – – Now I shall go and visit
Madam Vesterlund – she was in service with my parents,
was faithful and good-natured, and after she'd been
stealing for ten years she became the old retainer. (*Sits at
the table.*) Here are Gustavsson's wreaths of bearberry
twigs – which he sells as cranberry twigs – just as sloppily
bound as they used to be forty years ago – everything he
did was either careless or stupid, and that's why things
went badly for him. His self-knowledge excused him
much. What a fool I am! he would say, pulling off his hat
and scratching his head. – There's a myrtle – (*He taps the
pot.*) unwatered of course – he always forgot to water the
flowers, the fool...and then he expected them to grow!
(*The PAINTER comes into view.*)

What painter is this? I suppose he's from The Swamp as
well, and maybe has a thread in my weave!
(*The PAINTER has begun to stare at the STRANGER.*)
(*Stares back.*) Well, does he recognise me?

PAINTER: Is – it – Herr Arvid?

STRANGER: Was and is, if being is to be perceived.
(*Pause.*)

PAINTER: I ought really to be angry with you.

STRANGER: Do be, by all means! But let me know the
reason why! Things can normally be sorted out.

PAINTER: Do you remember...

STRANGER: I have, unfortunately, a remarkable memory!

PAINTER: Do you remember a boy called Robert?

STRANGER: Well yes, a big rascal who was good at
drawing!

PAINTER: (*Slowly.*) Well, he was to go to the Academy to be
a painter, an artist. But that was in the days when – colour-
blindness was fashionable. Yes, Herr Arvid, you were a
technician then and were to examine my eyes before the
guv'nor, your father, would agree to send me to painting
school... So you took two tangles of yarn from the dye
works; the one was reddish, the other green; and then you
asked me. I called the red one green and vice versa; and
with that my career was ruined...

STRANGER: Quite as it ought to have been!

PAINTER: No! – Because in actual fact, I could tell the colours apart, but it was the *names* I didn't know. I didn't discover that until I was thirty-seven years old…

STRANGER: That's a sad story; but I didn't know any better, and you'll have to forgive me!

PAINTER: How can I!

STRANGER: Want of knowledge is forgivable! – Listen to me now! I was going to join the navy; was examined in sailing as a cadet and was sort of seasick; I was turned down! But I don't mind the sea; the seasickness was because I had drunk too much. And with that my career was crushed and I chose another…

PAINTER: What's the navy got to do with it! I dreamed of Rome and Paris…

STRANGER: Oh well, one dreams of so much when one is young, and when one is old too! And besides, it was all so long ago, what's the point of talking about it now!

PAINTER: Listen to him! Do you think you can give me back the life I lost…

STRANGER: No, I can't! but I don't owe it to you anyway! The business with the coloured yarn I learnt at school, and you ought to have known the names of the colours. – Now get lost – one dauber less in the world can only be a service to humanity! – Here's Madam Vesterlund!

PAINTER: Listen to you talk! But you'll get yours!

●

(*FRU VESTERLUND comes in.*)

STRANGER: Good morning, Madam Vesterlund; it's me, Herr Arvid, don't be afraid; I've been in America, how are things going along? I'm extraordinarily well, and there's been a fire here, your husband is dead, he was a policeman, a really decent fellow, I liked him for his good nature and friendly manner. He was a harmless wit, who never wounded anyone; I remember one time…

FRU VESTERLUND: Oh my God! Is it my Arvid, who I nursed…

STRANGER: Yes, well that wasn't me, that was my brother, but no matter, it's just as good. I spoke of your husband who died thirty-five years ago, he was a kind man, a particularly good friend of mine...

FRU VESTERLUND: Yes, he died – (*Pause.*) – but I don't know if he was a particularly good man. – You're maybe mixing him up with someone else, Mr Arvid...

STRANGER: I'm not mixing him up... I remember old man Vesterlund well, and I liked him very much...

FRU VESTERLUND: (*Slowly.*) It's shameful to stand here and say it, but, he didn't have the best of natures.

STRANGER: Herr Vesterlund?

FRU VESTERLUND: Oh well...he had a way of getting in with people, but he never meant what he said...or he said it back to front.

STRANGER: What? Didn't mean what he said? You mean he was false?

FRU VESTERLUND: It's a shame to say it, but I think...

STRANGER: Perhaps he wasn't altogether honest?

FRU VESTERLUND: Well! He – was – a bit, well, he didn't mean what he said! Well, Mr Arvid, how have things been for you?

STRANGER: I can see it all now! – Think, what a villain! And I've gone around for thirty years speaking well of him, missing him, almost grieved his passing, I bought a wreath for his coffin out of my tobacco money...

FRU VESTERLUND: What is it then? What happened?

STRANGER: What a crook! (*Pause.*) Well! He tricked me one Shrove Tuesday; he said if you take away every third egg from the hens they would lay all the more. I did so, and was punished – nearly ended up before the magistrates... But I never suspected him as being the informer... He went into the pantry – The maids would come and empty the washing up bowls at all times of day – contrary to regulations[14], he never reported them!

---

14 Stockholm City Council, in 1859, restricted the disposal of waste water into the gutter to between the hours of 11pm and 7am.

– I can see him now in his true colours; and here I am
getting angry at someone who's been in the grave for
thirty-five years! – So he was satirical, and I didn't
realise it then! I do now though!

FRU VESTERLUND: Yes, he could be a little satirical, that
I *do* know!

STRANGER: It's coming back to me now... This
blackguard I've been speaking well of for thirty years!
And I went to his funeral, drank my first rum toddy...
And I remember how he used to flatter me, called me
The Professor! Squire! Ugh! – – – There's the
stonecutter! Go in now, Madam, otherwise there'll be a
row when he gets out his bills; go now Madam! We'll
meet again!

FRU VESTERLUND: (*Goes in.*) No, we won't meet again,
one should never meet again – it's never like it was
before, and they just turn a man's life to rubble. What
did you have to go and say all that for, when I had
everything sorted out... (*Goes.*)

●

(*The STONECUTTER comes in.*)

STRANGER: Come on!

STONECUTTER: You what?

STRANGER: Come on then!

(*STONECUTTER stares.*)

See my tiepin? – I bought it in London, in Charing Cross.

STONECUTTER: I'm no thief!

STRANGER: No, but you practise the ancient art of
rubbing out! You erase things!

STONECUTTER: It's true, but it was a villainous contract,
it was strangling me.

STRANGER: Why did you sign it?

STONECUTTER: Because I was in distressed circumstances.

STRANGER: That's a motive.

STONECUTTER: But now I've got my revenge!

STRANGER: That's nice!

STONECUTTER: And now *they* have to turn up.[15]

STRANGER: Did we never fight as children?

STONECUTTER: No, I was too young!

STRANGER: Haven't we ever lied to each other, or stolen something, or ruined each other's careers, or seduced each other's sisters?

STONECUTTER: No, but my father worked for the excise, and your father was a smuggler...

STRANGER: There, see! Always something!

STONECUTTER: And when my father failed to make any sequestrations he got the sack.

STRANGER: Are you going to take revenge for your father being an idiot?

STONECUTTER: Why did you say just now there was dynamite in the cellar?

STRANGER: You're lying again, sir! I said there could be dynamite in there, and of course, anything is possible.

STONECUTTER: Anyway the student has been charged! Do you know him?

STRANGER: Very little; his mother on the other hand was a maid in your house. She was both beautiful and kind. I went and proposed to her; in the meantime she became pregnant.

STONECUTTER: Aren't you the father then?

STRANGER: Oh no! But since paternity can never be denied, I am a sort of stepfather!

STONECUTTER: Then sir, you have been lied about?

STRANGER: Of course! It's very common...

STONECUTTER: And I was one of those who gave evidence against you...on oath!

STRANGER: I can well believe it; but what matter? Nothing matters! – Now let's stop tearing up the tracks otherwise we'll come back to the cat that killed the rat that ate the malt that lay in the house that Jack built!

STONECUTTER: But what about me – I've committed perjury...

15 I do not know what this line refers to.

STRANGER: Yes, that's not very nice, but these things happen...

STONECUTTER: It's terrible! Isn't it terrible to be alive?

STRANGER: (*With his hand before his eyes.*) Yes! It is, beyond all description, terrible.

STONECUTTER: I don't want to live anymore...

STRANGER: You have to. (*Pause.*) Have to! (*Pause.*) Now listen, the student has been charged, can he be released?

STONECUTTER: Hardly! – I'll tell you something, while we're having a nice chat: he is innocent, but cannot get his release; for the only witness who can prove his innocence, must by doing so prove his guilt – in something else.

STRANGER: Her with the hairpins?

STONECUTTER: Yes!

STRANGER: The old one or the young one?

STONECUTTER: You'll have to work that out for yourself; but it isn't the cook.

STRANGER: Imagine such a web! – But who put the lamp there?

STONECUTTER: His worst enemy.

STRANGER: His worst enemy lit the fire?

STONECUTTER: Ah now, that I wouldn't know! – Only the bricklayer knows that!

STRANGER: Who's the bricklayer?

STONECUTTER: He's the oldest in the building, some kind of relation to Madam Vesterlund, knows all the building's secrets; he has some secret or other with the guv'nor; he won't be a witness.

STRANGER: Who is the guv'nor's wife, my sister-in-law?

STONECUTTER: Yes! – She was the teacher in the house when the previous mistress ran off!

STRANGER: Is she of good character?

STONECUTTER: Character? Well now, I don't rightly know what that is. Do you mean what is her profession? Name and character it says in the census, but there it doesn't mean character, it means occupation.

STRANGER: I mean temperament!

STONECUTTER: Oh I see, well, a temperament changes to and fro doesn't it; with me it depends on who I'm talking to; with a decent person, I'm decent, and with a nasty one I'm like a wild animal.

STRANGER: But we were talking about the lady's temperament in general.

STONECUTTER: Well, nothing really; like most people; she's angry if you tease her; becomes nice once again; you can't always be in the same mood.

STRANGER: I mean, is she of a cheerful disposition or is she melancholy?

STONECUTTER: When things go well she's happy, when they go against her she's sad or angry, like all of us.

STRANGER: Yes, but what is her nature?

STONECUTTER: Yes, well it all comes to the same thing! – But as an educated person one has a polite manner, although, that is to say, she can be as crude as anyone else, when she has a mind to it.

STRANGER: This is making me none-the-wiser!

STONECUTTER: (*Pats him on the back.*) No, folk don't make you wise!

STRANGER: You're superb! – Well what do you think of the factory owner, my brother?
(*Pause.*)

STONECUTTER: Well, he's got a good way about him! More than that I don't know, because what he hides, I can't see!

STRANGER: Excellent! – Nevertheless! He's always got blue hands, but you know they're white underneath.

STONECUTTER: But you'd have to scrub them first, and he wouldn't allow it.

STRANGER: Fine! – Who are those young people coming along here?

STONECUTTER: The gardener's son and my daughter, who were meant to be getting married this evening, but have postponed it because of the fire. – I'm off now, because I don't want to embarrass them. – You know what I mean, a father-in-law such as I. – Farewell! (*Goes.*)

(*STRANGER withdraws to behind the tavern, but remains visible to the audience.*
ALFRED and MATILDA enter hand in hand.)

ALFRED: I had to come and see where the fire was – I had to –

MATILDA: What is there to look at?

ALFRED: I have suffered so much pain in this house, that I've wished fire upon it many times...

MATILDA: Yes, I know it stood casting its shadow over the garden, and now things will grow better, as long as they don't build another bigger house...

ALFRED: It's lovely and open here, fresh air and sunlight, and I've heard there's going to be a street...

MATILDA: Then you'll move perhaps?

ALFRED: Yes, we're all going to move, and I like that, I like new things, I'd like to emigrate...

MATILDA: Eugh! No! Do you know that our pigeons nested on the roof here, and when the fire started last night, they flew up and around at first, but then when the roof fell in they plunged down right into the fire... They couldn't be pushed from their old home!

ALFRED: But we must get away from here – away! My father says the earth around here has been sucked dry...

MATILDA: I heard that the cinders from the fire are going to be driven out to the allotments to improve the soil...

ALFRED: You mean the ashes...

MATILDA: Yes, it's meant to be good to sow seeds in the ashes...

ALFRED: New soil is better...

MATILDA: But your father, the gardener, he's ruined...

ALFRED: Not at all, he's got money in the bank! – Of course he complains, so does everyone...

MATILDA: Has he... Isn't he ruined because of the fire?

ALFRED: Not a bit! He's a cunning old devil, even though he calls himself an idiot.

MATILDA: What am I to believe?

ALFRED: He's got money to lend to the bricklayer here... and others.

MATILDA: I don't know where I stand. Am I dreaming? –
We've been crying all morning over your father's
misfortune, and over our postponed wedding...

ALFRED: You poor little thing! But the wedding will be
this evening...

MATILDA: Isn't it postponed?

ALFRED: It's been put back by two hours, until father can
get a new coat.

MATILDA: And we've been crying...

ALFRED: Wasted tears! So many tears!

MATILDA: It grieves me, they were unnecessary, though...
imagine father-in-law being so mischievous...

ALFRED: Oh yes, he's a big joker, to put it mildly. – He
always says he's tired, but it's just laziness, he's so lazy,
so, so lazy...

MATILDA: Don't speak any more ill of your father – let's
go away from here – I have to get dressed, and put
up my hair – and to think that your father isn't the man
I thought he was – going around fooling people, tricking
people like that! – Maybe you're like that too – no-one
knows who you really are!

ALFRED: You'll find that out later!

MATILDA: When it's too late!

ALFRED: It's never too late...

MATILDA: You're all so nasty in this building... And now
I'm afraid of all of you...

ALFRED: But not of me?

MATILDA: I don't know what to believe... Why didn't you
tell me before, that father-in-law was well off...

ALFRED: I wanted to test you, and see if you liked me as a
poor man.

MATILDA: That's what people say, afterwards, that they
were only testing; but now I can never trust anyone
again...

ALFRED: Go and get dressed now! I'll order the carriages.

MATILDA: Are we to have carriages?

ALFRED: Of course! – Closed carriages!

MATILDA: Closed carriages? This evening? Oh what fun!
Come on, come on! Quickly! Closed carriages!

ALFRED: (*Takes her by the hand and they skip out.*) Here I am!
— Hopla!

●

STRANGER: Bravo!

●

(*The INSPECTOR comes in, speaks softly to the STRANGER,
who replies in the same way, for about half a minute, after
which the INSPECTOR goes.*)

●

DYER'S WIFE: (*Comes in, dressed in black, stares at the
STRANGER for a long time.*) Are you my brother-in-law?
STRANGER: Yes. (*Pause.*) Don't I fit the descriptions or the
depictions?
WIFE: Frankly: no!
STRANGER: One usually doesn't; and I must admit, the
description I just now received of your person in no way
corresponds to the original.
WIFE: Yes, people do one another such injustice, and they
re-draw each other after their own image...
STRANGER: And they go about like theatre directors,
attributing roles to one another; some accept their role,
and others decline it, preferring to improvise...
WIFE: What part have you played then?
STRANGER: The Seducer! – Not because I've been one;
I have never seduced anyone, neither young girl nor
married woman, but I was once in my youth seduced,
and that's how I got the role. Strangely enough it was
forced upon me so I took it; and for twenty years I have
gone about with the seducer's guilty conscience...
WIFE: You were innocent then?
STRANGER: Why yes!
WIFE: How singular! My husband to this day still speaks of
the Nemesis which befell you, because you seduced
another man's wife.
STRANGER: I can well believe it. – But your husband is an
even more interesting case: he has put together a false

character for himself by lying; isn't it true that he is cowardly in all of life's struggles?

WIFE: Yes, he certainly is cowardly.

STRANGER: And boasts of his bravery which is nothing but brutality.

WIFE: You do know him well don't you!

STRANGER: Yes and no! – So, I suppose you have lived in the belief that you married into a respectable family that always distinguishes itself?

WIFE: I have thought so, until this morning...

STRANGER: Then it all fell to pieces! – What a web of lies, mistakes and misunderstandings! And this one is supposed to take seriously!

WIFE: Do you?

STRANGER: Sometimes! These days very seldom. I am like a sleepwalker on the edge of the roof. – I know I'm asleep, but I am awake – and I'm just waiting to be woken up.

WIFE: They do say you've been to the other side...

STRANGER: I have been over the river, but I don't remember any more than that – than that it is everything it was supposed to be! That's the difference!

WIFE: When nothing bears even touching, what is there to cling to?

STRANGER: Don't you know?

WIFE: Tell me! Tell me!

STRANGER: Grief gives you patience. Patience brings experience, experience brings hope; but hope doesn't let itself be disappointed.

WIFE: Hope!

STRANGER: Yes, hope!

WIFE: Don't you ever think it's fun to be alive?

STRANGER: Yes, of course; but even that is an illusion. Let me tell you, sister-in-law, that when you are born without a membrane over your eyes, then you see life and people as they are...and you would have to be a pig to thrive here in this mire. – When you've had your fill of illusions, then your eyes turn in upon themselves and

you look into your soul. And there you really find
something to look at...

WIFE: What do you see there?

STRANGER: Oneself! But when you've seen yourself, you
die.

(*The WIFE holds her hands in front of her eyes.*
Pause.)

WIFE: Will you help me?

STRANGER: If I can!

WIFE: Try!

STRANGER: Wait now! – No, I can't! – He is wrongly
accused; only you can set him free, but you can't. It's a
net that isn't set out by man...

WIFE: But he's not guilty.

STRANGER: Who is guilty?

(*Pause.*)

WIFE: No-one! – – – It was arson.

STRANGER: I know!

WIFE: What shall I do?

STRANGER: Suffer! It will pass! Even suffering is vanity.

WIFE: Suffer?

STRANGER: Suffer! But in hope!

WIFE: (*Holds out her hand.*) Thank you!

STRANGER: And take as comfort –

WIFE: What?

STRANGER: That you are not suffering innocently.

(*The WIFE bows her head and goes.*
The STRANGER walks into the ruins.)

●

DYER: (*Comes in, happy.*) Haunting the ruins?

STRANGER: Ghosts like ruins – Happy now?

DYER: Yes. I'm happy now.

STRANGER: And brave?

DYER: Who and what is there for me to hear?

STRANGER: I observe from your happiness, that you are
unaware of a particular circumstance... Do you have the
courage to suffer a reverse?

DYER: What's all this now?

STRANGER: You've grown pale?

DYER: Me?

STRANGER: A big reverse!

DYER: Out with it!

STRANGER: The police inspector was here just now, and he informed me...between ourselves...

DYER: What?

STRANGER: That the insurance premium was paid two hours too late...

DYER: Christ... What did you say? – But I sent my wife with the money!

STRANGER: But she sent the book-keeper...and he arrived too late!

DYER: Then I'm ruined!

(*Pause.*)

STRANGER: Are you crying?

DYER: I'm ruined!

STRANGER: Yes! Can't you bear it?

DYER: What am I to live on? Whatever shall I do?

STRANGER: Work!

DYER: I'm too old; I have no friends...

STRANGER: Maybe you'll get some now! An unhappy person is always likeable; I had my best moments in misfortune.

DYER: (*Wild.*) I'm ruined!

STRANGER: But in times of happiness and prosperity I was all alone; envy couldn't hide itself beneath friendship...

DYER: I'll sue the book-keeper!

STRANGER: Don't!

DYER: He'll pay for this...

STRANGER: You haven't changed! What's the point of living, when you haven't learnt anything!

DYER: I'll sue him, he's a villain, he hated me because I gave him a clip round the ear once...

STRANGER: Forgive him – as I forgave you, when I let you have my inheritance.

DYER: What inheritance is that?

STRANGER: Incorrigible! Merciless! Cowardly! False! –
Go in peace brother!

DYER: What inheritance are you talking about?

STRANGER: Listen, Rudolf, my brother, my mother's son
in any event, you had the stonecutter put away because
he erased...well...you rubbed out something in my
Christopher Columbus book, *The Discovery of America*
book.

DYER: (*Struck.*) What? What? What? Columbus?

STRANGER: Yes, *my* book which became yours!
(*DYER is silent.*)
Yes! And I understand why you put the student's lamp in
the wardrobe, I understand it all, but do you know that
the dining table wasn't made of ebony?

DYER: Wasn't it?

STRANGER: It was made of maple!

DYER: Maple?

STRANGER: The house's honour and pride, valued at two
thousand kronor!

DYER: That too? That was humbug too!

STRANGER: Yes!

DYER: Usch!

STRANGER: The debt is settled. The case is dismissed, the
matter can't be resolved, the parties withdraw...

DYER: (*Staggers out.*) I'm ruined!

STRANGER: (*Picks up his wreath from the table.*) I had
intended to go out to the cemetery with this wreath, to
my parents' grave; but I'll lay it here, on the ruins of my
parental home! My childhood home! (*Offers a silent
prayer.*) And so, out into the wide world again. Wanderer!

The End.

Opus 3

THE GHOST SONATA

Spök-Sonaten

(1908)

Characters

THE OLD MAN
Director Hummel

THE STUDENT
Akenholz

THE MILKMAID
(a vision)

CONCIERGE's WIFE

CONCIERGE

THE DEAD MAN
a consul

THE DARK LADY
the Dead Man's daughter with the Concierge's wife

THE COLONEL

THE MUMMY
the Colonel's wife

THE DAUGHTER
the Old Man's daughter

THE NOBLEMAN
called Baron Skanskorg[1]
fiance to the Concierge's daughter

JOHANSSON
servant to the Old Man

BENGTSSON
Colonel's footman

THE FIANCEE
Hummel's former fiancee
a white-haired old lady

---

1 Pronounced corry.

Corner of the façade of the ground floor and first floor of a modern house. The corner is formed by a rounded room on the ground floor and by a balcony with a flagpole on the first.

Through the open window of the round room can be seen, when the blinds are up, a white marble statue of a woman, surrounded by palms, brightly lit by the rays of the sun. In the window to the left there are potted hyacinths (blue, white, pink).

A blue silk quilt hangs over the balcony rail along with two white pillowcases. The windows to the left are hung with white sheets[2]. It is a clear Sunday morning.

In front of the house is a green bench; to the right in the foreground a street fountain; to the left a poster column. Upstage left, the entrance of the building, where the bottom of the staircase is visible, a staircase of white marble, a bannister of mahogany with brass. Laurels stand in large bowls on the pavement on either side of the doorway. The corner of the round room faces a side road, which seems to lead upstage. To the left of the entrance is a ground floor window with an angled mirror set up to reflect onto the street.

As the curtain goes up several church bells are ringing in the distance. The entrance doors are open; a woman dressed in dark clothes stands motionless on the steps. The CONCIERGE's WIFE is sweeping the entrance hall then she polishes the brasses on the doors, then she waters the laurels.

In a wheelchair by the poster column sits the OLD MAN reading a newspaper. He has white hair, a beard and glasses.

The MILKMAID comes in from the corner with bottles in a wire basket. She is dressed in summer clothes with brown shoes, black stockings and a white beret; she takes off the beret and hangs it on the fountain; she wipes the sweat from her brow, drinks from the scoop, washes her hands, straightens her hair, looks at her reflection in the water.

The bell of a steamer rings, and the bass of an organ in a nearby church pierces the silence now and then.

2 A sign of mourning.

After a couple of minutes' silence, when the girl has finished, the STUDENT comes in from the left. He is unshaven and he hasn't slept. He goes straight up to the fountain.

Pause.

STUDENT: May I use the scoop?
    (*The MILKMAID pulls the scoop towards her.*)
    Haven't you finished soon?
    (*The MILKMAID looks at him in horror.*)
OLD MAN: (*To himself.*) Who's he talking to? – I don't see
    anyone! – Is he mad? (*Continues watching them in
    amazement.*)
STUDENT: What are you looking at? Do I look that awful?
    – I didn't sleep last night, and naturally you think I've
    been out on a binge...
    (*The MILKMAID as before.*)
    Drinking punch? – Do I smell of punch?
    (*The MILKMAID as before.*)
    I'm unshaven, I know... Let me have a drink of water,
    girl, I've earned it! (*Pause.*) Right then! I'll have to tell
    you; I've been bandaging the wounded and tending the
    sick all night. I was there when that house collapsed last
    night...you know.
    (*The MILKMAID dips the scoop and gives him a drink.*)
    Thank you!
    (*The MILKMAID is motionless.*)
    (*Slowly.*) Would you do me a great favour? (*Pause.*) The
    thing is, my eyes are inflamed as you can see but my
    hands have been touching the wounded and dead bodies,
    so I can't safely touch my eyes... Would you take a clean
    handkerchief and dip it in this fresh water and bathe my
    poor eyes? – Would you? – Would you be the Good
    Samaritan?
    (*The MILKMAID hesitates, but does as he asks.*)
    Thank you, my friend! (*Takes out his purse.*)
    (*The MILKMAID makes a gesture of refusal.*)
    I'm sorry, how thoughtless, but I'm half asleep...

OLD MAN: (*To the STUDENT.*) Excuse me for addressing you, but I hear you were present at the accident yesterday evening... I was just reading about it in the paper...

STUDENT: Is it in the paper already?

OLD MAN: Yes, all of it; and your picture is here too, but they regret, they were unable to find out the brave student's name who...

STUDENT: (*Looks at the paper.*) Really! That is me! Well!

OLD MAN: Who were you talking to just now?

STUDENT: Didn't you see?

(*Pause.*)

OLD MAN: Would it be impertinent – to ask – your esteemed name?

STUDENT: What for? I don't like publicity – if you get praise, it's soon followed by criticism – denegration is developed to such a height – and anyway, I don't want payment...

OLD MAN: You are wealthy perhaps?

STUDENT: Not at all...the opposite! I'm destitute.

OLD MAN: Wait...I think I've heard that voice before... I had a friend in my youth with pronunciation like yours. I've only met one person with that pronunciation and that was him; you are the second – is it possible that you are related to Arkenholz the wholesaler?

STUDENT: He was my father.

OLD MAN: Strange are the ways of fate... I have seen you as a little child, in such painful circumstances...

STUDENT: Yes, they say I was born into this world right into bankruptcy.

OLD MAN: Yes, exactly!

STUDENT: May I ask you name perhaps?

OLD MAN: I am Director Hummel...

STUDENT: Are you...? Then I remember...

OLD MAN: You've often heard my name mentioned in your family?

STUDENT: Yes!

OLD MAN: And perhaps with a certain resentment?

(*The STUDENT keeps silent.*)

Yes, I can imagine it – I suppose they said it was I who ruined your father? – Everyone who is ruined by careless speculating thinks they have been ruined by the one person they were unable to fool. (*Pause.*) In fact your father stripped me of seventeen thousand kronor, which amounted to my entire savings at the time.

STUDENT: It's strange how a story can be told in two such conflicting ways.

OLD MAN: You don't, I suppose, think I am lying?

STUDENT: What am I to believe? My father didn't lie!

OLD MAN: That is true, a father never lies...but I am also a father, consequently...

STUDENT: What are you trying to say?

OLD MAN: I saved your father from wretchedness, and he rewarded me with all the dreadful hate that comes from a debt of gratitude...he taught his family to speak ill of me.

STUDENT: Perhaps you made him ungrateful by poisoning the help you gave him with unnecessary humiliation.

OLD MAN: All help is humiliating, sir.

STUDENT: What do you want from me?

OLD MAN: I don't want the money; but if you can do me some small service, I will consider myself well paid. You find me a cripple. Some say it is my own fault; others blame my parents. Myself I like to think it is the fault of life itself and its snares. If you avoid one trap you get caught in another – anyway, I can't go up and down the stairs, I can't ring bell-pulls, so I say to you: help me!

STUDENT: What can I do?

OLD MAN: Firstly: push my wheelchair, so I can read the playbills; I want to see what's being played tonight...

STUDENT: (*Pushes the wheelchair.*) Don't you have a servant with you?

OLD MAN: Yes, but he's gone on an errand...he'll be back soon... Are you a medical student?

STUDENT: No, I'm studying languages, but I don't know what I'm going to be...

OLD MAN: Aha! – Any good at arithmetic?

STUDENT: Yes, tolerably.

OLD MAN: Good! – Would you like a job perhaps?

STUDENT: Yes, why not?

OLD MAN: Fine! (*Reading the posters.*) They are giving the *Valkyrie* as a matinee... The colonel and his daughter will be there, and since he always sits on the end of the sixth row, I'll sit you next to him... Would you go away and telephone and book a ticket on the sixth row number eighty two?

STUDENT: Am I to go to the opera this afternoon?

OLD MAN: Yes! You are to do as I tell you, so you shall fare well! I want you to be happy, rich and admired, your debut yesterday as the brave rescuer will bring you praise tomorrow and then your name will be worth something.

STUDENT: (*Goes to the telephone kiosk.*) This is a strange adventure...

OLD MAN: Are you a sporting man?

STUDENT: Yes, that's my misfortune...

OLD MAN: Then we'll turn it to good fortune! – Go and telephone now. (*He reads the paper.*)
(*The DARK LADY has come out onto the pavement and is talking to the CONCIERGE's WIFE; the OLD MAN listens, but the audience can't hear.*
The STUDENT returns.)
Finished?

STUDENT: It's done.

OLD MAN: Do you see this house?

STUDENT: Yes, I've noticed it... I came past here yesterday. The sun was reflecting on the window panes – and, imagining all the beauty and luxury inside – I said to my friend: If one only had an apartment there on the fourth floor, a beautiful young wife, two beautiful children, and a private income of twenty thousand kronor...

OLD MAN: You said that? Did you? You see! I also love this house...

STUDENT: Do you speculate in property?

OLD MAN: Mm, yes! But not in the way you mean...

STUDENT: Do you know the people who live here?

OLD MAN: All of them. At my age one knows everyone, their fathers and forefathers; and one is always related to them in some way – I've just turned eighty – but no-one knows me, not properly – I am interested in people's destinies...

(*The blinds in the round room are pulled up: the COLONEL can be seen inside in civilian clothes; after looking at the thermometer, he withdraws into the room and stops in front of the marble statue.*)

Look, there is the colonel whom you will sit next to at dinner...

STUDENT: Is that – the colonel? I don't understand any of this, but it's like a fairy story...

OLD MAN: My whole life is like a book of fairy stories, sir; but although the stories are all different they connect by a thread, and the theme recurs regularly.

STUDENT: Who is the marble statue in there?

OLD MAN: His wife, naturally...

STUDENT: Was she really so adorable?

OLD MAN: Y-yes, yes!

STUDENT: Tell me!

OLD MAN: We cannot judge a person, my dear child! – And if I tell you that she left him, that he beat her, that she came back and remarried him, and that now she's sitting inside there like a mummy, worshipping her own statue, you will think I am mad.

STUDENT: I don't understand!

OLD MAN: I'm sure you don't! – And then there is the hyacinth window. That's where his daughter lives...she's out riding but she'll be home soon...

STUDENT: Who is the dark lady, talking to the concierge's wife?

OLD MAN: Well, you see that's a bit complicated, but it has to do with the dead man up there, where you can see the white sheets...

STUDENT: Who was he...?

OLD MAN: He was just a human being, like us, but what was most noticeable was his vanity... If you were a Sunday's Child,[3] you would see him come out through the door in a minute to look at the consulate's flag at half mast – he was a consul you see, he liked crowns, and lions, those fuzzy hats and coloured ribbons.

STUDENT: You talked of being a Sunday's child – they say I was born on a Sunday...

OLD MAN: No! Were you...? I could have guessed you were... I saw it in the colour of your eyes...then you can see what others cannot, have you noticed that?

STUDENT: I don't now what others see, but sometimes... well, one doesn't like to talk about it!

OLD MAN: I was almost certain of it! But you can tell me... I – understand such things.

STUDENT: Yesterday, for example...I was drawn to that obscure little street where that house collapsed... I got there and stopped in front of the building, which I'd never seen before...and I noticed a crack in the wall and heard the floorboards splitting; I ran forwards and snatched up a child who was walking beneath the wall...the very next second that house collapsed... I was saved, but in my arms, where I thought I had the child, there was nothing...

OLD MAN: Well, I must say...I thought so, but... Explain to me one thing: Why were you gesticulating just now by the fountain? And why were you talking to yourself?

STUDENT: Didn't you see the milkmaid I was talking to?

OLD MAN: (*In horror.*) Milkmaid?

STUDENT: Of course, the one who gave me the scoop.

OLD MAN: I see, so that's how it is? Oh well, I can't see, but there are other things I can do...

(*A white-haired WOMAN sits by the window with the mirror.*)

Look at that old woman in the window! Do you see her? – Good. She was my fiancée once, sixty years ago... I was twenty. – Don't worry, she doesn't recognise me! We see each other every day, without it making the least

3 According to legend, a Sunday's Child could be gifted with second sight.

impression on me, even though we once swore eternal fidelity, eternal!

STUDENT: How imprudent you were in those days! We don't talk about that sort of thing to the girls now.

OLD MAN: Forgive us, my boy, we didn't know any better! – But you can see that woman was once young and beautiful?

STUDENT: I can't tell. Well, yes, she has a beautiful expression. I can't see her eyes...

(*The CONCIERGE's WIFE comes out with a basket and strews fir twigs on the ground.*)

OLD MAN: Yes, the concierge's wife! – The dark lady over there is her daughter by the dead man, and that's how her husband got the job as concierge...but the dark lady has a suitor, an aristocrat, who expects to be rich, that is, he is getting divorced from his wife who is giving him a fine house just to get rid of him. This aristocratic suitor is the dead man's son-in-law; it's his bedclothes you can see being aired up there on the balcony... It's rather complicated, isn't it?

STUDENT: It's horribly complicated!

OLD MAN: Yes, it is, inside and out, and yet it seems so simple.

STUDENT: But who was the dead man, then?

OLD MAN: You just asked that, and I answered; if you could see around the corner to where the service entrance is, you'd see a crowd of poor people he helped...when it was convenient for him...

STUDENT: He was a charitable person, then?

OLD MAN: Yes...sometimes.

STUDENT: Not always?

OLD MAN: No! That's what people are like! Come along, sir, push the chair a little, push it into the sun, that's it, I'm so terribly cold. When you can't ever move, your blood congeals – I shall probably die soon, I know, but I have a few things left to accomplish before then – take my hand, feel how cold it is.

STUDENT: (*Recoils.*) It certainly is cold!

OLD MAN: Don't leave me, I'm tired, I'm lonely, but I haven't always been like this you see; I have an endless life behind me – endless – I have made people unhappy, and people have made me unhappy, I suppose the one cancels out the other – but before I die I would like to see you happy... Our fates are bound together through your father – and more besides...

STUDENT: Let go of my hand, you are draining all my strength, you're freezing me! What do you want?

OLD MAN: Patience, and you will see and understand... Here comes the young lady...

STUDENT: The Colonel's daughter?

OLD MAN: Yes, daughter! Look at her! – Have you ever seen such a work of art?

STUDENT: She's like the marble statue in there...

OLD MAN: It is her mother!

STUDENT: You're right – I've never seen such a woman of woman born. Happy is the man who can get her to the altar!

OLD MAN: You can see it! – Not everyone can appreciate her beauty... Well, so it is written!

●

(*The YOUNG LADY comes in from the left wearing a modern English riding suit, walks slowing to the door without looking at anyone. She stops and says a couple of words to the CONCIERGE's WIFE; then goes into the house. The STUDENT has his hands in front of his eyes.*)

OLD MAN: Are you crying?

STUDENT: In the face of hopelessness, there is only despair!

OLD MAN: I can open doors and hearts if only I can find an arm to my will... Serve me, and you will prevail...

STUDENT: Is it a kind of pact? Am I to sell my soul?

OLD MAN: No, not sell! – You see I have *taken*, all my life; now I have a yearning to give, give! But no-one wants to receive... I am rich, very rich, but I have no heirs, except a scoundrel who torments the life out of me... become my son, be my heir while I'm still alive, enjoy it, so I can watch you, at a distance at least.

STUDENT: What shall I do?

OLD MAN: Go and listen to the *Valkyrie* first!

STUDENT: That's already settled – what else?

OLD MAN: This evening you will sit in there in the round room!

STUDENT: How will I get in there?

OLD MAN: By going to the *Valkyrie*!

STUDENT: Why have you chosen me to be your medium? Did you know me before?

OLD MAN: Yes, naturally! I've had my eye on you a long time... But look up there, on the balcony...the maid running up the flag to half mast on account of the consul...and now she's turning the bedclothes...see that blue blanket? – That was for two to sleep under, now it's for one...

(*The YOUNG LADY, who has now changed her clothes, is watering hyacinths in the window.*)

That is my little girl, look at her, look! – She talks to the flowers, isn't she just like a blue hyacinth herself? ...She gives them water to drink, just pure water, and they transform the water into colours and fragrance... here comes the Colonel, with the newspaper! – He's showing her all about the collapsed house...he's pointing to your portrait! She's not indifferent...she's reading about your exploits... I think it's clouding over, what if it rains? It'll be just marvellous sitting here, if Johansson doesn't come back soon...

(*It clouds over and darkens; the OLD WOMAN at the mirror closes the window.*)

Now my fiancée is closing the window...seventy-nine... that's the only kind of mirror she uses, because in it she sees not herself but only the outside world, and from two directions; but the world can also see her, she hasn't thought of that... A beautiful old woman by the way...

(*The DEAD MAN in a shroud comes out through the door.*)

STUDENT: My God! What is it?

OLD MAN: What can you see?

STUDENT: Can't you see it, in the doorway? The dead man?

OLD MAN: I can't see anything, but I was expecting it! What's he doing?

STUDENT: He's walking out on the street... (*Pause.*) Now he's turning his head and looking at the flag.

OLD MAN: What did I tell you? He's come to count how many wreaths there are, and to read the visiting cards... Woe betide anyone whose card is missing!

STUDENT: Now he's turning the corner...

OLD MAN: He's going to count the poor at the service entrance...the poor are such a good decoration, 'followed by the blessings of the many', yes, but he won't get my blessing! – Between you and me, he was a villain!

STUDENT: But charitable...

OLD MAN: A charitable rogue, who always had his eyes upon a fine funeral for himself... When he felt the end approaching, he swindled the state out of fifty thousand kronor...now his daughter is in someone else's marriage, and is worrying about the inheritance...that villain hears everything we say, and he's welcome! – Here comes Johansson!

(*JOHANSSON comes in from the left.*)

Report!

(*JOHANSSON speaks inaudibly.*)

I see, not at home? You are an oaf! – And the telegraph office? – Nothing! ...Go on! ...Six this evening? Good! ...Special Edition? – With his full name? Student, Arkenholz, born...parents...perfect... I think it's going to rain... What did he say? ...I see, really! – He didn't want to? – Well, he has to! – Here comes the aristocrat! – Push me around the corner, Johansson, so I can hear what the poor people are saying... And Arkenholz must wait for me here...you understand? – Hurry up, hurry up!

(*JOHANSSON pushes the wheelchair around the corner. The STUDENT stays, watches the YOUNG LADY who is now raking the earth in the flower pots.*)

●

ARISTOCRAT: (*In mourning; talks to the DARK LADY who was walking on the pavement before.*) Yes, what can one do? – We must wait!

DARK LADY: I can't wait!

ARISTOCRAT: Is that how it is? You'd better go and stay in the country then!

DARK LADY: I don't want to.

ARISTOCRAT: Come over here, otherwise they'll hear what we're saying.
(*They move towards the poster column and continue the conversation inaudibly.*)

●

JOHANSSON: (*Comes in from the right; to the STUDENT.*) The master said don't forget that other matter.

STUDENT: (*Slowly.*) Listen – tell me first: who is your master?

JOHANSSON: Well! He's so many things, he's been everything.

STUDENT: Is he sane?

JOHANSSON: What is sane? – All his life he has been looking for a Sunday's Child, so he says, but that might not be true...

STUDENT: What does he do, is he a miser?

JOHANSSON: He likes to dominate... He goes around all day in his chariot like Thor...looks up at buildings, pulls them down, opens up streets, builds over squares; but he breaks into houses as well, crawls in through the windows, wreaks havoc on people's destinies, kills his enemies and never forgives. – Can you imagine sir, that this cripple was once a Don Juan, though he always lost his women?

STUDENT: How can the two go together?

JOHANSSON: He's so cunning he makes them leave him when he's tired of them... Anyway, now he's like a horse-thief at a human market, he steals people, in a variety of different ways... He stole me, literally out of the hands of justice... I'd made a mistake, well...
he was the only one knew about it; instead of getting me

locked up he made a slave out of me. I work just for my
food, and it's not such good food either...

STUDENT: What does he intend in that house?

JOHANSSON: Ah, well, that I wouldn't like to say! It's so
complicated.

STUDENT: I think I'll get out of this...

(*The YOUNG LADY drops her bracelet out the window.*)

JOHANSSON: Look, the young lady has dropped her
bracelet out the window.

(*The STUDENT goes cautiously to pick up the bracelet, and
hands it to the YOUNG LADY who thanks him stiffly; the
STUDENT returns to JOHANSSON.*)

So, you're thinking of leaving? That's not as easy as you
might think, once he's got his net over your head... And
he's not afraid of anything between Heaven and Earth...
Yes, one thing, or rather, one person.

STUDENT: Wait now, I think I know!

JOHANSSON: How could you know?

STUDENT: Let me guess! – Is it...a little milkmaid he is
afraid of?

JOHANSSON: He always turns away, when he comes
across a milk cart...and he talks in his sleep; apparently
once he was in Hamburg...

STUDENT: Can one believe what that man says?

JOHANSSON: You can believe him – every word!

STUDENT: What's he doing around the corner now?

JOHANSSON: He's listening to the poor people... He sows
words like seeds, plucks out bricks one at a time until
the house falls down...figuratively speaking... You see,
I'm an educated chap and I've been a bookseller... Are
you off now?

STUDENT: I don't like to be ungrateful... That man saved
my father once, and now he asks only a small favour in
return...

JOHANSSON: What's that?

STUDENT: I'm to go and see the *Valkyrie*...

JOHANSSON: That I don't understand... But he's always
thinking up new tricks... You see, now he's talking to the
policeman...he's always hanging around the police,

roping them in, getting them involved in his own
interests. He ties them to him with false hopes and
promises, and meanwhile he's getting secrets out of
them. – You wait, before the night is out he'll be invited
into the round drawing room.

STUDENT: What does he want there? What's between him
and the colonel?

JOHANSSON: Well...I can only guess, I don't know! You'll
have to see for yourself, when you get there!

STUDENT: I'll never be let in there...

JOHANSSON: That depends on you! – Go and see the
Valkyrie...

STUDENT: Is that the way?

JOHANSSON: Yes, if he says so! – Look, look at him in his
chariot drawn by the beggars in triumph. They don't get
paid a single öre, just a hint that they'll be treated to
something at his funeral!

OLD MAN: (*Comes in, standing up in his wheelchair, pulled by
a beggar, followed by others.*) Three cheers for the noble
youth, who in danger of his own life saved so many at
yesterday's accident! Hail Arkenholz!
(*The BEGGARS take off their hats without cheering.*
The YOUNG LADY at the window, waves her handkerchief.
The COLONEL stares out of his window.
The OLD WOMAN stands up by her window.
The MAID on the balcony, raises the flag to full mast.)
Applause, citizens! It is Sunday, but the ass at the well
and the ear of corn in the meadow give us absolution,
and even though I am not a Sunday's Child I have the
gift of prophesy and the gift of healing, for I have
brought a drowned person back to life...yes, it was in
Hamburg, one Sunday morning like today...
(*The MILKMAID comes in, seen by the STUDENT and the
OLD MAN; she stretches up her arms as if she is drowning,
her eyes fixed upon the OLD MAN.*)
(*Sits, then shrinks with fear.*) Johansson, take me away!
Quickly! – Arkenholz, don't forget the *Valkyrie!*

STUDENT: Is that all?

OLD MAN: We'll have to see, we'll have to see!

●

Inside the round drawing room: upstage, a white tilestove with a mirror; an ornamental clock and candlesticks; to the right a hall through which can be seen a green room with mahogany furniture; to the left a statue shaded with palms, perhaps hidden by curtains; upstage left a door to the hyacinth room, where the YOUNG LADY is sitting reading. We can see the COLONEL's back, as he sits writing in the green room.

The servant, BENGTSON, in livery, comes in from the hall with JOHANSSON, in white tie and tails.

BENGTSON: Now, Johansson, you will serve at table while I take their coats. Have you done it before?

JOHANSSON: I'm pushing a chariot around all day, as you know, but in the evenings I serve at parties and it's always been my dream to come into this house...
They're strange people, aren't they?

BENGTSON: Y-yes, you could say they're a bit unusual.

JOHANSSON: Is it a musical evening, or what?

BENGTSON: It's just the usual Ghost Supper, as we call it. They drink tea and don't say a word, or the colonel talks on his own; and they nibble at fancy biscuits, all of them at once, so they sound like rats in an attic.

JOHANSSON: Why is it called the Ghost Supper?

BENGTSON: They look like ghosts... And they've been doing it for twenty years, always the same people, saying the same things, or else they keep quiet to avoid feeling ashamed.

JOHANSSON: Isn't there a lady of the house as well?

BENGTSON: Yes, but she's gone barmy; she sits in a wardrobe because her eyes can't stand the light... She's in here. (*Indicates a jib-door in the wall.*)

JOHANSSON: In there?

BENGTSON: Yes, I said they were a bit unusual...

JOHANSSON: What does she look like?

BENGTSON: Like a mummy...want to see her? (*Opens the jib-door.*) There she is!

JOHANSSON: Jesus Chr–

●

MUMMY: (*Crowing.*) What are you opening the door for? Haven't I said it is to be closed...?

BENGTSON: (*Baby talk.*) Ta, ta, ta, ta! Be nice now Polly and you'll get something tasty! – Pretty Polly!

MUMMY: (*Like a parrot.*) Pretty Polly! Ooh, is Jacob there? Kurre! Kurre!

BENGTSON: She thinks she's a parrot...and she could well be. (*To the MUMMY.*) Whistle for us, Polly!
(*MUMMY whistles.*)

JOHANSSON: I've seen a lot, but never the likes of this!

BENGTSON: You see, when a house gets old, it gets mouldy, and when people sit together for a long time torturing each other, they go crazy. The lady of this house – quiet Polly! – this mummy, has sat here for forty years – same husband, same furniture, same relations, same friends... (*Closes the door on the MUMMY.*) As to what's gone on in this house – well, I don't know, do I... You see this statue?...it's her when she was young!

JOHANSSON: Oh my God! Is this the mummy?

BENGTSON: Yes! – Makes you cry, doesn't it! – But this lady, by the power of imagination, or something else, has taken on some of the characteristics of a parrot – she can't bear cripples, or sick people... She can't bear her own daughter, because she is ill...

JOHANSSON: Is the young lady ill?

BENGTSON: Didn't you know?

JOHANSSON: No...! And the colonel, who is he?

BENGTSON: You'll see!

JOHANSSON: (*Contemplates the statue.*) It's horrible to think... How old is she now?

BENGTSON: No-one knows...but it is said that when she was thirty five she looked nineteen and she led the colonel to believe that she really was... Here in this house... Do you know what that black Japanese screen is for, beside the *chaise longue*? – It's called the Death Screen, they put it up when someone is going to die, just like in the hospitals...

JOHANSSON: What a terrible house! And this is where the student longed to come, as if it were paradise...

BENGTSON: What student? Oh him! The one that's coming tonight... The colonel and the young lady met him tonight at the opera, and they were both quite taken with him. Hmm... But now it's my turn to ask questions: Who is his patron? That old man in the wheelchair...?

JOHANSSON: Yes, yes! – Is he coming too?

BENGTSON: He's not invited any way.

JOHANSSON: He'll come uninvited! If necessary...!

●

(*OLD MAN in the hall, wearing a frock coat, top hat, crutches, creeping forward listening.*)

BENGTSON: A right old crook, isn't he?

JOHANSSON: Fully fledged!

BENGTSON: He looks like the devil himself!

JOHANSSON: And he must be a magician as well! – since he can walk through closed doors...

OLD MAN: (*Comes and takes JOHANSSON by the ear.*) You crook! – Watch out! (*To BENGTSON.*) Announce my arrival to the colonel!

BENGTSON: Yes, but we're expecting company here...

OLD MAN: I know! But my visit is more or less expected, if not exactly longed for...

BENGTSON: I see! What was the name? Director Hummel?

OLD MAN: Precisely!

(*BENGTSON goes through the hall to the green room, closing the doors.*)

(*To JOHANSSON.*) Clear off!

(*JOHANSSON hesitates.*)

Clear off!

(*JOHANSSON goes into the hall.*)

(*Inspects the room; stands in front of the statue amazed.*)

Amalia! It's her... It's her! (*He wanders about the room touching things; straightens his wig in front of the mirror; returns to the statue.*)

MUMMY: (*From inside the wardrobe.*) Pretty Polly!

OLD MAN: (*Starts.*) What was that? Is there a parrot in the room? I can't see one!

MUMMY: Is Jacob there?

OLD MAN: A ghost!

MUMMY: Jacob!

OLD MAN: This is frightening...! Is this the kind of secret they were hiding inside this house? (*He stares at a portrait on the wall, his back turned to the wardrobe.*) There he is! ...Him!

MUMMY: (*Comes up behind the OLD MAN, pulls his wig. A voice like a parrot.*) Who's a funny fella?

OLD MAN: (*Jumps.*) Lord God Almighty! Who is it?

MUMMY: (*In a human voice.*) Is it Jacob?

OLD MAN: Yes, my name is Jacob, certainly...

MUMMY: (*With emotion.*) And my name is Amalia!

OLD MAN: No, no, no... Lord Je–

MUMMY: Yes, this is what I look like! – And I used to look like that! It's edifying to be alive – I live mostly in the wardrobe to avoid having to see and be seen... But you, Jacob, what are you looking for here?

OLD MAN: My child! Our child...

MUMMY: She's in there.

OLD MAN: Where?

MUMMY: There, in the hyacinth room!

OLD MAN: (*Looks at the YOUNG LADY.*) Yes, that's her! (*Pause.*) What does her father say? I mean the colonel? Your husband?

MUMMY: I was angry with him once, and told him...

OLD MAN: Well?

MUMMY: He didn't believe me. He just said, 'That's what all women say when they want to murder their husbands.' – It was a terrible crime nevertheless. It's made a fake out of his whole life, and his family tree. I read the peerage registry sometimes, and then I think: she's walking around with a false birth certificate just like a kitchen maid. She could end up in prison.

OLD MAN: There are many who do that; remember you gave the wrong year of your birth.

MUMMY: It was my mother, she made me...it wasn't my fault...! But you were the most to blame for our crime...

OLD MAN: Your husband provoked that crime when he took my fiancée from me! – I was born unable to forgive without having punished first – I considered it my overwhelming duty...I still do!

MUMMY: What are you looking for in this house? What do you want? How did you get in? – Is it about my daughter? If you go near her you must die!

OLD MAN: I mean her well!

MUMMY: But you must spare her father!

OLD MAN: No!

MUMMY: Then you must die, in that room, behind the screen!

OLD MAN: Maybe...but I can't let go once I bite into something...

MUMMY: You want to marry her to the student; why? He is nothing, and he has nothing.

OLD MAN: He'll become rich, through me.

MUMMY: Are you invited here this evening?

OLD MAN: No, but I intend to get myself invited to the Ghost Supper here!

MUMMY: Do you know who's coming?

OLD MAN: Not precisely.

MUMMY: The Baron...who lives above us, and whose father-in-law was buried this afternoon...

OLD MAN: The one who's getting divorced so he can marry the concierge's daughter...the one who was once your – lover!

MUMMY: And your former fiancée is coming, whom my husband seduced...

OLD MAN: What a lovely collection...

MUMMY: God, if only we could die! If only we could!

OLD MAN: Why do you keep company with each other, then?

MUMMY: Crimes and secrets and guilt bind us together! – We've broken with each other and parted so many times, it's endless, but we're always drawn together again...

OLD MAN: I think the colonel is coming...

MUMMY: Then I shall go into Adèle... (*Pause.*) Jacob, think what you are doing. Spare him!
(*Pause. She goes.*)

●

COLONEL: (*Comes in; cold, reserved.*) Please sit down!
(*The OLD MAN sits down slowly. Pause.*)
(*Looks fixedly at him.*) Is it you who have written this letter?
OLD MAN: Yes!
COLONEL: Your name is Hummel?
OLD MAN: Yes!
(*Pause.*)
COLONEL: Then I now know that you have bought up all my remaining promissory notes. Accordingly I am in your hands. What do you want now?
OLD MAN: I want to be paid, one way or another.
COLONEL: In what way?
OLD MAN: It's very simple – let's forget about the money, just allow me to be a guest in your house!
COLONEL: If you are satisfied with so little...
OLD MAN: Thank you!
COLONEL: And then?
OLD MAN: Dismiss Bengtson!
COLONEL: Why should I do that? My faithful servant, who has been with me all his life – he has the Fatherland's Medal for faithful service – why should I dismiss him?
OLD MAN: All those fine things, that's just your idea of him – He's not really what he seems to be!
COLONEL: Who really is?
OLD MAN: (*Recoils.*) True! But Bengtson must go!
COLONEL: Do you wish to run my home?
OLD MAN: Yes! Since I own everything you see – the furniture, curtains, cutlery, linen...and more besides!
COLONEL: What more?
OLD MAN: Everything! Everything you can see I own, it is mine!

COLONEL: Very well, it's yours! But my nobility and my good name remain my own!

OLD MAN: No, not even that! (*Pause.*) You are not a nobleman!

COLONEL: For shame!

OLD MAN: (*Takes out a paper.*) If you read this excerpt from the heraldic register, you will see that the family whose name you bear, died out a hundred years ago!

COLONEL: (*Reads.*) Certainly I have heard such rumours before, but I have the name from my father... (*Reads.*) It's right; you are right... I'm not a nobleman! – Not even that! – Then I will take off my signet ring. – It's true, it belongs to you... Here!

OLD MAN: (*Puts the ring in his pocket.*) Let's continue! – You are not a colonel either!

COLONEL: Am I not?

OLD MAN: No! For the sake of your name you were provisionally commissioned colonel in the American volunteer services, but after the war in Cuba and the reorganisation of the army all previous titles were withdrawn...

COLONEL: Is that true?

OLD MAN: (*Reaches for his pocket.*) Would you like to read about it?

COLONEL: Not, it's not necessary...! Who are you, that you have a right to strip me naked in this way?

OLD MAN: You'll see! But as regards stripping you naked...do you know who you are?

COLONEL: Aren't you ashamed?

OLD MAN: Take off your wig and look in the mirror, but take out your teeth as well and shave off your moustaches, let Bengtson undo your corset, and we'll see if servant XYZ recognises himself; the one who was a sponger at a certain kitchen...

(*The COLONEL reaches for the servants' bell on the table.*) (*Stops him.*) Don't touch the bell, don't call Bengtson, because then I'll have him arrested... Here come the guests – keep calm now, and we'll just carry on playing our old roles as usual!

147

COLONEL: Who are you? I recognise your expressions, the tone of your voice...

OLD MAN: Don't ask questions, just be quiet and obey!

●

STUDENT: (*Comes in, bows to the COLONEL.*) Colonel, sir!

COLONEL: Welcome to my house, young man! Your noble behaviour at the accident has set your name on everyone's lips, and I count it an honour to receive you in my home...

STUDENT: Colonel, sir, my low birth... Your distinguished name, your noble descent...

COLONEL: May I introduce Student Arkenholz, Director Hummel... Do please go in and say hello to the ladies, I must just finish a conversation with Mr Hummel...
(*The STUDENT is shown into the hyacinth room where he remains visible in shy conversation with the YOUNG LADY.*)
A superb young man, he's musical, he sings, writes poetry... If he were an aristocrat and of equal birth I wouldn't have anything against...well...

OLD MAN: What?

COLONEL: My daughter...

OLD MAN: Your daughter! – Talking of your daughter, does she always sit in there?

COLONEL: She has to be in the hyacinth room when she is not outside! It's a peculiarity of hers... This is Miss Beaty von Holsteinkrona...a charming woman...with a royal pension and an income perfectly suited to her position and circumstances...

OLD MAN: (*To himself.*) My fiancée!

●

(*FIANCÉE is white-haired, mad-looking.*)

COLONEL: Miss Holsteinkrona, Director Hummel...
(*FIANCÉE curtsies and sits.*)

●

(*ARISTOCRAT comes in, secretive, in mourning, sits down.*)

COLONEL: Baron Skanskorg...

OLD MAN: (*Aside without standing up.*) The jewel thief,
I believe... (*To the COLONEL.*) Let the mummy in, and
our gathering will be complete...

COLONEL: (*At the door of the hyacinth room.*) Polly!

●

MUMMY: (*Comes in.*) Krr-krr!

COLONEL: Shall I let the young people in too?

OLD MAN: No! Not them! They will be spared...
(*They all sit dumbly in a semicircle.*)

COLONEL: May we have in the tea?

OLD MAN: What's the point of that! None of us likes tea.
So let's not sit here shamming.
(*Pause.*)

COLONEL: Shall we converse then?

OLD MAN: (*Slowly with pauses.*) Talk about the weather,
which we already know, ask how we all are, which we
know; I prefer silence. You can hear thoughts and see the
past; silence doesn't hide anything, but words do. I read
the other day that the differences between languages
originate from primitive man's attempts to hide tribal
secrets from each other. Languages are therefore codes,
and whoever finds the key can understand any language;
but that doesn't mean you can't discover secrets without
a key, particularly where paternity has to be proved;
but proof before a court, that's another thing, two false
witnesses amount to absolute proof as long as they agree,
but in the case I'm talking about you don't take along
any witnesses; nature itself has given us a sense of shame
which seeks to hide what needs to be hidden; but we drift
into situations without wanting to, and opportunities
offer themselves now and then, when the most secret
things are revealed; the mask is pulled from the
deceiver, and the criminal is exposed...
(*They all look at each other in silence.*)
How quiet it's gone!
(*Long silence.*)

Here, for example, in this esteemed house, in this
charming home where beauty and education and wealth
are combined...

(*Long silence.*)

All of us sitting here, we know what we are...don't we...?
I don't need to say it...and you all know me, even
though you pretend ignorance... In there once again sits
my daughter, *mine*, you know that too... She had lost the
will to live without knowing why...but she wilted in the
air here, air that breathed crime and deceit and all kinds
of falsehood...therefore I sought out a friend for her, in
whose presence she could feel the light and warmth that
comes from a noble deed...

(*Long silence.*)

That was my mission in this house; to remove the weeds,
reveal the crimes, settle the accounts so that the young
may start afresh in this house which I give to them.

(*Long silence.*)

I now give you leave to depart each of you in turn;
whoever stays I will have them arrested!

(*Long silence.*)

Listen. The clock ticks like deathwatch beetle inside the
wall! Do you hear what it says? 'Time! Time!' – – –
When it strikes in a little while, then your time is up,
then you can go but not before. But it shakes its fist first,
before it strikes! – Listen, it's warning you; 'the clock
can strike' – – – I too can strike...

(*He brings down his crutch upon the table.*) Do you hear?
(*Silence.*)

MUMMY: (*Goes up to the pendulum and stops it; then clearly
and gravely.*) But I can halt the passing of time – I can
turn the past into nothing, undo what's been done; but
not with bribery, not with threats – but through suffering
and remorse – – – (*Goes to the OLD MAN.*) We are
wretches, we know that; we have transgressed, we have
erred like everyone else; we are not what we seem, we
are at bottom better than ourselves, for we detest our
faults. But that you, Jacob Hummel, with your false
name, to sit in judgement upon us, shows you to be

worse than we poor wretches! You are not what you seem
to be, either! – You are a stealer of men, you stole me
once with false promises; you murdered the consul who
was buried today, you strangled him with his promissory
notes; you have stolen the student by binding him to an
imaginary debt of his father's, who never owed you an
öre...

(*OLD MAN has tried to stand up and interrupt, but has
now shrunk back into his chair and shrinks more and more
during the following speech.*)

There is a dark part of your life which I don't really
know about, but can guess... I think Bengtson knows
about it! (*Rings the bell.*)

OLD MAN: No, not Bengtson! Not him!

MUMMY: So he does know! (*Rings again.*)

(*The little MILKMAID appears in the doorway, unseen by
everyone except the OLD MAN who is horror struck. The girl
disappears when BENGTSON enters.*)

Bengtson, do you know this man?

BENGTSON: Yes, I know him and he knows me. Things
can change as we know, I have been his servant, another
time he was mine. So, he was a sponger in my kitchen
for two whole years – since he had to be away by three
o'clock dinner was made ready by two, everyone had to
eat warmed-up leftovers after this ox! – but he drank the
juice from the meat as well so we had to make it up with
water – he sat out there like a vampire sucking all the
vitality out of the house, so we became like skeletons –
and he nearly had us all locked up when we accused the
cook of being a thief. Later I met this man in Hamburg
under another name. He was a money lender, a blood-
sucker; but there he was accused of having lured a girl
out onto the ice to drown her, because she witnessed a
crime he was afraid would be discovered...

MUMMY: (*Puts her hand over the OLD MAN's face.*) It's you!
Hand over the promissory notes and the will!

(*JOHANSSON, visible in the hall doorway, is watching the
goings-on with great interest, since he is now free from
thralldom.*

The OLD MAN takes out a bundle of papers and throws them on the table.)

(Strokes the OLD MAN on the back.) Pretty Polly! Is Jacob there?

OLD MAN: *(Like a parrot.)* Jacob is there! – Kaka? Dora!

MUMMY: Can the clock strike?

OLD MAN: *(Clucking.)* The clock can strike! *(Imitates the cuckoo clock.)* Cuckoo, cuckoo...! Cuckoo!

MUMMY: *(Opens the cupboard door.)* Now the clock has struck! – Get inside the wardrobe where I have sat for twenty years lamenting our misdemeanour. – There's a rope in there, just like the one you strangled the consul with, up there, and with which you thought to strangle your benefactor... Go!

(OLD MAN enters the wardrobe.)

(Closes the door.) Bengtson! Put the screen across! The Death Screen!

(BENGTSON puts the screen in front of the door.)

It is finished! – God have mercy on his soul!

ALL: Amen!

(Long silence.

In the hyacinth room the YOUNG LADY is sitting beside a harp with which she accompanies the STUDENT's recitation.)

STUDENT: *(After a prelude.)* I saw the Sun, it was as if
I'd seen the Hidden One;
A man receives as he has given,
Blessed is he who does good.
For your Deeds of Anger
Remedy no Evil;
Comfort those you have harmed,
Your kindness is its own reward.
No one is afraid who had done no wrong;
Goodness is an innocent thing.

●

A room decorated in a somewhat bizarre style, with oriental motifs. Hyacinths of all colours are everywhere. On the tilestove sits a Buddha with a slice of a root in his lap, and out of it has grown the stalk of

an Askalon plant with its spherical cluster of star-shaped petals!
Upstage right, a door to the round room where the COLONEL and
the MUMMY can be seen sitting idly silent; part of the Death
Screen is also visible. Left, a door to the kitchen and pantry. The
STUDENT and the YOUNG LADY (Adèle) are at the table; she at
the harp, he standing.

YOUNG LADY: Sing to my flowers!

STUDENT: Is that the flower of your soul?

YOUNG LADY: It is my one and only! Do you love the
hyacinth?

STUDENT: I love it above all others. Its maiden-like shape,
slim and straight which rises up from the root and rests
on the water then sinks its pure white roots into the
colourless liquid; I love its colours; the innocent and
pure snow-white, the sweet honey-yellow, the young pink
and the mature red, but above all the blue, dew-like blue,
the deep-eyed, the faithful... I love them all more than
gold or pearls, have loved them since I was a child
and admired them, since they possess all the qualities
I lack...but...

YOUNG LADY: What?

STUDENT: My love is unrequited, because these beautiful
flowers hate me...

YOUNG LADY: Why?

STUDENT: Their scent, so strong and pure, of the first
breezes of spring, that have drifted across the melting
snow, confuses my senses and numbs me, dazzles me and
forces me from the room, brings woe to my heart with
poison darts and sets my head on fire! Don't you know
the story of this flower?

YOUNG LADY: Tell it!

STUDENT: But first its meaning. The root is the Earth that
rests on the water or lies on the soil; now the stalk shoots
up, as straight as the world's axis and at its top, the six-
pointed starflower.

YOUNG LADY: Above the earth the stars! It's so grand!
Where did you get it from, how did you see it?

STUDENT: Let me think! – In your eyes! – It's a model of the cosmos... That's why Buddha sits holding that root. It's the Earth, and he's watching with his brooding eyes to see it grow upwards and outwards, transforming itself into a sky. – The poor Earth is to become heaven! That's what Buddha is waiting for!

YOUNG LADY: Now I can see it – isn't the snowdrop a six-pointed star too, like the hyacinth lily?

STUDENT: Exactly! – Then snowdrops are falling stars...

YOUNG LADY: And the snowdrop is a snow star...grown out of the snow.

STUDENT: But Sirius, the biggest and most beautiful of all stars in the firmament; it's a yellow and red narcissus, with its yellow and red chalice and six white beams of light...

YOUNG LADY: Have you seen the Askalon root[4] in bloom?

STUDENT: Oh yes, I have! – It bares its flower in a ball, a sphere like the globe of the sky, strewn with white stars...

YOUNG LADY: Yes. Oh God, so grand! Whose thought was that?

STUDENT: Yours!

YOUNG LADY: Yours!

STUDENT: Ours! – We have given birth to something together; we are married...

YOUNG LADY: Not yet...

STUDENT: What remains?

YOUNG LADY: Waiting, trials, patience!

STUDENT: Good! Test me! (*Pause.*) Tell me! Why do your parents sit so quietly in there, without saying a single word?

YOUNG LADY: Because they don't have anything to say to each other because the one doesn't believe what the other is saying. My father once put it like this: What's the point in talking, we can't deceive each other anyway?

STUDENT: What a horrible thing to have to hear...

4 The shallot.

YOUNG LADY: Here comes the cook... Look at her, so big and fat...

STUDENT: What does she want?

YOUNG LADY: She wants to ask me about dinner. You see I'm looking after the house while my mother is ill...

STUDENT: Do we have to be involved in the kitchen?

YOUNG LADY: We have to eat... Look at the cook, I can't...

STUDENT: Who is that enormous woman?

YOUNG LADY: One of the Hummels, family of vampires; she's eating us up...

STUDENT: Why isn't she dismissed?

YOUNG LADY: She won't go! We just can't beat her! We've got her for our sins... Can't you see that we're wasting away, we're being consumed...

STUDENT: Don't you get any food then?

YOUNG LADY: Yes, we get plenty of different dishes, but all the strength has gone out of them... She boils away the meat and gives us the strands of dry meat and water, while she drinks the stock herself. Everything she touches becomes dry; it's as if she absorbs moisture with her eyes. We get the grouts after she's drunk the coffee, she drinks from the wine bottles and fills them again with water...

STUDENT: Get rid of her!

YOUNG LADY: We can't!

STUDENT: Why?

YOUNG LADY: We don't know! She won't go. Nothing gets the better of her – she's taken all our strength!

STUDENT: Can I get rid of her?

YOUNG LADY: No! It has to be as it is! – She's here now! She's going to ask what it is to be for dinner, I'll answer this and that; she'll raise objections, and in the end it will be what she wants it to be.

STUDENT: Let her decide herself, then!

YOUNG LADY: She doesn't want to.

STUDENT: This is a strange house. It's bewitched!

YOUNG LADY: Yes! – but now she's turned back, when she caught sight of you!

●

COOK: (*In the doorway.*) No, that wasn't why! (*She sneers so that her teeth are visible.*)

STUDENT: Get out woman!

COOK: When it suits me. (*Pause.*) Now it suits me! (*Disappears.*)

YOUNG LADY: Don't get carried away! Practise being patient; she's part of the trials we go through in this house! But we have a housemaid too! Whom we tidy up after!

STUDENT: I'm sinking! *Cor in aethere.*[5] Sing!

YOUNG LADY: Wait!

STUDENT: Sing!

YOUNG LADY: Patience! – This room is called the Room of Trials – it's beautiful to see, but consists purely of defects...

STUDENT: Unbelievable; but one can overlook it! It's beautiful, but a little cold. Why don't you light the fire?

YOUNG LADY: Because it smokes.

STUDENT: Can't you clean the chimney?

YOUNG LADY: It doesn't help...! Do you see the writing desk there?

STUDENT: Extraordinarily beautiful!

YOUNG LADY: It wobbles; every day I put a slice of cork under the leg, but the housemaid takes it away when she sweeps, so I have to cut a new one. The pen is all covered in ink every morning and so is the blotting paper; I have to clean up after her every day the sun comes up. (*Pause.*) What's the worse thing you know?

STUDENT: Counting the washing! Ugh!

YOUNG LADY: That's what I have to do! Ugh!

STUDENT: What else?

YOUNG LADY: To have my sleep disturbed and have to get up and fasten the catch on the window...because the housemaid has forgotten.

STUDENT: And what else!

5 'Hearts on high' (Latin); invoking higher powers.

YOUNG LADY: To climb up on a ladder and mend the damper chord on the tilestove after the housemaid has pulled it off.

STUDENT: And what else!

YOUNG LADY: To sweep up after her, dust after her, to light the tilestove after her, she just puts the wood in! To watch the damper, dry the glasses, *re*-lay the table, pull the corks, open the windows to air the rooms, to *re*-make my bed, to wash out the water jug when it's green with algae, to buy matches and soap, which are always missing, to dry the lamp glass and clip the wicks so the lamps won't smoke and won't go out; when there are visitors I have to fill the lamps myself...

STUDENT: Sing!

YOUNG LADY: Wait! – First hardship, the labours necessary to keep everything unclean in life away from you.

STUDENT: But you can afford to have two servants!

YOUNG LADY: It's no help, even if we had three! It's troublesome to live and I get tired sometimes... Imagine another nursery!

STUDENT: The greatest of joys...

YOUNG LADY: The most costly... Is life worth so much trouble?

STUDENT: It depends on the payment one expects for the hardship... I wouldn't shrink from anything to win your hand.

YOUNG LADY: Don't talk like that! – You can never have me!

STUDENT: Why?

YOUNG LADY: You mustn't ask.

(*Pause.*)

STUDENT: You dropped your bracelet out the window...

YOUNG LADY: Because my hand has become so thin...

(*Pause.*

The COOK is seen with a Japanese bottle in her hand.)

There's the one who's eating me, and all of us!

STUDENT: What's she got in her hand?

YOUNG LADY: It's the bottle of colouring with the
scorpion lettering on it! It's the soya, that turns water
into soup, to replace the sauce, which you cook cabbage
with, and which turtle soup is made from.

STUDENT: Get out!

COOK: You suck the nourishment out of us and we from
you; we take the blood and you get the water back –
with the colouring. – It's colouring! – I'm going now,
but I'll stay anyway as long as I like! (*Goes.*)

STUDENT: Why has Bengtson got a medal?

YOUNG LADY: It's on account of his great merits.

STUDENT: Has he no faults?

YOUNG LADY: Yes, great faults, but you don't get medals
for those.
(*They smile.*)

STUDENT: You have many secrets in this house...

YOUNG LADY: Like everyone else...let's keep ours!
(*Pause.*)

STUDENT: Do you love honesty?

YOUNG LADY: Yes, to a degree!

STUDENT: A furious craving comes over me sometimes to
say everything I think; but I know that the world would
collapse if one were to be really honest. (*Pause.*) I was at
a funeral the other day...in the church – it was very
solemn and beautiful!

YOUNG LADY: Was it Director Hummel's?

STUDENT: My false benefactor, yes! – At the head of the
coffin stood an elderly friend of the deceased carrying
the funeral mace.[6] The priest, particularly, made a great
impression on me with his dignified bearing and his
moving words. – I cried, we all cried. – Afterwards we
went to a restaurant... And there we found out that the
funeral mace had been in love with the deceased's son...
(*YOUNG LADY looks fixedly at him to discover his meaning.*)
And that the deceased had borrowed money from his
son's admirer... (*Pause.*) The very next day the priest was

6 A ceremonial rod decorated with flowers and carried at the head of a
funeral procession.

arrested for embezzelling the church funds! – Charming, isn't it?

YOUNG LADY: Ugh!

(*Pause.*)

STUDENT: Do you know what I think about you?

YOUNG LADY: Don't say, I shall die!

STUDENT: I must, otherwise I shall die…!

YOUNG LADY: In the asylum you say everything you think…

STUDENT: Exactly! – My father ended up in a mad house…

YOUNG LADY: Was he ill?

STUDENT: No, he was healthy, but he was mad… It broke out suddenly under the following circumstances: He was, as we all are, surrounded by a certain circle of acquaintances, which, for simplicity's sake he called friends; they were a crowd of villains of course, as people are for the most part. But he had to have some company, he couldn't just be alone. Anyway, one doesn't tell people what one thinks of them, not normally, and neither did he. He knew well enough how false they were, he could feel their essential faithlessness…but he was a wise man and well brought up, so he was always well mannered. But one day he held a large party – it was in the evening; he was tired from the day's work, and from the strain of on the one hand, keeping silent, and on the other gossiping with his guests…

(*YOUNG LADY is horrified.*)

Well, he bangs on the table for silence, catches up his glass to make a speech… Then opened the floodgates, and in one long lecture, denuded the whole company one after the other, and told them how false they were. Then, exhausted, he sat right in the middle of the table and told them all to go to hell!

YOUNG LADY: Usch!

STUDENT: I was there, and I'll never forget what happened then…! Father and Mother fought, the guests made a rush for the door…and father was taken to the madhouse where he died! (*Pause.*) Keeping silent for too long creates stagnant water which then rots, and it's like that in this house too. There's certainly something rotten here! And I thought it was paradise, when I saw you coming in here the first time... I stood there on that Sunday morning and looked in; I saw a colonel who wasn't a colonel, I had a generous benefactor who was a bandit and had to hang himself, I saw a mummy that wasn't one, and a maid...and talking of maids, where is virginity? Where is beauty? In nature and in my mind when it's in its Sunday best! Where is honour and faith? In fairy tales and in children's games! Where is something that fulfils its promise?... In my imagination! – Now your powers have poisoned me and I have given you back the poison – I asked if you would live with me as my wife, we made up poems, sang songs, played music and then the cook came in... *Sursum Corda!*[7] Try once more to play fire and purple from your golden harp, try, I beg you, I'm on my knees... Alright, I'll do it myself! (*He takes up the harp but the strings make no sound.*) It's deaf and dumb! Imagine! The most beautiful flowers so poisonous, the most poisonous? It's a curse upon the whole of creation, and upon life... Why won't you be my bride? Because you are sick at the very source of life... I can feel the vampire in the kitchen sucking my blood, I think it is Lamia[8] suckling its children. It's always in the kitchen where children get the buds of their hearts cut, if it doesn't happen in the bedroom... There are poisons which deaden the sight, and poisons which open your eyes – I was born with the latter, because I can't see ugly things as beautiful, nor call evil good, I can't! Jesus Christ descended into hell; that was his wanderings upon

7 Latin: 'Lift up your hearts!'; first words of a prayer of thanksgiving.

8 Lamia: in Greek mythology, a demon with the head and breasts of a woman and the body of a snake, who lured away children from their mothers in order to feed upon their blood.

the earth, in the madhouse, the house of correction, the mortuary; and the lunatics killed him, when he wanted to set them free, but the bandit they let go, the bandit always wins sympathies! – Woe! Woe! To all of us. Saviour of the world, save us, we are lost!

(*The YOUNG LADY has collapsed, she is dying, she rings, BENGTSON comes in.*)

YOUNG LADY: Get the screen! Quickly – I'm dying!

(*BENGTSON returns with the screen which he erects in front of the YOUNG LADY.*)

STUDENT: The deliverer is coming! Welcome, pale one, gentle one! – Sleep you beautiful, unhappy, innocent girl, guiltless of your suffering, sleep without dreams, and when you wake again...may you be greeted by a sun that doesn't burn you, in a home without dust, by a family without shame, a love without blemish... You wise, gracious Buddha, sitting waiting for heaven to grow out of the earth, grant us patience in our trials, and purity of will, so that all our hope won't come to nothing!

(*The harp strings sigh; the room is filled with a white light.*)

I saw the sun,
it was as if
I'd seen the Hidden One;
a man receives as he has given,
blessed is he who does good,
Do not seek to atone your deeds of anger
with greater wickedness;
Comfort those you have harmed,
Your kindness is its own reward.
He has nothing to fear who has done no wrong,
Goodness is an innocent thing.

(*Whimpering can be heard from behind the screen.*)

You poor little child, child of this world of delusion and guilt, suffering and death; the world of eternal change, misjudgement and pain! God in heaven keep you safe on your journey...

(The room disappears; Boecklin's[9] 'Toten-Insel' forms the background; feint music, peaceful, pleasant, full of sorrow, can be heard from off the island.)

The End.

9 Arnold Boecklin (1827–1901), Swiss painter of landscapes and mythological subjects. 'Toten-Insel', the Island of Death, was one of Strindberg's favourite paintings.

Opus 4

THE PELICAN

Pelikanen

(1907)

Characters

The MOTHER
Elise, a widow

The SON
Frederik, a law student

The DAUGHTER
Gerda[1]

The SON-IN-LAW
Axel, married to Gerda

MARGERET
a servant

1 Pronounced Yerda.

A drawing room; door upstage to dining room; door to balcony, partially visible. Secretaire, writing desk, chaise longue with crimson plush counterpane; a rocking chair.

The MOTHER comes in, in mourning, sits down listlessly in an armchair; listening anxiously every few moments. Outside Chopin's Fantasie Impromptu (œuvre postume), *Opus 66, is playing.*

MARGERET, the cook, in from the upstage door.

MOTHER: Close the door, please.

MARGERET: Is Madam alone?

MOTHER: Close the door, please. – Who is that playing?

MARGERET: Terrible weather this evening, wind and rain...

MOTHER: Close the door, please, I can't bear that smell of carbolic and fir twigs...

MARGERET: I know, Madam, that's why I said the master should have been taken to the chapel straight away...

MOTHER: It was the children who wanted the funeral at home...

MARGERET: Why does Madam stay here, why don't you move?

MOTHER: The landlord won't let us, so we can't budge... (*Pause.*) Why have you taken the cover off the red chaise longue?

MARGERET: I had to put it in the wash. (*Pause.*) You know, Madam, the master took his last breath on that sofa: but in that case why don't you get rid of it...

MOTHER: I can't touch anything until the inventory has been made...so I'm stuck here, incarcerated, and I can't be in the other rooms...

MARGERET: Whyever not?

MOTHER: Memories...all the unpleasantness, and that horrible smell... Is that my son playing?

MARGERET: Yes! He doesn't like it in here; he's restless; and he's always hungry, he says he's never been properly full up...

MOTHER: He was always frail from the day he was born...

167

MARGERET: A bottle-fed baby should have especially good food after it's been weaned...

MOTHER: (*Sharply.*) Well? Has there ever been anything lacking?

MARGERET: Not exactly, but Madam oughtn't to have always bought the cheapest and worst food; and sending the children off to school with only a cup of chicory and a slice of bread, it's not right.

MOTHER: My children have never complained about their food...

MARGERET: Didn't they? Not to you Madam, they never dared, but when they got older they used to come out to me in the kitchen...

MOTHER: We have always lived in modest circumstances...

MARGERET: Oh no, you haven't! I read in the paper the master was taxed for twenty thousand kronor sometimes...

MOTHER: The money went!

MARGERET: Alright! But the children are frail. Miss Gerda, I mean Mrs Gerda, she's gone twenty now and she's still not properly developed...

MOTHER: What are you going on about?

MARGERET: Ah well. (*Pause.*) Shall I light the fire for you Madam, it's cold in here?

MOTHER: No, thank you, we can't afford to burn our money...

MARGERET: But the young master has been cold all day, he has to either go out or keep himself warm by the piano...

MOTHER: He's always been cold...

MARGERET: And why's that?

MOTHER: Be careful, Margeret... (*Pause.*) Is there someone out there?

MARGERET: No, there's no-one out there...

MOTHER: Do you think I'm afraid of ghosts?

MARGERET: How should I know... But I won't be staying here too much longer... When I came here it was as if I was doomed to watch over the children... I wanted to leave when I saw how the servants were mistreated, but I couldn't, or I wasn't allowed to... Now Miss Gerda is married, I think my mission is over, and soon it's going to be my day of liberation, but not yet...

MOTHER: I don't understand a word you are saying – the whole world knows how I have sacrificed myself for my children, how I have kept this house and done my duties. You're the only one who accuses me of anything, but I don't care. You can leave when you like, I don't intend having any more servants, when Gerda and Axel have moved into this appartment...

MARGERET: Good luck to you Madam...it's not in the nature of children to be grateful, and mothers-in-law aren't usually so welcome if they don't bring money with them...

MOTHER: Don't worry... I'll pay my way, and help around the house besides...anyway my son-in-law is different from other sons-in-law...

MARGERET: Is he?

MOTHER: Yes he is! He doesn't treat me like a mother-in-law, more like a sister, or even a friend...

(MARGERET pulls a face.)

I know why you're pulling faces; I like my son-in-law, there's nothing wrong with that, and he deserves to be liked...my husband didn't like him, he was envious, if not jealous, yes, he did me the honour of being jealous, even though I'm not young any more... Did you say something?

MARGERET: I didn't say anything! – But I thought someone was coming... It's the young master, that was his cough; shan't I light the fire?

MOTHER: It's not necessary.

MARGERET: Madam! – I have frozen, I have starved in this house, never mind that now, but let me have a bed, a proper bed, I'm old and tired...

MOTHER: It's a fine time to ask now, when you're leaving...

MARGERET: True! I forgot! But for pity's sake, burn all my bed linen that people have died on, so this house isn't put to shame in front of whoever comes after me, if there'll be anyone!

MOTHER: There won't be anyone!

MARGERET: Well, if there is she won't last long... I've seen fifty housemaids come and go...

MOTHER: Because they were bad people. All of you are!

MARGERET: Thanks very much! – – – Well! Your turn is coming! Everyone has their turn, it comes to us all.

MOTHER: I'll have had enough of you soon?

MARGERET: Yes, soon! Very soon! Sooner than you think! (*Goes.*)

●

(*The SON comes in with a book, coughing. He stammers slightly.*)

MOTHER: Close the door, please.

SON: What for?

MOTHER: Are you answering me back? – What do you want?

SON: Can I sit here and read, it's so cold in my room.

MOTHER: You, you're always cold.

SON: When you sit, you feel it more, if it's cold! (*Pause. Pretends to read first.*) Is the inventory finished?

MOTHER: Why do you ask that? Can't we get the mourning over first. Aren't you mourning your father?

SON: Yes...but – well, he's alright – I hope he rests in peace, the peace he was granted at last. But that doesn't stop me wanting to know how I stand – if I'm going to make it to the exam without borrowing...

MOTHER: Your father left nothing, you know that, debts maybe...

SON: But the business must be worth something?

MOTHER: There is no business where there is no stock, no goods, do you understand!

SON: (*Thinks first.*) But the firm, the name, the customers...

MOTHER: You can't sell customers...

(*Pause.*)

SON: Yes, I've heard you can!

MOTHER: Have you been to a solicitor? (*Pause.*) Is that how you mourn your father!

SON: No, it isn't! – But you have to take each thing separately. – Where's my sister and her husband?

MOTHER: They came home from their honeymoon this morning, and now they're staying in a boarding-house!

SON: At least they'll get enough to eat then!

MOTHER: You're always talking about food; have you ever had reason to complain about my food?

SON: No, not at all!

MOTHER: Tell me something! You remember how I was forced to live separated from your father before he died. You stayed here alone with him – did he ever say anything about how his business was doing?

SON: (*Reading his book.*) No, nothing in particular!

MOTHER: Can you explain why he left nothing, when he was earning twenty thousand a year?

SON: I don't know anything about father's business; but he did say the household was very expensive to run; and then he bought this new suite of furniture recently!

MOTHER: He said that did he? Did he have debts do you think?

SON: I don't know! He did have, but he paid them.

MOTHER: Where did the money go? Did he make a will? He hated me, and several times he threatened to leave me penniless. Perhaps he's hidden away some savings? (*Pause.*) Is there anyone out there?

SON: No, not that I can hear!

MOTHER: Dealing with the funeral and the business has made me nervous. – By the way, do you know your sister and your brother-in-law will have this flat, and you'll have to look for a room in town!

SON: Yes, I know.

MOTHER: You don't like your brother-in-law do you?

SON: No, not very much!

MOTHER: But he's a good boy, and clever! – You should like him, he deserves to be liked!

SON: He doesn't like me – and besides, he was unkind to father.

MOTHER: Whose fault was that?

SON: Father wasn't unkind...

MOTHER: Wasn't he?

SON: Now I think I heard someone out there!

MOTHER: Light a couple of lamps! But only a couple!
(*The SON turns on a couple of electric lamps.*)
(*Pause.*)
Wouldn't you like to take your father's portrait onto your room? This one hanging on the wall?

SON: What for?

MOTHER: I don't like it; the eyes are cruel.

SON: I don't think so!

MOTHER: Take it away then; you like it, you can have it!

SON: (*Takes down the portrait.*) Yes, I will then!
(*Pause.*)

MOTHER: I'm expecting Axel and Gerda... Do you want to see them?

SON: No! Not desperately...and I suppose I'll go into my room... As long as I can light the tilestove.

MOTHER: We can't afford to burn our money...

SON: We've heard that for twenty years! But we've been able to travel abroad on ridiculous trips just for show... and to eat in restaurants for a hundred kronor, the equivalent, that is, of four cords of firewood; four cords on one meal!

MOTHER: What nonsense!

SON: Yes, there have been some strange goings on, but I suppose it's all over now...just as soon as the settling up is done...

MOTHER: What do you mean?

SON: I mean the inventory, and that other...

MOTHER: What other?

SON: Debts, and unsettled business...

MOTHER: Oh yes?

SON: Meanwhile, can I buy myself some wool?

MOTHER: How can you ask for that now? You should start thinking about earning yourself some money soon...

SON: After my exam!

MOTHER: You'll have to borrow like everyone else!

SON: Who would want to lend me money!

MOTHER: Friends of your father!

SON: He didn't have any friends! An independent man can't have friends, since friendship consists of pledging oneself to mutual admiration...

MOTHER: You're so wise, aren't you, you must have learnt it from your father!

SON: Yes, he was a wise man – who was guilty of folly sometimes.

MOTHER: Listen to it! – Now, are you going to get married?

SON: No thanks! Maintain a companion for young gentlemen? be legal guardian to a flirt? Give your best friend, that is to say your worst enemy, an armoury of weapons to use against you... No, I'm too careful for that!

MOTHER: Whatever are you saying? – Go to your room – I've had enough of you for today! You've obviously been drinking?

SON: I always have to drink a bit, partly for my cough, partly so that I can feel as if I've eaten.

MOTHER: Is something wrong with the food again?

SON: Nothing wrong, but it's so light, it tastes of air!

MOTHER: (*Taken aback.*) Get out!

SON: And then the food has got so much salt and pepper in it, you get hungry from eating it! It's what you might call spiced air!

MOTHER: You're drunk! Go away!

SON: Yes... I'll go! I was going to say something, but that will do for today! – yes! (*Goes.*)
(*The MOTHER paces uneasily about the floor, pulls out drawers from the table.*)

●

(*The SON-IN-LAW hurries in.*)

MOTHER: (*Greeting him warmly.*) At last! There you are Axel! I've missed you! But where's Gerda?

SON-IN-LAW: She's coming later! How are you, how's everything going?

173

MOTHER: Sit down and let me ask you first, we haven't seen each other since the wedding. – Why have you come home so soon, you were meant to be away eight days, it's only three.

SON-IN-LAW: Well, it felt like a long time, you know what it's like, once you've finished with all the talking, it gets oppressive to be alone, and we were so used to your company, that we missed you.

MOTHER: Really? Yes, we three have stuck together through many storms and, well, I think I have been of some use to you.

SON-IN-LAW: Gerda is a child, she doesn't know the art of living. She has prejudices and she's stubborn, fanatical in some cases...

MOTHER: Well, what did you think of the wedding?

SON-IN-LAW: It went off very well! Very well. And what did you think of the verses?

MOTHER: Your verses to me do you mean? Yes, I doubt if a mother-in-law has ever had verses like that given to her on her daughter's wedding day... Do you remember the one about the pelican giving its blood to its young, you know I cried...

SON-IN-LAW: At first yes, but then you danced every dance, Gerda was nearly jealous of you...

MOTHER: Oh that wouldn't have been the first time; she wanted me to go dressed in black, 'in mourning' she said, but I didn't care for that; am I to obey my own children?

SON-IN-LAW: No, don't pay any attention, Gerda is an idiot sometimes; if I so much as look at another woman...

MOTHER: What? Aren't you happy together?

SON-IN-LAW: Happy? What's that?

MOTHER: I see, so you've been arguing already?

SON-IN-LAW: Already? When we were engaged we never did anything else... And now with me being discharged, and being made reserve lieutenant... It's priceless really, but it seems she likes me less as a civilian...

MOTHER: Why don't you wear uniform then? I must confess I hardly recognise you as a civilian. You're a completely different person...

SON-IN-LAW: I'm not allowed to wear uniform other than on duty and on parade days...

MOTHER: Not allowed?

SON-IN-LAW: Yes, it's a regulation...

MOTHER: Poor Gerda; she got engaged to a lieutenant, and she's married to a book keeper!

SON-IN-LAW: What can I do about that? One has to live! Talking of living, how's business?

MOTHER: Frankly, I don't know! But I'm beginning to suspect Fredrik.

SON-IN-LAW: Why?

MOTHER: He was saying such strange things this evening...

SON-IN-LAW: Sheep's head!

MOTHER: They're usually a shy lot. I'm not sure there's not a will or savings around here somewhere...

SON-IN-LAW: Have you checked?

MOTHER: I've looked in all his drawers...

SON-IN-LAW: In the boy's?

MOTHER: Of course, and I always search his waste paper basket, he writes letters and then tears them up...

SON-IN-LAW: Oh, that's not anything, but have you looked in the old man's secretaire?

MOTHER: Yes, naturally...

SON-IN-LAW: But properly? In all the drawers?

MOTHER: All of them!

SON-IN-LAW: But there's usually a hidden drawer in all secretaires.

MOTHER: I didn't think of that!

SON-IN-LAW: Let's have a look at it then!

MOTHER: No, don't touch it, it's been sealed by the solicitors.

SON-IN-LAW: Can't you get round the seal?

MOTHER: No! you can't!

SON-IN-LAW: Yes, look if you just loosen the planks at the back, all secret drawers are at the back...

MOTHER: We need tools for that...

SON-IN-LAW: No. We can do it without...

MOTHER: But Gerda mustn't know.

SON-IN-LAW: No, of course not...she'd only go telling tales to that brother of hers...

MOTHER: (*Closing the doors.*) I'll close the doors just in case...

SON-IN-LAW: (*Examining the back of the secretaire.*) Well, someone's been at it... The back's loose... I can get my hand in...

MOTHER: That boy... You see, I suspected him... Hurry, someone's coming!

SON-IN-LAW: There are some papers here...

MOTHER: Hurry up, someone's coming...

SON-IN-LAW: An envelope...

MOTHER: It's Gerda! Give me the envelope...quickly!

SON-IN-LAW: (*Gives her a large envelope which she hides.*) Here, look! Hide it!

●

(*A tug at the doors, followed by knocking.*)
Why did you lock the doors...we're done for!

MOTHER: Be quiet!

SON-IN-LAW: You idiot! – – – Unlock them! – Otherwise I will! – Get out of the way! (*He opens the doors.*)

GERDA: (*Comes in, dejected.*) Why have you locked yourselves in?

MOTHER: Aren't you going to say hello first, my child, I haven't seen you since the wedding; was it a good trip? Did you have fun? Tell me about it and don't look so gloomy!

GERDA: (*Sits on a chair, oppressed.*) Why did you lock the door?

MOTHER: Because it opens by itself, and I'm tired of nagging every time someone forgets to close it. We must think about how to furnish your apartment, you are going to live here, aren't you?

GERDA: We have to I suppose... I don't mind either way – what about you, Axel?

SON-IN-LAW: Yes, it's alright here and your mother will be comfortable here too, so...as long as we all get along...

GERDA: But where will you sleep, Mama?

MOTHER: Here, my child, I'll just put a bed in!

SON-IN-LAW: You're going to put a bed in the drawing room?[2]

GERDA: (*Pricks up her ears.*) Are you talking to me?

SON-IN-LAW: No, I'm talking to your mother... Oh it will sort itself out...we'll all have to chip in...and with the money your mother gives us we can live...

GERDA: (*Brightening.*) And I'll get some help with the housekeeping...

MOTHER: Of course, my child...but I don't want to wash up!

GERDA: How could you even imagine it! Anyway, it's going to be fine, as long as I have my husband to myself! They're not allowed to look at him...they did of course at the boarding-house, and that's why our honeymoon was so short...but whoever tries to take him, shall die! So now we know!

MOTHER: Let's go and start moving the furniture...

SON-IN-LAW: (*Stares at the MOTHER.*) Good! But Gerda can start here...

GERDA: Why? I don't want to stay here alone...when we've moved in, then I'll be calmer...

SON-IN-LAW: Alright, since we're afraid of the dark, we can go all three of us...

(*All three go.*)

●

(*The stage is empty; the wind whistles in the window frame and the tilestove; the upstage door starts slamming, papers from the writing table fly about the room; a potted palm standing on a console moves about furiously; a photograph falls from the wall. The SON's voice: 'Mama!'. Then 'Close the window'. Pause. The rocking chair moves.*)

---

2 In the original he uses the familiar form, 'du', where he would be expected to use the polite form, 'ni'. I think this familiarity is better conveyed by the actor than in a translator's contrivance.

MOTHER: (*Comes in, frantic, a paper in her hand. Which she is reading.*) What is it? The rocking chair moved!

SON-IN-LAW: (*Following her.*) What is it? What does it say? Let me read it! Is it the will?

MOTHER: Close the door! We'll all be blown away. I have to open the window because of this smell. It isn't a will – it's a letter to the boy, full of lies about me and – you!

SON-IN-LAW: Let me read it!

MOTHER: No, it will only poison you, I'll tear it up, thank God it never fell into his hands... (*She tears it up and throws it in the tilestove.*) Imagine, he's speaking from the grave – he isn't dead! I can never live here – He says I murdered him... I didn't! He died of a stroke, that's what the doctor said...but he says other things too, all lies! He says I ruined him! Axel, get us out of this flat soon, I can't bear it here! Promise me! – Look at the rocking chair!

SON-IN-LAW: It's the draught!

MOTHER: Let's get away from here! Promise!

SON-IN-LAW: I can't... I was depending on an inheritance since you all hinted at one, otherwise I wouldn't have got married – now we'll just have to take things as they are, and you'll have to think of me as a tricked son-in-law – and a ruined one! We'll have to stick together if we are to be able to live; we'll have to save and you'll have to help us!

MOTHER: You mean, I'm to be employed as a maid in my own home? I won't!

SON-IN-LAW: There's no choice...

MOTHER: You're a scoundrel!

SON-IN-LAW: Mind your tongue, old woman!

MOTHER: Your maid!

SON-IN-LAW: Think what it was like for your maids who had to starve and freeze, you won't have to do that!

MOTHER: I have my annuity...

SON-IN-LAW: That's not enough for a garret, but here it's enough for the rent, if we stay put...and if we don't stay put, I'm going!

MOTHER: Leave Gerda? You never loved her...

SON-IN-LAW: You know that better than I do... You rooted her out of my mind, you squeezed her aside, except from the bedroom, which she was allowed to keep...and if there is a child, then you'll take that away from her too... She doesn't know anything yet, she's sleepwalking, but she's beginning to wake up. You'd better watch out when she opens her eyes!

MOTHER: Axel! We must stick together...we mustn't separate... I can't live alone, I accept everything – but not the chaise longue...

SON-IN-LAW: I don't want to spoil the apartment by having bedroom furniture in this room – so that's that!

MOTHER: But let me get another one...

SON-IN-LAW: No, we can't afford it, and this one is very attractive!

MOTHER: Urgh! It's a slaughtering block!

SON-IN-LAW: Rubbish...but if you don't like it, all that remains for you is the garret and loneliness, the mission-house and the workhouse.

MOTHER: I give in!

SON-IN-LAW: Very wise...

(*Pause.*)

MOTHER: But just think, he's written to his son that he died murdered.

SON-IN-LAW: There are many ways of murdering...and your way had the advantage of not being punishable by law!

MOTHER: Our way, you mean! Because you were there and you helped, you goaded him into a fury and brought him to desperation...

SON-IN-LAW: He stood in my way and wouldn't move aside! So I had to give him a shove...

MOTHER: The only thing I reproach you with is that you lured me away from my home... and I can't forget that first evening, in your house, when we were sitting at dinner together, and we heard those terrible cries from below, in the plantation, we thought they came from the prison yard or the madhouse...do you remember? It was him walking about in the tobacco plots in the dark and

179

the rain, roaring out his soul with longing for his wife
and child...

SON-IN-LAW: Why do you bring that up now? And how
do we know it was him anyway?

MOTHER: It was in his letter!

SON-IN-LAW: So, what is it to us? He was no angel...

MOTHER: No, he wasn't, but he had human feelings, yes,
sometimes; a little more than you have...

SON-IN-LAW: Your sympathies are turning around...

MOTHER: Don't be angry now! We must keep the peace!

SON-IN-LAW: We have to, we're doomed...

(*Hoarse cries from within.*)

MOTHER: What is it? Do you hear! It's him...

SON-IN-LAW: (*Roughly.*) Which him?

(*The MOTHER listens.*)

Who is it? – The boy! He must have been drinking
again!

MOTHER: Is it Fredrik? It sounded so like him – I thought
– – – I can't bear it! What's the matter with him then?

SON-IN-LAW: Go and have a look! The scoundrel is
drunk! I expect!

MOTHER: Is that what you call him? He is my son, at
least!

SON-IN-LAW: Yes, he's your son! (*He takes out his watch.*)

MOTHER: What are you looking at the time for? Don't
you want to stay until evening?

SON-IN-LAW: No thanks, I don't drink tea water or eat
rancid anchovies...or eat porridge...and anyway I have a
meeting...

MOTHER: What meeting?

SON-IN-LAW: Business, that doesn't concern you! Do you
intend to start behaving like a mother-in-law?

MOTHER: Are you leaving your wife alone on the first
evening in your new home?

SON-IN-LAW: That doesn't concern you either! – – –

MOTHER: Now I know what lies ahead for me – and my
children! Off come the masks –

SON-IN-LAW: That's right, off they come!

Same set. Outside is playing Goddard's 'Berceuse', from Jocelyn. *GERDA sits at the writing table.*

Long pause.

SON: (*Comes in.*) Are you alone?

GERDA: Yes! Mama is in the kitchen.

SON: Where's Axel then?

GERDA: He's at a meeting... Sit down and talk, Fredrik, keep me company!

SON: (*Sits.*) Yes, I believe we've never really talked before, we avoided each other, we had nothing in common...

GERDA: You were always on father's side, and I was always on mother's.

SON: Perhaps that will change now! – Did you ever know your father?

GERDA: That's a strange question! But I only ever saw him through Mama's eyes...

SON: But surely you saw that he loved you!

GERDA: Why did he want to stop my engagement?

SON: Because he didn't think your husband was the kind of support you needed!

GERDA: He got his punishment, when Mama left him.

SON: Was it your husband persuaded her to leave?

GERDA: It was both of us! So that Father should know how it felt to be separated from someone, since he wanted to separate me from my fiancé.

SON: And that shortened his life... Believe me, he only wanted what was best for you!

GERDA: You stayed with him, what did he say? How did he take it?

SON: I can't describe his suffering...

GERDA: So what did he say about her?

SON: Nothing!... Anyway, after what I've seen, I'm never getting married. (*Pause.*) Are you happy, Gerda?

GERDA: Yes! When you get what you want, you are happy!

SON: Why has your husband left you here on your first evening?

GERDA: He had a business meeting!

SON: The restaurant?

GERDA: What? Are you sure?

SON: I thought you knew!

GERDA: (*Cries into her hands.*) Oh God, my God!

SON: I'm sorry, I've hurt you!

GERDA: Hurt me, yes! Hurt! I wish I could die!

SON: Why didn't you stay longer on your honeymoon?

GERDA: He was worried about business, he wanted to see
Mama, he missed her, he can't be away from her...
(*They stare at each other.*)

SON: I see. (*Pause.*) Was it a pleasant trip otherwise?

GERDA: Oh yes!

SON: Poor Gerda!

GERDA: What do you mean?

SON: Well, you know how curious mother is, she can use a
telephone better than anyone!

GERDA: What? Has she been spying?

SON: She always spies...she's probably behind the door
now listening to this conversation...

GERDA: You always think the worst of our mother.

SON: And you always think the best! I wonder why that is?
You know what she's like...

GERDA: No! I don't and I don't want to...

SON: Ah! So you don't want to know; you have some
interest in not knowing...

GERDA: Stop it! I'm sleepwalking, I know, but I don't want
to be woken up! I couldn't bear to live!

SON: Don't you think we're all sleepwalking then? – I'm
studying law as you know, court proceedings. So, I'm
reading about big criminals, they can't explain how it all
happened...they thought what they were doing was right,
up until the moment they were caught and then they
woke up! If it isn't a dream, it has to be a sleep!

GERDA: Let me sleep! I know I'll wake up eventually, but
don't let it be now! Ugh! All those things I don't know
but only suspect! Do you remember as a child...people
said one was wicked if one simply told the truth...

'You are so wicked,' they always said to me, if I said that
something bad was bad...so I learned to keep quiet...
then I was liked for my nice manners; so I learned to say
things I didn't mean and then I was ready to step out
into life.

SON: One is almost expected to gloss over people's faults
and weaknesses, it is true... but then to sneak and
flatter... It's difficult to know how one is meant to be...
sometimes it's your duty to speak up...

GERDA: Quiet!

SON: All right, I'll be quiet!
(*Pause.*)

GERDA: No, keep talking, but not about that! I can hear
your thoughts in the silence!... When people come
together they talk, talk endlessly just to hide their
thoughts...to forget, to numb themselves... They like to
hear all about others, but everything about themselves
they hide!

SON: Poor Gerda!

GERDA: Do you know what hurts me most? (*Pause.*) It is to
see that life's greatest happiness is just emptiness!

SON: Now you've said something!

GERDA: I'm cold, light the fire!

SON: Are you cold too?

GERDA: I've always been cold and hungry!

SON: You too! It's strange here in this house! – But if I go
out now to fetch wood for the fire – there will be hell to
pay!

GERDA: Perhaps there's already a fire made up; Mama
usually puts wood in just to fool us...

SON: (*Goes to the tilestove and opens its grates.*) Yes! There's
plenty of wood in here! (*Pause.*) But what's this? – A
letter! Torn up, we can use it to light the fire...

GERDA: Fredrik, don't light it, we'll get nagged into
eternity, come and sit down again and we can talk...
(*The SON goes and sits, putting the letter on the table beside
him.*
Pause.)
Do you know why Father hated my husband like he did?

183

SON: Yes, your Axel came and took his daughter and his wife away from him, so he was left all alone; and the old man noticed that someone was getting better food than he was; you locked yourselves into the drawing room and read, and played music, but always something Father didn't like; he was squeezed out, eaten out of his own home, and that's why he ended up going around the bars.

GERDA: We didn't realise what we were doing...poor Father! It's good to have parents with an irreproachable name and reputation, and we should be grateful...do you remember their silver wedding, such speeches and verses people made in their honour!

SON: I remember, but I thought it was farcical to celebrate a marriage as being happy when really it had been a dog's life...

GERDA: Fredrik!

SON: I can't help it, you know the way they lived...don't you remember when Mama tried to jump out of the window and we had to hold her back?

GERDA: Be quiet!

SON: There were reasons behind it all we don't know about...and when they were getting divorced, and I was looking after the old man, he often seemed to want to talk, but the words never got off his tongue... I dream about him sometimes...

GERDA: So do I! And when I see him...he is thirty years old, he looks at me in a kindly way, full of meaning, but I don't understand what he wants...sometimes Mama is there; he's not angry with her, because he loved her, despite everything, right up until the end. You remember what beautiful things he said about her at their silver wedding, how he thanked her, despite everything...

SON: Despite everything! That says a lot, and yet not enough.

GERDA: But it was beautiful! She had one great merit though...she looked after her home!

SON: Yes, that's the big question!

GERDA: What do you mean?

SON: You see. You stick together! As soon as housekeeping is mentioned, you're all suddenly on the same side...it's like freemasonry, or a Camorra... I've even asked old Margeret, who is my friend, about this household's economy, I've asked why one never gets enough to eat here, and that talkative person is suddenly silent, silent and angry...can you explain that?

GERDA: (*Short.*) No!

SON: Now it seems you are a freemason too!

GERDA: I don't know what you mean.

SON: Sometimes I wonder if father fell victim to that Camorra, which he must have discovered.

GERDA: Sometimes you talk like a madman...

SON: I remember Father used that word Camorra occasionally, as a joke, but in the end he kept quiet...

GERDA: It's horribly cold in here, like a grave...

SON: Then I'll light the tilestove, whatever it costs! (*He picks up the torn-up letter, without thinking, then his eyes light upon it and he begins to read.*) What's this? (*Pause.*) 'To my son'!... In Father's handwriting! (*Pause.*) It's to me! (*He reads. Falls into a chair and continues in silence.*)

GERDA: What are you reading, what is it?

SON: It's horrible! (*Pause.*) It's absolutely terrible!

GERDA: Tell me what it is!
(*Pause.*)

SON: This is too dreadful... (*To GERDA.*) It's a letter from my dead father, to me! (*Reads on.*) Now I'm waking up from my sleep! (*He throws himself onto the chaise longue and cries, but puts the letter in his pocket.*)

GERDA: (*Kneeling beside him.*) What is it? Fredrik? Tell me what it is. – My little brother – are you ill, tell me, tell me!

SON: (*Sitting up.*) I can't live anymore!

GERDA: Tell me then!

SON: It's too incredible... (*Recovering himself, getting up.*)

GERDA: It might not be true!

SON: (*Annoyed.*) He wouldn't lie from the grave...

GERDA: Maybe he was tormented by hallucinations...

SON: Camorra! Is it you again; then I'll tell you! – – –
Listen!

GERDA: I feel as if I know already; but I still don't
believe it!

SON: You don't want to believe it! – But here it is anyway!
She who gave us life was a thief!

GERDA: No!

SON: She stole the housekeeping money, faked the bills,
bought the worst food for the highest prices, she ate in
the kitchen in the morning and then let us have the
diluted warmed-up leftovers, she skimmed the cream off
the milk, that's why we children are such failures, always
ill and hungry; she stole from the firewood money, so we
had to freeze. When Father found out about it he warned
her, and she promised it would get better but she carried
on, discovering new ways such as the soya and the
cayenne pepper!

GERDA: I don't believe a word!

SON: Camorra! – But here comes the worst! That ruffian, who
is now your husband, Gerda, he never loved you, he loved
your mother!

GERDA: Oh!

SON: When Father found out, and when your husband
borrowed money from our mother, then the villain
crowned the whole thing off by proposing to you! That's
the general outline, I leave you to work out the details...

GERDA: (*Crying into her handkerchief, then.*) I knew this
already, and yet I didn't know...it never reached...inside
my mind, because it was too much!

SON: What can be done now, to save you from
humiliation?

GERDA: Run away!

SON: Where to?

GERDA: I don't know!

SON: The other words, wait and see how things develop!

GERDA: You're defenceless against your own mother; a
mother is holy...

SON: The devil she is!

GERDA: Don't say that!

SON: She is as cunning as an animal, except that her self-love blinds her sometimes...

GERDA: Let's escape!

SON: Where to? No, stay until the villain drives her out of the house! – Sssh, the villain is coming home! – Sssh! – Gerda, now you and I will be freemasons! I'll give you the password: 'He beat you on your wedding night'!

GERDA: Remind me often! otherwise I'll forget! I'd so like to forget!

SON: Our lives are ruined...nothing to respect, or look up to...you can't just forget...let's live to get redress for us, and for Father's memory!

GERDA: And find justice!

SON: Justice? Revenge!

●

(*The SON-IN-LAW comes in.*)

GERDA: (*False.*) Well, how do you do! – Was it fun at the meeting, was the food nice?

SON-IN-LAW: It was cancelled!

GERDA: Was it closed, did you say?

SON-IN-LAW: I said it was cancelled!

GERDA: And are you going to see to things at home now?

SON-IN-LAW: You're very amusing this evening! But then Fredrik is such jolly company!

GERDA: We've been playing freemasons!

SON-IN-LAW: Be careful!

SON: Then we can play Camorra instead! Or Vendetta!

SON-IN-LAW: (*Uneasy.*) You're talking very strangely, what have you been up to? Secrets, is it?

GERDA: You don't tell us your secrets, do you? Or maybe you don't have any?

SON-IN-LAW: What's happened? Has someone been here?

SON: Gerda and I have been clairvoyants. We've had a visit from a departed spirit.

SON-IN-LAW: Can we finish with this joke now, before it gets nasty! It suits you though, Gerda, to be a bit merrier, you're usually so glum. (*He goes to stroke her chin but she pulls away.*) Are you afraid of me?

GERDA: (*In an outburst.*) Not a bit! There are feelings that are like fear but are something else, there are gestures that say more than the expressions on your face, and words that hide what neither gestures nor expressions can show...

(*The SON-IN-LAW is taken aback, runs his fingers along a bookshelf.*

The SON stands up from the rocking chair which continues to rock by itself until the MOTHER comes in.)

Here comes Mother with the porridge!

SON-IN-LAW: Is it...

●

MOTHER: (*Comes in, sees the rocking chair moving; she is afraid, but then calms herself.*) Do you want to come and have some porridge?

SON-IN-LAW: No thanks! If it's oats, then go and give it to the bloodhounds, if you've got any, and if it's rye, you can put it on your boils...

MOTHER: We are poor, we have to save...

SON-IN-LAW: You're not poor when you've got twenty thousand!

SON: You are, if you lend it to someone who doesn't pay it back!

SON-IN-LAW: What? Is the boy mad?

SON: He has been perhaps!

MOTHER: Are you coming?

GERDA: Come! Let's go in. Cheer up, gentlemen! I'm going to give you beef and sandwiches...

MOTHER: You?

GERDA: Yes, me, in my own house.

MOTHER: Listen to her!

GERDA: (*Indicates the door.*) Come along, gentlemen!

SON-IN-LAW: (*To MOTHER.*) What's going on?

MOTHER: Owls in the moss!

SON-IN-LAW: So it seems!

GERDA: Come along, gentlemen!

(*They all move towards the door.*)

MOTHER: (*To SON-IN-LAW.*) Did you see the rocking chair move? His rocking chair!

SON-IN-LAW: No, I didn't. But I saw something else!

●

(*Same set. A waltz, 'Il me disait' by Ferraris, is playing. GERDA is sitting with a book.*)

MOTHER: (*Comes in.*) Recognise it?

GERDA: The waltz? Yes!

MOTHER: Your wedding waltz, that I danced until dawn!

GERDA: Me? – Where's Axel?

MOTHER: What's that got to do with me?

GERDA: Oh dear! Have you been arguing already?

(*Pause. Makes a grimace.*)

MOTHER: What are you reading, my child?

GERDA: The recipe book! But why doesn't it say how long things should be cooked?

MOTHER: (*Abashed.*) It depends so much, tastes vary, some people do it this way, some that...

GERDA: I don't understand that; food should be served freshly cooked, otherwise it's just warmed up and therefore ruined. Yesterday, for example, you roasted grouse for three hours; for the first hour the apartment was filled with a wonderful aroma of game; then it went quiet in the kitchen; and when the food was served it lacked aroma and tasted only of air! Explain that!

MOTHER: (*Abashed.*) I don't understand it!

GERDA: Explain then why there was no juice, who ate that up?

MOTHER: I don't understand at all!

GERDA: But I've been making enquiries, I've found out a good deal...

MOTHER: (*Interrupts.*) I know all that, you won't teach me anything, but I'll teach you the art of housekeeping...

GERDA: You mean with soya and cayenne pepper, I know that already, and when there's a dinner party choose dishes that no-one eats so that it's left over for the following day...or invite visitors when the larder is full of pigswill... I know all that now, and that's why from this day I'm taking charge of the household!

MOTHER: (*Furious.*) Am I to be your maid?

GERDA: I'll be yours and you'll be mine, we'll help each other! – Here comes Axel!

●

SON-IN-LAW: (*Comes in, with a heavy cane in his hand.*) Well? What do you think of the chaise longue?

MOTHER: It's all right...

SON-IN-LAW: (*Threatening.*) Don't you like it? Is there something wrong?

MOTHER: Now I'm beginning to understand!

SON-IN-LAW: Oh really! – – – Well, meanwhile, and since we can never get enough to eat in this house, Gerda and I intend to eat alone.

MOTHER: And what about me?

SON-IN-LAW: You're as fat as a barrel, so you don't need much; you ought to slim for the sake of your health, as we have had to do... Meanwhile, go out Gerda, a moment; meanwhile you can light the tilestove!
(*GERDA goes out.*)

MOTHER: (*Shaking with anger.*) There's wood there...

SON-IN-LAW: Oh no, there are a few sticks, but you're going to go and fetch some firewood, enough to fill the stove!

MOTHER: (*Lingers.*) Is one to burn one's money?

SON-IN-LAW: No, but wood has to be burnt to give warmth! Quick!
(*The MOTHER lingers.*)
One, two – three! (*He bangs his cane on the table.*)

MOTHER: I think the firewood has run out...

SON-IN-LAW: Either you are lying, or you have stolen the money...because a load of wood was bought the day before yesterday!

MOTHER: Now I can see who you are...

SON-IN-LAW: (*Sits in the rocking chair.*) You would have seen that long ago, if you hadn't duped my youth with your age and experience... Quickly! go out and fetch the firewood, otherwise... (*He lifts his cane.*)

(*The MOTHER goes out and returns with firewood.*)

Now light it properly, and don't just pretend! – One, two, three!

MOTHER: How like the old man you are now, sitting in his rocking chair!

SON-IN-LAW: Light it!

MOTHER: (*Cowed but furious.*) I'm going to, I'm going to!

SON-IN-LAW: Now keep an eye on the fire while we go out into the dining room and eat...

MOTHER: What do I get then?

SON-IN-LAW: The porridge Gerda put out for you in the kitchen.

MOTHER: With the blue skimmed milk...

SON-IN-LAW: Since you've eaten up the cream, it's right and just!

MOTHER: (*Sullen.*) Then I'm leaving.

SON-IN-LAW: You can't, because I'm locking you in!

MOTHER: (*Whispers.*) Then I'll jump out the window!

SON-IN-LAW: If you like! You ought to have done it a long time ago and four people's lives would have been spared! Light the fire now! – Blow on it! That's it! Sit here now until we come back. (*He goes.*)

(*Pause.*

The MOTHER first stops the rocking chair; then listens by the door; then she takes wood out of the tilestove and hides it under the chaise longue.)

●

(*SON comes in, slightly drunk.*)

MOTHER: (*Jumps.*) Is that you?

SON: (*Sits in the rocking chair.*) Yes!

MOTHER: How are you?

SON: Bad, I'll be finished soon!

MOTHER: It's just your imagination! – Don't rock like that! – Look at me, I've reached an age, a certain age…and yet I've lived a life of work and drudgery and duty to my children and my house, haven't I?

SON: Huh! – And the pelican, who never gave its heart blood, it says in the encyclopedia that it's a lie.

MOTHER: Have you any complaints, tell me!

SON: Listen, mother, if I was sober I wouldn't answer honestly, because I wouldn't have the strength, but now I can tell you I read father's letter, which you stole and threw in the tilestove…

MOTHER: What are you taking about, what letter was that?

SON: Always a lie! I remember when you taught me to lie for the first time, I could hardly talk; do you remember?

MOTHER: No, I don't remember it at all! Don't rock!

SON: And when you lied to me for the first time? – I remember also as a child I had hidden under the piano, and a lady came to visit you; you sat and lied to her for three hours, and I had to listen to it!

MOTHER: That's a lie.

SON: But do you know why I'm so wretched? You never breast fed me, I had a nurse maid and a bottle instead; and when I was older I had to go with her to her sister who was a prostitute; and there I witnessed the mysterious acts, which otherwise only dog owners provide children in the spring and autumn on street corners! I told you, I was four, what I'd seen in that house of shame. You said it was a lie and beat me for being a liar though I spoke the truth. The maid, encouraged by your approval, initiated me at five years old into further mysteries, I was only five years old… (*He sobs.*) And then I began having to starve and freeze like father and us others. Now finally I find out that you stole the housekeeping money, and the money for firewood… Look at me, pelican, look at Gerda who has no chest! – How you murdered my father, you know yourself, by driving him to desperation, which isn't punishable by law; how you murdered my sister, you know best yourself, but now she knows too!

MOTHER: Don't rock! – What does she know?

SON: What you know, but I can never say! (*Sobs.*) It's terrible that I've said all this, but I must; I feel as if when I get sober I'll shoot myself; so I keep on drinking; I daren't be sober...

MOTHER: Tell more lies now!

SON: Father once said in anger, that you were one great perversion of nature...that you never, like other children, learned to speak but to lie...that you always shirked your responsibilities so you could have a good time. And I remember that when Gerda was lying ill, at death's door, you went to the Opera for the evening. I remember your words: 'life is hard enough without making it any harder'! And that surer, three months, you were with father in Paris having a good time, the household went into debt. Gerda and I lived here in town, shut up with two maids in this flat; in our parents' bedroom a fireman was staying with the housemaid and that intimate pair used the conjugal bed –

MOTHER: Why haven't you spoken of it before?

SON: You've forgotten that I did, and I was punished for telling tales, or lying, as you alternately called it, for as soon as you heard a true word, you called it a lie!

MOTHER: (*Walks around the room like a wild animal that has just been captured.*) I've never heard the like from a son to a mother!

SON: Yes, it is a little unusual and it's completely against nature, I know that, but it had to be said once. You were sleepwalking and couldn't be woken and therefore you couldn't change either. Father said 'if you were put on the rack, you wouldn't be able to confess to any crime or that you had lied'...

MOTHER: Father! You think he didn't have any faults?

SON: He had great faults; but not in his relationship with his wife and children! – But there are other secrets in your marriage, which I imagined, but never wanted to admit to myself... Father took those secrets with him to the grave, partly!

MOTHER: Have you said enough now?

SON: Now I shall go out and drink... I can never sit the examination, I don't believe in Justice; laws seem to be made by thieves and murderers to set the criminal free; one person telling the truth is not evidence, but two false witnesses are full proof! At half past eleven my case is righteous, but after twelve it is no longer; a slip of the pen, an inadequate margin can land me in jail though I am innocent. If I show mercy to a crook, he accuses me of infringing his honour. My contempt for life, humanity, society and myself is so boundless, that I can't be bothered to live anymore... (*He walks to the door.*)

MOTHER: Don't go!

SON: Are you afraid of the dark?

MOTHER: I'm nervous!

SON: The two go together!

MOTHER: And that chair is driving me mad! It was always like two knives when he sat there...hacking at my heart.

SON: You haven't got one!

MOTHER: Don't go! I can't stay here, Axel is a villain!

SON: I thought so too until just now! Now I think he is the victim of your criminal tendencies... Yes, he was the young man who was seduced!

MOTHER: You must keep bad company!

SON: Bad company, yes. I've never been in good company!

MOTHER: Don't go!

SON: What can I do here? I'd only torment you to death with my talking.

MOTHER: Don't go!

SON: Are you waking up?

MOTHER: Yes, I'm waking up now like out of a long, long sleep! It's dreadful! Why couldn't I wake up before?

SON: If you couldn't, it must have been impossible! And if it was impossible, it wasn't your fault!

MOTHER: Say those words again!

SON: You couldn't be any different!

MOTHER: (*Slavishly kisses his hand.*) Say more!

SON: I can't anymore! – Alright, I'll ask you: not to stay here to make bad worse!

MOTHER: You're right! I'll go, out!

SON: Poor Mama!

MOTHER: Have you sympathy for me?

SON: (*Sobs.*) Yes, of course I have! How often have I said of you: 'she is so wicked, you have to feel sorry for her!'

MOTHER: Thank you! – Go now, Fredrik!

SON: Can't this be helped?

MOTHER: No, it's hopeless!

SON: Yes, it is! – It's hopeless! (*He goes.*)

    (*Pause.*)

●

MOTHER: (*Alone; her arms folded across her breast a long while. Then she goes to the window, which she opens and looks down below; retreats into the room and makes to jump out, but pulls herself back when there are three knocks on the door upstage.*) Who is it? What was it? (*She closes the window.*) Come in. (*Door upstage opens.*) Is someone there? (*The SON can be heard bawling somewhere in the apartment.*) It's him. In the plantation. Isn't he dead? What shall I do, where shall I go? (*She hides behind the secretaire.*) (*A wind blows about as before, causing paper to fly about.*) Close the window, Fredrik! (*A potted plant blows down.*) Close the window! I'm freezing to death and the fire's going out in the stove! (*She turns on all the electric lights; closes the door which blows open again; the rocking chair is moved by the wind; she goes round and round the room, until she throws herself headlong onto the chaise longue and hides her face in the cushions.*)

●

(*'Il me disait' is playing outside.*
The MOTHER lying as before on the chaise longue hiding her head.
GERDA comes in with the porridge on a tray, which she puts down, then she turns off all the electric lights except one.)

MOTHER: (*Wakes, stands up.*) Don't turn the lights out!

GERDA: Yes, we have to save money!

MOTHER: Are you back so soon?

GERDA: Yes, he didn't think it was any fun without you there.

MOTHER: How nice!

GERDA: Here's your supper!

MOTHER: I'm not hungry.

GERDA: Yes, you are hungry, but you don't eat porridge!

MOTHER: Yes, sometimes!

GERDA: No, never! But not for that but for your wicked smile every time you tortured us with porridge oats, you enjoyed our suffering...and you gave the same to the dog!

MOTHER: I can't eat blue milk, it makes me cold!

GERDA: Since you skimmed off the cream for your eleven o'clock coffee! – Here you are! (*Serves the porridge on a gueridon.*) Eat it. Let me watch you!

MOTHER: I can't!

GERDA: (*Leans down and takes the sticks of firewood out from under the chaise longue.*) If you don't eat it, I'll tell Axel you've stolen the firewood.

MOTHER: Axel, who was missing my company...he won't do me any harm! Do you remember at the wedding, when he danced with me...to 'Il me disait'! There it is. (*She hums to the second reprise which is playing now.*)

GERDA: It would be wiser of you not to remind me of that infamy...

MOTHER: And I received verses, and the most beautiful flowers!

GERDA: Shut up!

MOTHER: Shall I recite the verses to you? I know them by heart. 'In Ginnistan... Ginnistan is a Persian word for the Garden of Eden, where the gracious Peri live on aromas... Peri, they are geniuses or fairies which are so created that the longer they live, the younger they become.'

GERDA: Oh my God, do you think you are a Peri?

MOTHER: Well, that's what it says here, and Fabror Victor has proposed to me; what would you think, if I remarried?

GERDA: Poor Mama! You're still sleepwalking, as we all have been, but will you never wake up? Don't you see how people smile at you? Don't you understand, when Axel insults you?

MOTHER: Does he? I think he's always more polite to me than he is to you...

GERDA: Even when he raises his stick to you?

MOTHER: To me? It was to you, my dear child!

GERDA: My dear mother, have you lost your mind?

MOTHER: He missed my company this evening, we always have so much to talk about, he's the only one who understands me and you are just a child...

GERDA: (*Takes her mother by the shoulders and shakes her.*) Wake up, for God's sake!

MOTHER: You're not fully grown yet, but I am your mother and I've nourished you with my blood...

GERDA: No, you gave me a bottle and a rubber dummy in my mouth, and then I had to go to the side-board and steal, but there was only hard rye bread which I ate with mustard, and when it burned my throat I cooled it with the vinegar bottle; the cruet stand and the bread basket – that was the larder!

MOTHER: I see, you stole as a child already! How charming, and aren't you ashamed to tell me? To think what children I have sacrificed myself for!

GERDA: (*Cries.*) I could forgive you for everything; but not for stealing my life from me – yes, he was my life because with him I began to live...

MOTHER: It's not my fault he preferred me! Perhaps he found me, what shall I say? more pleasing...yes, he had better taste than your father, he never appreciated me before he had rivals – – – (*Three knocks on the door.*) Who's that, knocking?

GERDA: Don't speak ill of father! I don't think my life is long enough to regret how I have offended against him, but you will pay the penalty for that! Do you remember when I was a tiny, tiny child, you taught me to say wicked, hurtful things that I didn't understand? He was wise enough not to punish me for shooting the arrow, because he knew who had stretched the bow! Do you remember when you taught me to lie to him and say I needed new books for school, and when we had swindled him out of the money, we shared it! – How could I forget such a past? Is there no drink that extinguishes the memory without choking all the life out of you? If only I had the strength to walk away from it all, but I am like Fredrik, we are powerless, victims with no wills of our own, your victims...and you, so callous you can't suffer for your own crimes!

MOTHER: Do you know about my childhood? Have you any idea what a bad home I had, what wickedness I learnt there? It seems to be hereditary, but who did it start with, the first parents? It said so in the children's books and it seems to fit... So, don't blame me, and I won't blame my parents, who could blame theirs, and so on. And besides, it's the same in every family, you just can't see it from outside...

GERDA: If that's so, then I don't want to live, but if I am forced to, then I want to pass through this misery deaf and blind, but in the hope that what comes after is better...

MOTHER: You exaggerate so, my dear, if you have a child, you'll have other things to think about...

GERDA: I won't have any children...

MOTHER: How do you know that?

GERDA: The doctor has explained it.

MOTHER: He's made a mistake...

GERDA: There, you lied again... I am infertile, incomplete, like Fredrik, and so I don't want to live...

MOTHER: How you talk...

GERDA: If I could be as wicked as I want to be, you would be no more! Why is it so difficult to be wicked? When I lift my hand against you, I beat myself! – – –

(*The music stops suddenly; the SON is heard bawling outside.*)

MOTHER: He's been drinking again!

GERDA: Poor Fredrik...what is he going to do?

•

SON: (*Comes in, half drunk.*) There's...smoke...in – the kitchen!

MOTHER: What did you say?

SON: I think... I... I think there's...a fire!

MOTHER: A fire? What are you taking about?

SON: Yes, I... think...there's a fire!

MOTHER: (*Runs upstage and opens the doors but is met by the red glow of a fire.*) Fire! – How will we get out! – I don't want to burn! – I don't want to! (*Walks round in circles.*)

GERDA: (*Takes her brother in her arms.*) Fredrik! Escape, the fire is on top of us, run!

SON: I can't!

GERDA: Run! You must!

SON: Where?... No, I don't want to...

MOTHER: I'd rather go out the window...
(*Opens the balcony and stumbles out.*)

GERDA: Oh, God, help us!

SON: It was the only thing!

GERDA: You did it!

SON: Yes, what else could I do? – There was nothing else! – Was there anything else?

GERDA: No! Everything must burn, otherwise we'll never get out of here! Hold me in your arms, Fredrik, hold me tight, little brother; I am happier than I've ever been; it's getting light, poor Mama, she was so wicked, so wicked...

SON: Little sister, poor Mama, do you feel how warm it is, it's so good, I'm not cold anymore. Can you hear it crackling out there, everything is burning, all the old wickedness, the nasty, ugly...

GERDA: Hold me tight, little brother, we won't burn, we'll suffocate from the fumes, can you feel how good it smells, it's the palms burning and Papa's laurel wreath. Now the linen cupboard, it smells of lavender, and now the roses! Little brother! Don't be afraid, it's soon over, my dear, dear – don't fall, poor Mother! who was so wicked! Hold me tighter, hug me, as Papa used to say! It's like Christmas Eve, when we were allowed to eat in the kitchen, and dip bread in the stew, the only day we could get full up, like Papa said, feel that smell, it's the larder burning with the tea packet and the coffee, and the spices, the cinnamon and the cloves...

SON: (*Ecstatic.*) Is it summer? The clover must be in bloom, summer holidays are starting, do you remember when we went down to the white steamboats, and stroked them, when they were freshly painted and waiting for us. Papa was happy then, he was really alive, he said, and the textbooks were finished with! This is how life should always be, he said, it must have been him who was the pelican, because he plucked his feathers and gave them to us. He always had worn knees in his trousers and a worn-out velvet collar, while we went about like little aristocrats... Gerda, hurry up, the steamboat bell is ringing, Mama is sitting in the saloon, no, she's not here, poor Mama! She's gone, is she still on the beach? Where is she? I can't see her, it's no fun without *Mama*. Here she comes! – Now the holidays can begin!

(*Pause.*

Upstage door opens. There is a strong red glow. The SON and GERDA sink to the floor.)

The End.

Opus 5

THE BLACK GLOVE

Svarta Handsken

(1907)

Characters

YOUNG WIFE

THE OLD MAN

ELLEN

KRISTIN

THE CARETAKER

CHRISTMAS GNOME

CHRISTMAS ANGEL

OLD WOMAN

ACT ONE

The Entrance hall of an apartment building

Upstage a hall door with a letterbox and name plate; to the right an icebox: to the left a bench.

Above the door there is a stained-glass window with a heart design.

A black glove lies on the floor of the hall.

An OLD MAN comes in from the left, out of breath he sits on the bench.

He catches sight of the glove, which he takes up with his stick.

OLD MAN: What's this? – A glove? Black, female, size six; it belongs to the little lady in there, I can tell that from the marks left by the rings; on the left hand two smooth and one ring-finger with the cut diamond; a beautiful hand, but a little too firm a grip, a silken paw with sharp nails; I'll put it on the icebox, it can be found there! (*The CARETAKER comes in from the left.*)
Ah, greetings! Happy Christmas!

CARETAKER: Happy Christmas, sir! It is you isn't it, the curator?

OLD MAN: Yes, it's me; and I am indeed the preserver of birds, fish, and insects, but I cannot preserve myself – if I put arsenic under my skin it wrinkles, and my hair falls out like off a seal-skin trunk, my teeth too, are going their ways...

CARETAKER: It's like with all this electricity we've got here, it has to be mended all the time...

OLD MAN: It is unfortunate that we should sit in the dark over Christmas, can't you get it to work?

CARETAKER: It seems there's been a short circuit, but we'll soon sort that out. – Let's see now... (*He pushes a fuse plug in; the hearth and the coloured window lights up.*)
There you see, we've got light in the hall...

OLD MAN: You go around bringing light into this house...

205

CARETAKER: And yet myself, I live down in the basement in the dark, because we've only got an old paraffin lamp…

OLD MAN: It's good to live for others! – By Christ, that heart is pretty!

CARETAKER: It's pretty alright, but the colour's a bit strong! Not to say glaring!

OLD MAN: That's the little lady for you! If only she was as good as she is beautiful!

CARETAKER: What glove is that?

OLD MAN: It was lying here in the hall, perhaps you would take care of it?

CARETAKER: I'll take it with me and hang it in my little cubby hole down there, until the owner turns up! – Now I must continue my way upwards.

OLD MAN: And I shall sit a little longer and rest after all my eighty years… Merry Christmas!

CARETAKER: (*Turns out the heart and goes out to the right.*) Merry Christmas!

●

(*ELLEN comes in from the right, opens the icebox and removes a small crate of milk bottles.*)

OLD MAN: Good morning, Ellen, and Merry Christmas!

ELLEN: Merry Christmas!

OLD MAN: How is the little girl, and the young lady, her mother?

ELLEN: Oh well, those two together, they twitter like a couple of canaries – you can hear them from here! But that's just them two… Madam doesn't treat the rest of us any good though! Neither me or the caretaker got any Christmas box, because she said we was animals…

OLD MAN: But you mustn't tell me things like that, I'm not part of your household – people will say that I'm a gossip…

ELLEN: Talking of canaries, have you stuffed that one of Madam's yet?

OLD MAN: Yes! I have! – But – (*He grinds his jaw.*) – she won't pay for it! – You see, now I'm gossiping!

ELLEN: No, she doesn't want to pay for work done – and when the master wanted to give us girls something extra for the move in from the country – she went wild. – And when he gave us it all the same, why she turned on the plumbing and the electrics all night. – And when she still didn't get her own way, she went sick – dying she was; and the master had to send for the professor; when *he* came and said it was nothing but a carry on, she wanted to take poison, and threatened to turn on all the gas taps and blow up the building!

OLD MAN: Oh! God preserve us! Do you really have that kind of a to-do in there?

ELLEN: Yes, but betweentimes she's a perfect angel – yes, you should just see her playing with her little girl, or sitting sewing Christmas presents, like she's doing right now! – It's quite as if she was possessed by evil spirits when it's going on; and I'm sure she can't help it, poor little thing!

OLD MAN: That's very nice of you Ellen, I rather think she's ill! You see I haven't seen that sort of thing before... They're too well off, that's the problem. The husband does nothing at all, because he's rich!

ELLEN: But he's busy all day spending all his money; and this year he's bought three bits of furniture for the drawing room, one of them's in black pear-wood with silver inlaid, and the whole lot went up in the attic. – Like you say: they're too well off!

•

KRISTIN: (*Comes in from the right; she speaks mildly.*) What are you standing there for Ellen? Madam is quite beside herself, her ring's gone missing...

ELLEN: What ring?

KRISTIN: Her best ring, with the blue stone, that cost two thousand kronor – and since you weren't there she thought –

ELLEN: What did she think?

KRISTIN: That you had run away and taken the ring with you.

ELLEN: No, I've never heard the like, me? What do you think Kristin?

KRISTIN: I know you're innocent, Ellen; when you know a person, you can say without thinking about it: she is innocent, or she is guilty.

OLD MAN: Are you quite sure about that?

KRISTIN: You can't swear to it, but you can still be sure.

ELLEN: So that's what I'm in for is it?

KRISTIN: It's a fixed idea madam has...

ELLEN: But she can see I haven't run away!

KRISTIN: It doesn't help!

ELLEN: And if the ring turns up, she'll be angry with me because I was innocent! And because she was wrong! I've a good mind to up and leave!

KRISTIN: Don't do that, because then she'll be convinced you've taken it, and she'll go for the police.

ELLEN: What a nice Christmas it's going to be!

OLD MAN: (*Gets up.*) You'll have a good Christmas, my dear girls, but after you've been tested – so far rain has always been followed by sunshine – and I'm sure it will here too! Ellen is an honest girl, but she must learn patience!

ELLEN: Haven't I learnt that already?

OLD MAN: Yes, but you haven't finished the course yet! – And now I shall bid you once more and with all my heart and with complete confidence: Merry Christmas, my children! (*Goes out right.*)

●

ELLEN: If only a clear conscience always helped!

KRISTIN: It helps a good deal! Come in now, but be nice and patient, when the storm breaks!

ELLEN: How can I?

KRISTIN: Look at the master, her husband! He's *also* suspected of taking the ring...

ELLEN: Him too?

KRISTIN: Him too! But he doesn't storm around, getting angry, only sad! – Come on now!

ELLEN: Him too! Then I'm not ashamed; and in that case I can bear it!

KRISTIN: Come on now!

(*They go in right.*)

•

CHRISTMAS GNOME: (*Comes in with a broom.*) I'll do the sweeping for Ellen and Kristin, because they've been good; but their neighbour's maid, Ebba, I'll sweep it all into her patch, because she's nasty; now I'll dust the bench, and the icebox, and rub the brass – but not Ebba's! – There!

Now we'll see what they're up to downstairs!

(*Turns on a torch; the upstage area is lit from behind. We can see into the cloakroom; a white icebox with a white mirror above it can be seen, a little white chair, and beneath this some children's galoshes; the lady of the house is standing in front of the mirror arranging her hair.*)

Yes, beautiful young mother, you can admire the gift you've been given all you like, but you mustn't idolise; you can love your little child, but you mustn't worship it! Now you shall have a Christmas card! (*He searches amongst a bunch of cards.*) Alpine rose, no; Violets, no; Snowberries, no; Mistletoe, no; Thistles, yes that's the one for you! The flower is beautiful but has thorns! (*Puts the Christmas card in the letterbox.*) Now let's hear what they're saying in the kitchen! (*He turns out the torch and listens at the door.*) Ellen is accused of having taken a ring! – She hasn't! Ellen wouldn't take a ring! Ebba might have done! I know them all in this house! All the gentry and all their maids. Ellen is crying! Now I shall look for the ring, from the cellar up to the attic, in the lift, in the shower, in the hoover, I know all the nooks and crannies...but first I'll just check they're keeping the fridge tidy! (*Takes a look and gropes about in the icebox.*) Approved!

●

CHRISTMAS ANGEL: (*Dressed in white with snowflake-shaped shapes stars on her head.*)

What are you doing, idiot?

You're eavesdropping, that's not very nice!

CHRISTMAS GNOME: What I do is always right!

I keep order in this house,

I do the sweeping, the beating, the comforting, the loving and the tidying up.

CHRISTMAS ANGEL: It's a very big house to keep watch over!

CHRISTMAS GNOME: It's a Tower of Babel, with all kinds of folk

and mother tongues; six storeys plus the lower ground;

three apartments on every floor,

a dozen cradles, seven pianos;

so many human destinies have been fulfilled;

stretching and straining,

in their hearts and minds, and in their natures, like the joists and the very stones of the building;

they hold together, but only just;

with neighbours, who don't know their neighbours,

they need forbearance and consideration;

and to tolerate each other's little whims.

One plays music after ten o'clock;

another gets up too early, one retires too late!

It can't be helped, there must be compromise;

listen to all the little noises in the stair-well!

The lift creaks, the water-pipes gurgle;

the heating hums like a kettle;

now someone's in the shower, another is vacuuming;

a door closes, a child screams!

Here are some newly-weds; there's a divorcée, here a widow,

all jumbled up, like their pianinos

making rhythms, from waltzes, to fugues and sonatas.

In the basement the same poverty as in the garret,

in the apartments, luxury, ostentation, solid assets and empty vacillation.

They struggle along, they storm ahead, they slip ahead –
one fine day they die, or get married, or divorced,
one of them may fight, complain, then make amends,
but when he sees that fighting is to no avail,
he finally makes up his mind –
to move – somewhere else!

CHRISTMAS ANGEL: Who lives in there?

CHRISTMAS GNOME: It's that young woman everyone's
talking about!

CHRISTMAS ANGEL: I know her then! –
Listen to the storm from the kitchen! –
So, my child, this is meant to be the season of goodwill?

CHRISTMAS GNOME: This is the day before Christmas
Eve,[1] so the kitchen is in a mess!
But there's another thing!
Poor Ellen has been falsely accused...

CHRISTMAS ANGEL: I know, and that's the last drop;
the cup of mercy is just about to overflow,
and the wine of anger will be pressed from sour grapes;
punishment, though, is not my domain,
I give comfort, succour, put things right;
You're the one to pull hair, you wield the hard hand...
Listen! That young woman, formed in beauty,
for the joy of mankind, to the honour of her maker,
she will be taught a lesson, short and sharp –
she has built her happiness upon her little child,
and upon that happiness she has built pride,
and with pride comes harshness and cruelty...
And so: take away the little child!
Let her feel the loss –
Don't worry! She'll get it back again tomorrow evening,
as a Christmas gift, but as a gift, mark you!
What are they to think? They can think what they like!
That it has gone astray, got lost!
But you mustn't tell any fibs!
An untrue word sows seeds like weeds!...

---

1 In Sweden, Christmas Eve is equivalent to our Christmas Day, i.e. the
main day of celebration.

CHRISTMAS GNOME: It's too cruel, she'll never survive it!
CHRISTMAS ANGEL: She'll come through it! I'll stand
by her!

And her heart, it isn't a bad one,
just a little poorly; and grief shall cure her –
Once the clear sun of happiness has begun to burn,
then the weeds and flowers alike, they wilt;
a little cloud gives a cooling shade.
And clouds bring rain, and rains new foliage...
Now it's clouding over! – Don't be too hard with her, though!
CHRISTMAS GNOME: (*Sadly.*) You don't need to tell me that! –
She's so beautiful!
CHRISTMAS ANGEL: Yes! And is about to become virtuous!
From that comes happiness! Lasting happiness! –
CHRISTMAS GNOME: But wait now, there's a poor wretch
up in the garret waiting for a present –
CHRISTMAS ANGEL: Who is this protégé of yours, tell me!
CHRISTMAS GNOME: A philosopher, who longs only for
the end!
CHRISTMAS ANGEL: Over life and death we have no power,
but if he deserves it, he shall have a gift this hour!
CHRISTMAS GNOME: He is brooding over the enigma
of Life...
CHRISTMAS ANGEL: Is that worth brooding over? –
CHRISTMAS GNOME: He's just an old fool, but he is kindly...
CHRISTMAS ANGEL: But what does he do up there in his
garret?
CHRISTMAS GNOME: He stuffs birds, dries fish, sticks
pins into worms,
and has a cupboard full of yellow paper,
which he searches, searches day and night!
He's searching for the enigma of life in that cupboard!
CHRISTMAS ANGEL: I know that type! Well, he'll get his
present! –

But now! Merry Christmas and, to work!
(*Curtain down momentarily.*)

End of Act One.

ACT TWO

In the entrance hall

The entrance hall. A white ice-box to the right, with a white mirror above it; on the lower ledge of this mirror a silver brush, on the upper ledge a glass of tulips; beneath the mirror a basket is hung, for gloves. On the ice-box is the CHRISTMAS GNOME's Christmas card with the thistle upon it. On the left a white chair, beneath the coat stand; under the chair a pair of small child's galoshes; on the hanger a white child's fur coat and a white bonnet. No other clothes can be seen.

Upstage the door to the drawing room stands open, and through the portiere of yellow silk can be seen the sewing table, upon which is standing an attractive lamp and a beautiful floral centre-piece; behind it we can see the lady of the house. She is dressed in white, a dress with a neckline cut only as low as the thorax; her black hair is set high upon her head in the Japanese fashion, so that her neck is visible. She is sewing a yellow silk, which may be a child's garment.

CHRISTMAS GNOME:
> *(In the hall, he takes the card from the icebox.)*
> There, my Christmas card with the piece of thistle! –
> A little weed amongst the wheat for you –
> it's prickly, like you, but has a beautiful flower! –
> Like you!
> The beautiful young mother! – See how her hands move
>   as she's picking flowers –
> and her head bent as if in meditation or prayer! –
> Now she smiles; for she hears the little child approaching –
> The tiny steps on the shiny parquet floor tiles,
> polished yesterday with beeswax and turpentine –
> so that it smells of pine forest in May, when the bream is
>   at play
> and it's time to open the green shutters of the summer
>   cottage.

A beautiful home where pretty people live –
in their beauty and purity, protected from the dirt of life –
Look at the flowers in the mirror! –
The turbans of the tulips, red and yellow,
concealing round cheeks, budding lips,
pressed together in chaste kisses,
given to their waterlily wives on cool mirrored pools –
Yes, the mirror! You can see the child's fingerprints
from when she tried to touch the image behind the glass,
thinking it might be another little girl!
There sits the dog, Rosa, on her mistress' chair
guarding her coats and boots.
Everything, everything to brighten a life and a home,
but never valued until it's gone –
out go the lights! Let dark the grief conceal,
and this deed I do now, it cannot bear the light –
(*He turns a switch on the wall, it goes dark.*)
But when the light is lit again then it shall be Christmas
in this house.

(*He hides behind the curtain on the right.*
The YOUNG WIFE rings a little bell.
ELLEN comes in with a lighted candle.
We can see the YOUNG WIFE scolding ELLEN.
ELLEN cries into her apron and goes out.
The YOUNG WIFE comes into the hall with the candle
which she puts down on the ice-box. There she finds the
Christmas card with the thistle, which she reads then tears to
pieces. – Then she looks into the mirror and adjusts her hair.
Now a piano can be heard from a neighbour who is playing
Beethoven's Sonata 31, *Opus 110,* L' intesso tempo di
arioso. *She listens. Then she takes the silver brush and begins*
to brush her child's clothes; plucking threads, dusting; she
discovers a loose button on the coat; takes the doll from the
chair and places it on the ice-box; sits down on the chair,
takes a needle and thread from her breast pocket and sews on
the button. Then she gets up and takes a black glove from the
glove basket; she looks for the other glove but without success;
she looks for the child's tiny galoshes under the chair; the odd

glove she tucks into her dress at the breast, and stands there forlorn.

The music changes to Beethoven's Funeral March. *She listens and is seized by fear. A rumbling noise comes from the icebox, as when lumps of ice are dislodged.*

The cry of a child! The YOUNG WIFE is horrified; wants to go, but stands petrified.

There is a knocking on a wall; the lift creaks; the water pipes hiss; human voices murmur through the walls.

KRISTIN comes in, white-faced, her arms raised and her hands clasped together, speaks to the YOUNG WIFE words we cannot hear, and rushes out.

The YOUNG WIFE wants to run after her, but cannot – falls to her knees beside the chair, and hides her face in the little child's coat which she strokes and embraces.

Curtain falls quickly.)

End of Act Two.

ACT THREE

The Caretaker's room

The caretaker's room. Upstage a coloured window lit from outside, but occasionally darkened by the lift as it passes up and down.

A table set for a Christmas dinner, with a white tablecloth and a little Christmas tree with wax candles; a small keg of ale, with fir twigs entwined around it, sits at the end of the table; buns, butter-dish, a pig's head, shoulder of mutton, salmon, a smoked goose, etc. A candelabra at the other end of the table; juniper twigs on the floor; on the wall a coloured print of the birth of Jesus; beneath this a black board with a lot of keys. An oil lamp burns.

The CARETAKER is sitting by the table, resting.

OLD MAN: (*Comes in carrying a decorative sheaf of corn for feeding the birds.*) Good day again, my fellow countryman, sitting alone?

CARETAKER: The old tree can't grow old if it is not also alone
    standing in the forest uncrowded by the young trees;
    and time has so effectively thinned out the space about me.
    (*Pause. He gestures the OLD MAN to be seated.*)
    Once the house was crowded, there wasn't any room –
    I'm not complaining, it was nice and warm there with
                           mother and children,
    but this isn't bad either, maybe it's better;
    everything is best, in its way and in its time...
    Now I sit in the shadow of my Christmas tree,
    remembering the past with a grateful mind;
    I have had these things, at least! How many have not had
                           them
    and sit reproaching themselves with the loss
    of what they never had, when it's too late to get them –

OLD MAN: Yes, I've had these things too – but I prefer to
                        forget about it –

CARETAKER: Take a seat, I should have said, as a
                    countryman of yours, from Bergslagen,[2] –
  I feel free – I too was born and bred in the mines,
  under the ground; that's why I like it best down here
  in the obscurity of the basement, of this tower of Babel –
  And to look through the coloured window panes,
  which is my sun, though darkened now and again,
  by the shadow of the lift which floats past like scattered
                                        cloud.
OLD MAN: Yes, in truth, you are like the Mountain King
  ruling over the elements –
  Master over the fire and the heating,
  apportioning the water, hot and cold;
  from the regions of darkness you send out the lighting;
  and with rarified and compressed air,
  you absorb the ashes and dust of the earth
  that has gathered on the feet of the human children, as
                                    they wander about.
  And with the laws of gravity you regulate the lift,
  so that the people rise and fall at your command.
CARETAKER: In truth my friend, you make too much of it...
OLD MAN: Oh no, because you are much else besides –
  I see you hold the keys to all the doors in the building,
  and everyone holds the key to your heart;
  you know all the destinies being woven here,
  you hear, you see through walls and floors,
  and this is where they all bring their confidences, their
                                worries and their sorrows...
CARETAKER: You do me too great an honour, doctor,
  but I can bear it, you won't spoil me, nor do you alarm me;
  just make me more content with this humble place;
  lighten my heavy heart,
  and transform this narrow hovel into a palace.
OLD MAN: Someone's talking out there in the lobby, I can
                            hear raised voices...

2 Pronounced Berry-Slahgen, an area in central Sweden, a mining district.

someone's screaming, someone's crying, so they'll be in
here soon;

and you'll have to sit in judgement,

investigate and advise, quieten them down when they
make their scenes!

CARETAKER: (*Listens.*) I know what it is; it's that lovely
Ellen –

on the third floor – the young wife's maid...

OLD MAN: I'll take this corn up to the birds

singing along to the weather vanes.

And so; Happy Christmas once again!

CARETAKER: The same to you, Doctor!

OLD MAN: One more thing! How did it go with that glove
you found?

CARETAKER: Oh yes! I've lost it here on the stairs
somewhere –

A grave matter; who could not do without *one* glove?

OLD MAN: I don't know about that, like seeks like.

(*Goes out.*)

●

ELLEN: (*Comes in, dressed to go out.*) Can I sit here with you
a while?

CARETAKER: Sit, my dear child!

ELLEN: I can't bear it any more; when the electricity went
off, I got the blame; and then I got blamed for the ring
again; she's reported me to the police. –

CARETAKER: And this is supposed to be Christmas? Your
household is the worst in the building – but first, let's
have some light – (*Takes out tools.*) My hammer, my
pincers – (*Takes keys from the board.*) My keys, so that I
can walk through closed doors –

ELLEN: I think the heating's broken too!

CARETAKER: The heating as well! What's going on up
there? It's only in your apartment that this kind of thing
keeps happening.

ELLEN: It's like a curse – I was scared, I heard a child call
out, and music came through the walls – Kristin is
leaving too, it's unbearable!

CARETAKER: Where is your master? Is there no master in the house?

ELLEN: I think he's gone away hunting – we haven't seen him for two days – he couldn't bear it either! But it's just like the professor said: they're too well off! Nothing to do, no appetite, no sleep; their only worry is how to spend all the money.

CARETAKER: Not by paying for work done, anyway! They don't like that.

ELLEN: Haven't they given you a Christmas box?

CARETAKER: Oh no! They were angry with me, because I asked her not to stand in the lift – I said it a little sharply of course, I was in a hurry.

ELLEN: Shsh, I can hear Kristin on the stairs! – She's more patient than I am, but even she is getting tired of it! –

CARETAKER: Just remember, for people like that, wealth isn't a blessing – that's a comfort to us poor folk, cold comfort of course – Where did they get their money from?

ELLEN: They inherited it I suppose – shsh now, she's coming! Something's definitely happened up there, in the haunted apartment! –

CARETAKER: Say rather, haunted building! There's so much peculiar goes on here – it's just as if all these machines here, bring something else with them – Ebba upstairs says she's seen the Christmas fairy sitting on the roof of the lift holding onto the cable –

•

(*The CHRISTMAS GNOME can be seen swapping round the keys on the board.*)

•

ELLEN: It's easy to believe in bad fairies. Sometimes you can't find something where you left it: or a door gets jammed, or hot water comes out of the cold tap...

CARETAKER: (*Listens.*) Is anyone there? I thought I heard the keys jangling on the board –
(*The CHRISTMAS GNOME hides.*)

219

(*Looks amongst the keys.*) I think the devil's been and jumbled up the keys – Here's number twenty-five where thirteen should be! And seventeen on eighty-one! We've got the grocer's postcard in the judge's box! And people are always talking on the stairs: quarrelling and crying, but when I go out there's no-one there. –

ELLEN: But this time it's Kristin – you can tell it's her!

CARETAKER: (*Pretends to open a door to the left.*) There's not a living soul out there –

ELLEN: You're scaring me! – And sometimes there's children's voices – sometimes it's pigeons on the roof – I think sometimes it's the professor sitting up there, up to his tricks – Who is he anyway?

CARETAKER: He's a strange fellow – but there's no harm in him –

ELLEN: Listen; didn't you find a glove on the stairs?

CARETAKER: Yes, the professor found one, and I was meant to take care of it but then I lost it!

ELLEN: You lost it! You should have heard the fuss they were making over that glove upstairs! Just like they did about the ring!

(*The telephone rings.*)

CARETAKER: (*On the telephone.*) – Yes, she's sitting right here! – No, that's impossible! She doesn't steal rings! We know Ellen! She doesn't take things – It's unjust! But I'll tell her! – Alright! (*Hangs up.*)

ELLEN: I know! – It was the police!

CARETAKER: Yes, my child! It was a summons to the station!

ELLEN: I'd rather drown myself!

CARETAKER: But go to the police station first!

ELLEN: No fear, you never come back!

CARETAKER: Look at me! – Ellen! – Don't always think the worst! – Go now in peace!

ELLEN: (*Looks at him and is won over.*) I'm going! – I looked into your eyes, I heard your voice – and I feel safe!

(*The CARETAKER leads her out.*)

And this hand gave me strength – It leads me, it supports me! – I'm going! (*She goes.*)

●

(*Pause.*)

(*An OLD WOMAN comes in with the black glove, and a small brown child's lace-up boot.*)

OLD WOMAN: Look what I found in the lift! Perhaps you can find the owner, Caretaker... You did get a Christmas box from me, didn't you?

CARETAKER: Yes thanks! Look, here's the missing glove. (*Puts it on the table with the boot.*)

OLD WOMAN: So, you've got a Christmas dinner and a tree – so much food – smoked pig's head! Very nice too, thank you very much!

CARETAKER: Should you rich folk envy the poor?

OLD WOMAN: You're not as poor as you look! And I'm not as rich as I look!... Take care of that glove now, it's as black as a funeral! – But it conceals a white hand and maybe something more! (*Goes.*)

CARETAKER: (*Dumbfounded.*) But this little boot, you see! A sloping heel, the sloppy devil –

●

(*The CHRISTMAS GNOME snatches away the glove and hides.*)

●

CARETAKER: Some little child, a girl or boy, you can't tell from the shoes because they can't tell right from left yet – good from bad – because they belong to Heaven – But later! Oh yes! – (*He goes to pick up the glove.*) But where's the glove? I put it here on the table! (*He searches.*) It's gone! (*Searches.*)

●

KRISTIN: (*Stands in the room, in despair.*) Imagine! Imagine! Just imagine!...

CARETAKER: What is it? Who is it? – Kristin!

KRISTIN: Just imagine! God help us! – The child has gone!

CARETAKER: Gone? What do you mean?

KRISTIN: She's gone! Someone has taken her...

CARETAKER: That's not possible; I would have seen!
I would have heard! That's what I'm here for, to guard
the house and the people in it!

KRISTIN: You don't know anything about it! Then I'm
going to the police! – Be kind to the mother. Here she
comes! She was sitting up there without heat or light...
It's all too horrible! Even for her! (*Out.*)

●

CARETAKER: What's all this? Not the work of man! And
that's why there's some hope! (*He puts the boot on the
table.*) Who's that? It's the poor little mother herself! (*He
withdraws to the right.*)

YOUNG WIFE: (*Comes in from the left, dressed as in the
previous act.*)
Where is this I've come to?
And where am I?
Where did I come from?
Who am I?
This must be a poor man's home! – but so many keys!
It must be a hotel –
No, a prison, an underground prison –
That's the moon shining, but it looks like a heart,
and the clouds march by in black –
Over there stands a forest, a pine forest,
a Christmas forest full of gifts, and with candles in it –
In a prison!? No, this is something else.
Is anyone here?

CARETAKER: (*Can be seen in the wings to the right, but only
by the audience. Aside.*)
She's beside herself, she's lost her memory –
A merciful thing, such a merciful thing! for one who is
suffering!

YOUNG WIFE: Wait! I remember! but my memory is
lagging behind.
While I went forwards to try to find something.

What was I looking for?
A glove I lost! It was black –
It's gone dark again!
But out in the darkness I can see some blue,
like the springtime sky, between white clouds
a mountain lake, between steep shores,
as blue as my sapphire that I've lost –
that someone has stolen –
I've lost a lot these past days –
I was cold and sat in the dark...
It's warm here though, but oppressive;
the weight of the tall tower up above,
and the heavy human destinies, around and around,
pressing me down into the earth,
squeezing my heart in this frail breast;
I wanted to speak but was left searching for the words;
I wanted to cry because I am in sorrow!
(*Catches sight of the boot.*)
What's this? – A little boot!
A little sock and a foot! In you go!
What was that? – Here's a candle
that's grown branches, it's grown
from the candlestick root, soon it will bloom,
three blue-white flowers with some red in them...
So candles can grow! Grow shoots, twigs!
What part of the world have I come to?
A buoy afloat in a pine forest,
a wild boar sticking its head up out of the waves,
and fish walking on dry land! –
(*Catches sight of the print of Jesus' birth.*)
What's this? – A cradle in a stable!
(*Begins to come round.*)
And the shepherd's brown cows looking wide-eyed,
at the little child – that – in the cradle – sleeps.
(*Wakes and screams.*)
O Lord Jesus, Saviour of the world, save me!
I perish! I per-ish! – A child this night is born, a child
has died! There's the caretaker, angry with me because

he didn't get a Christmas box; don't be angry with me!
Don't take revenge! I'll give you all my rings...

CARETAKER: (*Comes forward.*) I'm not angry, I wont take
revenge; your child will come back, a child can't get lost
in a city like this – come with me now, and we'll get
some heat and light in the meantime –

YOUNG WIFE: Say that again, a child can't get lost in a
city like this – I don't believe a word of it of course. –
but say it over and over –

CARETAKER: Come along with me, while I mend the
machines; you can go up and warm yourself, go to see
your old friend on the third floor. He knows how to talk
– I can't talk – and he can comfort you –

YOUNG WIFE: Do you mean the judge? He's angry with
me too isn't he?

CARETAKER: He's not angry with you, come along now...!

YOUNG WIFE: How kind of you not to take revenge.

CARETAKER: Dear me! Dear me! How wicked you are!

YOUNG WIFE: But my child! – My child! My child!

CARETAKER: Come!

End of Act Three.

ACT FOUR

The garret

The garret: Upstage two windows covered by pale green curtains; against the central column between the two windows stands a cabinet for manuscripts, with an attractive lamp above it; on the left an oak table covered in manuscripts; to the right an armchair.

CHRISTMAS GNOME: (*Comes in.*) Christmas eve
    morning is here! But here in the old philosopher's house
    no sign of any Christmas cheer.
    (*Draws back the curtain.*)
    He has, however, put a Christmas tree out on the balcony!
    For the sparrows and the pigeons,
    the sheaf of corn with it's thousand yellow beaks,
    one grain in each to feed the birds of heaven;
    they're still sleeping on the tin roofs,
    heads tucked under their wings –
    soon the morning breeze will shake the weather vanes
    a-top the chimney pots, above the stoves,
    where the hearty fires crackle,
    warming the coffee pots;
    there I'll be, running along the ledges,
    delighting in the smells,
    as the rays of the morning sun
    fall on the telephone wires.
    Then, when weather vanes sing
    and the pigeons coo in the cornices;
    the children shall leave their beds – – –

    What's he got here?
    On yellow leaves in their thousands
    he has gathered all his knowledge!
    Straw under seeds in the hotbeds –
    after threshing; no, like chaff
    where you have to search for the wheat –

and the grains have gathered here in the barn
of carved oak, where the harvest lies.
(*Opens the cabinet.*)
This is the index, the key to his wisdom,
to the riddle of creation he imagines he has found.
You old madman, classifying the universe –
I'll just stir the soup,
that you've scoured the world to concoct
and I'll create chaos once again
let you start from scratch!
(*He jumbles up the manuscripts.*)
Here we see the wiseman's spectacles!
With the years he became short-sighted –
now I'll give you a Christmas present,
that will make you long-sighted, far-sighted!
(*Exchanges the glasses for others which he takes out from his
pocket.*)
You shall have new eyes
to see what isn't visible
to mere mortals!
Where once you saw laws,
there you shall see the law maker,
and then you shall meet the Judge;
where once you saw nature
and the mischief of blind chance,
there you shall find creatures
of the same sort as yourself!

I hear the old boy has woken up;
perhaps he has stayed awake and kept a vigil
for the night is akin to daylight
for those who research in the dark!
He's coming, I'll stay,
then I'll make his acquaintance,
and he can make mine!
(*Retires to behind the right hand curtain.*)

OLD MAN: (*Comes in from the left; dressed in black, with a
white neckerchief, black silk skull-cap; long white hair and
beard.*)

Welcome life! Good morning toil!
For sixty years I have given order to the universe;
now the sun is rising on the day,
when I shall solve the riddle.
It's all lying there like the strata of the Earth
deposited slowly by fire and water,
by animal, vegetable and mineral,
elements, forces, measurements and number
I have heaved together the keystones
of the Tower of Babel's stairway to the heavens,
and with it I shall rise out of this vale of tears
and seize the mosque with its blue cupola
resting on the four points of the compass.

For sixty years, I have collected, and counted;
and once, halfway through, I found the riddle.
It happened one night, I wrote it on a piece of paper,
but it got buried, has since been lost.
It's there somewhere, but while I have searched
the haycock has grown to a haystack;
my own child has grown into a giant...
I am beaten back when I approach it,
I dig as you dig for treasure,
but the spade falls from my hand,
my head tires, my body is withering.
And I was often left lying for dead
when I tried to survey it all – – –

Now though, I feel the moment has come,
for in a dream last night I saw
the paper I've been searching for, a large, pale blue
regal, an English vellum –
(*Takes off his cuffs.*)
Now or never! It's you or me,
O pile of paper, surrender unto me your secret!
I am your master, you spirits,
None but I command thee!
(*Puts on his glasses and roots amongst his papers.*)

What's this? – What is this?
This isn't how I had ordered them,
alphabet and numbers have changed about,
a, b, c, d, h, r – I think the very Devil –
and numbers one, seven, four, ten, twenty-six – He has
been here!
Alpha, beta, pi; and the codes of my own devising – I've
forgotten it – it's gone from my memory – (*Carries on
searching.*) He's a clue – but there, right in the middle of
it, a blot of ink. I'll remove it! (*Takes out a penknife.*) I've
made a hole in the paper! – Fine! I'll search; if I go
through every scrap I'll find it! – (*Searches page by page.*)
The neighbours are beginning to play! Play on! – You
don't bother me, I've got all day! – And all night! I don't
eat anything – don't need any sleep! (*While the OLD
MAN is searching amongst his papers someone is playing a
piano: Beethoven's* Sonata 29, *Opus 106,* andante
sostenuto.)
How quickly I tire today! – I'll rest a while! (*He walks
exhaustedly to his armchair and falls into it; the music
continues.*) My eyesight is odd; what's near seems far
away and what's far away seems near; and my head is
empty! (*He closes his eyes; the music continues.*)
(*The OLD MAN wakes up and attacks the piles of paper once
more, but tires straight away and returns to the chair; attacks
it once more but is beaten back. Now he falls asleep in the
chair like a dead man.
The CHRISTMAS GNOME pushes an armchair in from
the right and sits himself down nonchalantly in front of the
OLD MAN.
The music stops; the OLD MAN wakes up.*)
Who's there? Are you real...

CHRISTMAS GNOME: To exist is to be perceived,
You have perceived me!
Therefore I am!

OLD MAN: (*Gets up.*)
But I want to feel you, I want to touch you!
Without that, for me, you don't exist!

228

CHRISTMAS GNOME:

　　You can't touch a rainbow either, but it exists!

　　And the mirages at sea and in the desert, they exist –

　　I am a mirage; don't come too close,

　　because then you'll no longer see me,

　　even though I'll still be here.

OLD MAN: In truth, your logic is good –

CHRISTMAS GNOME:

　　Well, then you shall have to believe your eyes –

　　(*OLD MAN mutters to himself in complaint.*)

　　You're grumbling, because I don't fit into your system;

　　and your system is your master,

　　and you are its servant...

OLD MAN: I have sovereignty over my system.

CHRISTMAS GNOME: Then you can tell me, briefly

　　the basic thought behind the multiplicity of facts

　　you have gathered, for otherwise you have gathered leaves,

　　raindrops, grains of sand, all alike

　　but all unlike!

OLD MAN: My thought, my idea, which unifies

　　the millions of phenomena we encounter –

CHRISTMAS GNOME: Let's hear it! I'm keen to learn!

OLD MAN: You little thief! You stole my thought from me;

　　it was clear in my head just now...

CHRISTMAS GNOME:

　　And now? It's gone clouded, like the clear ice

　　melting in the heat; it's turned to slush,

　　then water, evaporating away!

　　Evaporating! I shall condense it,

　　and state your theory, which you have forgotten.

　　(*Pause.*)

　　It is in the unity of the universe that you see the riddle

　　　　　　　　　　　　　　　　　of existence...

OLD MAN: Exactly! You're a sharp little fellow,

　　finding what I've been looking for for thirty years:

　　The unity of matter! That's the word!

CHRISTMAS GNOME:

　　So much for the system! Now for reality!

Consider now nature's duality! Let us see
if that theory isn't somewhat better!
(*Pause.*)
The wet element, water,
a unity, has two elements,
hydrogen, and oxygen. You can't dispute that;
magnetic force is divided into north and south;
electricity into positive and negative,
in plant seeds, a male and a female;
and highest up the chain, at it's top,
you find duality, for being alone
wasn't suitable for mankind;
and that's how man and woman came about:
Nature's duality established!
OLD MAN: You little devil! You've quite destroyed –
CHRISTMAS GNOME:
Your toy, you great fool; your chain broke
and the links are lying like a pile of scrap,
the rope you wound has come undone
and turned to oakum, on its way to the junk yard.
OLD MAN: Ha! Sixty years to blow a bubble!
A bubble that bursts with one puff of breath!
I don't want to live any longer!
CHRISTMAS GNOME:
If the bubble has burst, then you can blow some more,
they're only made of soap and water,
whipped up to look like something,
though it's really very little, almost nothing –
OLD MAN: Sixty years –
(*Wild, he gets up and throws the papers off left.*)
Out with you! Satan's illusions!
The rotten fruit of twenty thousand days of work!
Out! Out! You dry leaves that have consumed my tree.
You jack-o-lanterns, will-o-the wisps, which have led me
astray,
lured me into the swamp where I sank into the mire,
up to my neck; that lured me into the deserts
where thorny bushes lacerated my hands –

(*He empties the cabinet of its papers, but leaves a box.*)
Get out of here you false pilots, leading me aground,
you guides who took me down into Hell;
insolvent, destitute, I declare myself bankrupt
and sit empty-handed on the burned-out site –
(*Sinks down into his chair.*)
A mollusc, who had his shell crushed,
a spider whose web has been ripped apart,
a wild bird out on the ocean,
too far out to turn back and find the shore –
He flails about above the seething abyss –
Until, worn out, he falls – and dies!
(*Pause.*)
CHRISTMAS GNOME:
    Tell me! Do you want to start again? Be young once more?
OLD MAN: Be young? No thanks! Have the strength to
                                                    suffer –
    the strength to weave false dreams? No!
CHRISTMAS GNOME: Do you want gold?
OLD MAN: To buy what?
    I want nothing – Yes I do. To depart this life!
CHRISTMAS GNOME:
    Yes, alright! But as one reconciled to life first!
OLD MAN: Reconciled? – Tied to the stake once again?
    No. Unreconciled! Otherwise I'd never leave –
    'One more handshake, and one for the road!'
    'Oh do stay a little longer!' – And so you stay.
    No! Jump up on the box, whip up the nag
    and shake yourself free, you won't look back!
CHRISTMAS GNOME: You shook yourself free once, free
                                        from the comforts of life,
    from hearth and home, from wife and child,
    to run after the empty eggshell of honour.
OLD MAN: Half true – I left in time,
    to avoid seeing the others go, they'd already packed!
    When life betrayed me, when the ship was about to sink,
    I made for myself a life-buoy which I inflated
    with air. That much is true;

it kept me afloat, for a time, quite a long time,
then it burst, and I sank; is that my fault?

CHRISTMAS GNOME: (*Has taken the box from the cabinet.*)

Here's some flotsam the sea has tossed back –

OLD MAN: (*Powerless.*)

Leave my box alone! Don't wake the dead!

CHRISTMAS GNOME: You Sadducee! You didn't believe
in the resurrection – why do you fear the dead?

OLD MAN: Leave my box alone! You call up spirits!

CHRISTMAS GNOME:

So be it! Then you'll see that life is spirit,
but imprisoned in a body, a thing!
Observe! Now I call them forth!
I conjure them!
(*Opens the box.*)

OLD MAN: Ah! What an aroma! Is it Clover?

O rose-filled month of May, when the apple trees blossom,
the lilacs wave their shoots in the west wind
and the newly dug garden that just now was white
beneath the snow, now stretches out its black cloth
over seeds, sown to rise again.
(*Sinding's 'Frülingsrauschen' is playing.*)
I can see – a little cottage, white with green shutters,
a window is opened, the curtains flutter –
wine-red taffeta – inside, a mirror,
a gilded frame, moulded in the empire style –
and in the oval glass, like a mirage,
I see – the most beautiful thing life has to offer;
a young mother, dressing her child, –
combing its soft curls, washing the sleep
from its blue eyes, opening
and smiling at the sun, and at the mother with the pure
joy of living
the little foot stamps the floor boisterously
impatient as a foal to rush out –
Music! Sweet notes from young days,
half forgotten which rise up again –
The little river gliding beneath the alders,

232

a boat, midsummer garlands, baskets of wild strawberries,
and a fresh pike, floundering on the thwart –
(*The CHRISTMAS GNOME picks up a bridal posy and a
white veil.*)
What's this now! What have you got there?
A little garland, a crown for a little queen,
made of myrtle, and a veil of lace –
a morning mist in a fairy ring at sunrise –
Now I can see no more, my eyes are veiled –
O my God, all this that once was,
and is no more, and will never return!
(*Breaks down and cries.*)

CHRISTMAS GNOME:
All this was yours and you threw it away,
fresh flowers exchanged for dry leaves,
the warmth of life for cold reason,
you poor man – what have we here?
(*Shows a lady's black glove.*)

OLD MAN: A little glove! May I see! I don't remember –
How came that here! – Yes, wait. I've got it –
Yesterday morning, I found it on the stairs –

CHRISTMAS GNOME:
You can have it from me as a Christmas present –
It holds secrets, those thin fingers
have meddled in destinies, made mischief,
but the little hand reaches out favourably to you now.
If you give it to her as I expect you will,
then you shall have spread happiness, solved a riddle
of more value than the sphinx's riddle that holds you in
its grip –

(*Locks the box in the cabinet.*)

OLD MAN: If I can still make a mortal happy,
If I can receive a look of thanks,
if I can bring comfort, stir a heart,
then there is still a cure for despair!

CHRISTMAS GNOME: Burning down that dark old forest,
was the bravest and wisest thing you've done;
sow seeds now in the clearing, things grow well in ashes,

You've *some* harvests yet to come!
But if you can't enjoy them yourself,
then give them away, it is more blessed to give than to
receive!

It is sacrifices which please!
And now I shall return to my dark little shed,
and wish you a very, merry Christmas!
(*Disappears.*)

●

OLD MAN: (*Alone, he looks at the glove.*)
A little hand outstretched in the dark –
A glove thrown down, not in a challenge but in peace!
A small child's hand, soft and mild –
What secrets are you hiding?
Maybe you're only a decoy,
coming with a Christmas gift –
(*A knock on the door.*)
Come in, unknown friend, a Christmas gift awaits
whoever comes first! – Come in!

●

(*ELLEN comes in.*)
ELLEN: Forgive me doctor, for barging in,
but you are known to be a philanthropist –
I'm lost, abandoned, I'm in despair!
OLD MAN: (*Gets up.*)
May God comfort you, my child, sit down,
what has happened, is this about the ring?
ELLEN: I was there just now, and I'm still a suspect,
they're looking for me. I wanted to drown myself,
but I couldn't. Let me stay;
say something, say 'not guilty'.
OLD MAN: Calm yourself, and let me think –
what was it now – ah yes, a Christmas present,
from a stranger!
ELLEN: What, an old glove!
OLD MAN: Yes, I don't understand it, but it was lost
then found, then lost again, then found once more –

ELLEN: I think it's Madam's! Let me see the size!
   (*She turns the glove inside out; and the ring falls out.*)
   O my God! There's the ring!
   Then I'm saved! You didn't know it was there?
OLD MAN: I knew nothing! Dry your eyes.
ELLEN: You're so kind! I already knew you were kind to
                              animals, and flowers...
OLD MAN: Hush now! I've no part in this –
ELLEN: But you are a good man, to save another person...
OLD MAN: I was an instrument, nothing more!
ELLEN: You should be happy now, I wish I were you,
   to make a poor wretch happy –
OLD MAN: Go now and put right what you can,
   and celebrate with the rest of the household...
ELLEN: How can I? – The little child is gone.
   How can we celebrate in a house of mourning!
OLD MAN: The little child? I've heard that story –
   but believe me, Ellen, someone has been playing hide
                              and seek here.
   More I cannot say! But with another view of things –
   I suspect, I hope, I believe that before the day is out,
   we might each have endured a time of trial.
   (*Sinks back into his chair and falls asleep.*)

End of Act Four.

ACT FIVE

The nursery

The nursery. Upstage an attractive alcove curtain with a little table in front of it; on the table, two candles in silver candlesticks; between them a child's portrait with flowers; a mirror behind the candles, whose flame can be seen in the mirror. On the left a small, white cot with a blue canopy above it. On the right, a child's table, white, with a chair. On the chair is the doll 'Rosa'; on the table, Christmas gifts and a little Christmas tree. A white rocking horse, beside the bed.

The YOUNG WIFE comes in dressed in black, with a black pelisse; she wears a black veil which she tears up and drapes over the objects in the room; the Christmas tree, the doll, the rocking horse etc.

YOUNG WIFE: We have gone into mourning! But we have
been given something,
to fill the emptiness of longing;
we have been given coldness and the chill of it cools us;
we have been given darkness, and the darkness conceals,
like the blanket you want to crawl under
on a sleepless night, to escape the images of fear.
Are you missing your little mistress, Rosa?
With your pale cheeks and your cold hands;
shall the Christmas tree play a song of mourning for you?
(*She winds up a music box and puts it under the Christmas tree.*)
And Blanka,[3] with crêpe on your neck!
I remember last year, we went away
to mother and father out in the country,
you stood all alone here in this cold room
but Mary thought of you, she said;
'Poor Blanka is standing all alone and cold
and maybe she's afraid of the dark, in those dark rooms.'
When she came home, you'd caught a cold,
had a sore throat, and she looked after you

3 A typical nursery name for a horse, like Dobbin.

236

and tied her best stocking around your neck,
and kissed your white nose,
combed your mane, and tied a gold ribbon
on your forehead! Yes, you were alright then,
but now – now we are in such pain, all of us!
little bed, you stand empty now, like a lifeboat at sea
when the ship has sunk, bobbing around out of control.
Who shall I make the bed for?
My little life which is now dead?

I remember that last evening
when after your supper, you found crumbs
in your bed, and I had to change the sheets,
you thought it was sand strewn there
by the Sandman, after the stories I had told you.
I mixed your evening prayers with tales and rhymes
to sing on your pleasure trip
to the green woods and blue lakes of dreams.
And your eyelids closed like daisies
atop the roses of your cheeks, the reeds of your hair...
There no more! A little dent in the soft feather bed
is the only image left of your body.
There under the bed's blue canopy
now turned to black and overcast with clouds...
Where is my child? Where are you, answer me?
Have you flown off to the stars
to play with other children, yet unborn,
or perhaps dead ones, born again?
Have you gone in search of the fairy tales
to meet Tom Thumb, The Blue Bird,
Red Riding Hood, or little Soliman,
because you grew tired of us, and our quarrelling?
If I could only join you. I was never at home here.
It was always so promising, but never fulfilling,
it seemed to be, but it wasn't;
was a work of art perhaps, but made only of faults;
too much body and not enough soul,
and how hopeless, that you could never be,
never become, what you wanted to be!

(*Pause.*)

But it's dark! They've turned off the lighting.

(*Turns a light switch in vain.*)

And it's cold, they've denied me heat!

(*Puts her arm out behind the curtain as if looking for a tap.*)

And no water! My flowers are thirsty!

(*She rings the servants' bell.*)

No-one comes! They've all gone away!

Was I so very nasty? No-one knows

What they all know – think they know!

They all bowed down to me, no-one dared

tell me how I ought to be!

Yes, the mirror dared, but he was a bad friend.

That smooth glass, offered only compliments.

(*Pause.*)

What's this? – The glove I dropped!

And here, inside the finger, is my ring!

Then she wasn't guilty. Poor Ellen!

She shall avenge herself, I'll get her punishment,

then the last shall be worse than the first!

Prison? – I don't want that – I'll hide the ring –

(*Pause.*)

No! Yes! – What was that? Someone stroked my cheek!

Is anyone here? I heard whispering.

A child breathing in its sleep.

And now. It's the weather vane on the neighbours roof.

Quiet. Listen, it's singing up there in the chimney tops.

What's it saying? 'my Mary, Mary, Mary'

And then; 'Ellen Ellen!' – Poor Ellen!...

A bell is ringing! The ambulance!

What has happened here? What have I done?

No, fair's fair, when I have done wrong

I must go myself and take my punishment!

●

(*ELLEN comes in.*

The YOUNG WIFE falls to her knees before her.)

ELLEN: Get up, in Jesus' name. It makes me sad to see you, my poor dear madam, get up, I can't bear to see it; it's

238

nothing, just a mistake, just something we have to put up with; everything's so difficult, life is hard, almost impossible they say! There, there!

YOUNG WIFE: Ellen! Forgive me!

ELLEN: I have done, I have, dear little madam. Please, get up and I'll tell you something...

YOUNG WIFE: (*Gets up.*) Is it about....?

ELLEN: No, it isn't! It's about someone else! The old man up in the garret – he's passed away – content and reconciled with whatever it was he wished for. – But when we looked in his papers – we found his real name – And...

YOUNG WIFE: Then I know! – He's my long lost father!

ELLEN: Yes!

YOUNG WIFE: And he died without ever seeing his child again! – I want to see him again! – This strange house, where human destinies are piled up under the floorboards, one on top of the other, next to each other. – Where is my husband? Have you heard from him?

ELLEN: He'll be home for supper – but not before!

YOUNG WIFE: Christmas dinner? In the dark, and the cold and the drought; in the house of mourning with dead bodies laid to rest in the rooms – my poor husband! Now I shall go to my father! – How did he die, Ellen?

ELLEN: He burnt all his papers and said that it was all rubbish – and it was him who found the ring. – After making me so happy he said, 'Now I can die content, now I've been granted the favour of making someone happy!'

YOUNG WIFE: He was right! – I didn't love him; but I want to close his eyes and perform the last services – as is only right! Come with me, Ellen!

(*They go.*

Pause.

KRISTIN and the CARETAKER come in carrying tools. They walk slowly across the stage.)

CARETAKER: It will be alright, it will be alright!

KRISTIN: (*Indicates the little bed.*) Quiet! Quiet!
(*They creep out.*
The CHRISTMAS GNOME in the wings, to the right, the
CHRISTMAS ANGEL to the left.)

CHRISTMAS ANGEL: Now our weft is almost complete;
I've seen someone fall to her knees, and in lowered tones;
utter that word 'sorry' that can atone for everything!
Now it's said and done! –
Lay off your weeds of mourning! Let the time of rejoicing
begin!

(*The CHRISTMAS GNOME creeps about, removes the black*
gauze which he gathers in his hands.)

CHRISTMAS GNOME: I shall blow away the dust, sweep
and tidy,

polish the brass clouded as if by foul breath;
I'll water the flowers when the maid forgets,
so they don't thirst!
(*He waters the flowers beside the mirror.*)
I shall pleat the curtains nicely,
straighten the mat; I can make a mess sometimes,
but not here, and not today!
Little mother, beautiful young wife,
now you have suffered, don't forget the lessons you have
learned!

Tears of pain and remorse
have beautified your eyes, now clear and mild
but if you cry from anger you shall be ugly!
Now my angel! Can we say 'happy Christmas' now?

CHRISTMAS ANGEL: Here she comes, from her labour
of love,

having closed the eyes of her dead father –
who, in death, got back his child –
(*The CHRISTMAS GNOME goes to look in the bed, rocks*
it gently, lifts his finger as if to say 'she's asleep'.)
Now she has got hers back, in life, alive –
Go away now to your buttons and taps.

CHRISTMAS GNOME: I'll go and make everything ready
for the tableau!

(*They go off in separate directions.*
Pause, music: Sinding's 'Frülingsrauschen'.)

●

YOUNG WIFE: (*Comes in, as before in a pelisse.*)
O warmth, have you returned?
Are the west wind risen, and the winter sun?
Risen from the equator.
(*Bright lighting on the stage.*
Drops her pelisse to the floor.)
O God! – One word! – And there was light!
Have you opened up the heavens again,
that I might see a tiny face
smiling between white clouds,
small hands stretching out, a tiny mouth...
But hush!
(*She listens as if she heard a noise from the bed; she looks*
about her.)
And what has happened here! Has mourning been put
aside?
(*Goes to the bed; sees the child, which the audience, however,*
cannot see.)
Yes, the Lord took, and the Lord gave back again!
I am not yet worthy of your mercy –
(*On her knees beside the bed.*)
But when a mother can hold her child in her arms
then joy can find no words, finds only tears!
(*The CHRISTMAS GNOME can be seen in the wings to*
the right; takes off his cap and blows kisses to the mother and
child.)

The End.

THE GREAT HIGHWAY

a drama of the road
with seven stations

Characters

HUNTER

HERMIT

WANDERER

MILLER A

MILLER E

WIFE A

GIRL

SCHOOLMASTER

BLACKSMITH

PEOPLE

ONE OF THE PEOPLE

WAITRESS

ORGAN GRINDER

PHOTOGRAPHPER

EUFROSYNE

GOTTHARD

KLARA

JAPANESE

MÖLLER

MURDERER

CHILD

WOMAN

TEMPTER

The Scenes

1. *In the Alps.*
2. *Beside the windmills.*
3. *In Eseldorf.*
4. *A lane in the city.*
5. *In the park beside the crematorium.*
6. *At the final gate.*
7. *In the dark forest.*

The music in the dark forest is Chopin's *Nocturne 13*, Opus 48, and this is played up until the end of the play.

Scene 1 – In the Alps

In the Alps. A signpost with two arms; one pointing up the mountain, and one down. In the background, black storm clouds. Later the storm breaks.

HUNTER: (*Comes in, reading the signpost.*)
Where have I come to, and how far?

Yes, there the road goes up, that way down!
You always come down in the end, I want up.
But the signpost here throws up its arms,
as if to warn me of the upward path!
A danger then, many dangers
along the path, so steep and narrow!
It doesn't scare me, I love the danger.
But I shall rest first a while,
and breathe!
And think, and gather my thoughts;
and restore me to myself,
My self which has been stolen…

●

I was too long amongst the people
and put aside my soul,
my heart, my thought;
the rest they took, they stole –
pinioned me with friendliness,
and gifts I'd not desired;
yes, it was warm walking down there
from home to home, sitting at tables,
music and flowers, candles and glasses.
But the warmth grew to heat, and stifled me –

Then I cast off my moorings,
and dropped the ballast, all that weighed me down,
however dear – and see, I rose!
Here I can breathe, and my heart's cotyledon,
my feeble lungs, can expand;

no dust, no smoke, nor the breath of others
poisoning my blood.

                    White, pure snow
of sublimated steam! Diamonds of the first water
thou, lily blooms, by the cold made into stone,
heavenly flour sieved through the black cloth of cloud –
holy silence, pull your silken sheet
above the tired traveller's head
on his way to bed, whispering his prayers.

●

What's to the North? A rock of flint,
a cloud like the school's black board,
as yet unmarked – a rumble! The teacher's here!
And the class falls silent!
Silence in Nature, when the great teacher speaks!
Look there! – A bolt from east to west –
in inky fire he writes his name
on the blue black cloud! I know You,
eternal, invisible, visible,
stern, all-forgiving! –
And the mountain pines bow down,
and the stilly streams stand silent.
A mountain goat falls fearful to its knees,
bareheaded vultures crouch in capless pate
on the Alpen ridge; Nature trembles! –
I, called 'lord of creation',
a nickname, not of my choosing,
I bow my head in shame,
the feeblest of creatures before your almighty throne!

●

See, the cloud has burst! The veil is gone,
drawn all aside! What do I see?
Pretty Earth! Temptress,
luring me back down below –
Dressed in your jewels!
In hope's green and faith's blue,
and the rose-red hue of love.

The high pines painted by the sun's demise,
nocturnal, grave-bound cypresses,
a cliff with marble temples,
built to happiness or honour,
a cave, home to a grey sibyl,
who scares away the nymphs into the olive groves –

Here comes the sun! Glistening
in the frost's pink diamonds; the clouds edged
with silver, blue-black cloaks
all hung out in the wind to air!
What's stirring here? Who blocks the sun?
And draws his shadow-pictures in the snow?
A golden eagle, *Chrysaetos* with his golden chest!
Knight of the Air, in a golden coat of mail,
and chivalry's chain about your neck –

What? Are you falling down into the valley?
Have your wings tired, does your dorsal rudder
fail to keep an upward course?
Yes, he wants to go down! Down! Down to rest,
and breathe the warm human breath,
and catch the scent of clover fields –
for it's still summer down below...
Down there, the clouds drop pearls;
here brilliants and table-cut stones;
there brooks babble, here they are struck dumb,
here desolate fields of snow, though with white
flowers –
there white daisies...
Up here, and down there! Here and there,
a man is driven, to Just as Good and Just as Bad!

●

HERMIT: Whither thou? *Quo Vadis*, wanderer?[1]
You've come half way and turn around.
Excelsior! was your motto up till now.

1 These were St Peter's words to Christ when, according to legend, he met
Him on the *Via Appagia*; Jesus' reply was 'To Rome to be crucified again.'

HUNTER: It is so still!

HERMIT: What do you seek up here?

HUNTER: My own self, which I lost below!

HERMIT: What you lost below
    you cannot surely regain up here?

HUNTER: So right you are! But if I go down,
    I lose still more, and never find what I have lost.

HERMIT: You want to save your skin...

HUNTER: Not my skin, my soul...

HERMIT: You have no love for people...

HUNTER: Yes, all too much, therefore I fear them too...

HERMIT: To love is to give; give!

HUNTER: They don't want to receive, just take;
    they take not just the gift but the giver too!

HERMIT: But the shepherd sacrifices himself for his
                         flock...

HUNTER: Yes, ashes to ashes, but the spirit belongs to God.

HERMIT: You fence well with your tongue, you ought to
                        wield a pen!

    In any case, your life is half done;
    don't expel the foetus, premature birth
    can't make you a man, can't make you human;
    live out your life, go back down, it's not dangerous;
    the highway will cover you with dust, brush it off;
    ditches run along its sides, fall into them!
    But get up again. There are fences,
    jump over them, creep under them, lift the latches;
    you'll meet people; take them in your arms,
    they don't bite and if they do, the bite isn't dangerous,
    if you get soaked, let it run off!
    Give away your coin, you'll get it back,
    there's nothing to gain up here,
    for stone is but stone, and snow is snow –
    but people, that's another matter.

HUNTER: I know that well enough, if only I could
    remain an observer, sit in the stalls,
    but I want to get up on the stage, and react, and take part;
    and then I take a role, I lose myself,
    and forget who I am...

HERMIT: Who are you?

HUNTER: Nice! Let us stop there...
  Truth to tell, it's getting cold for me up here.

HERMIT: And the air is somewhat thin, and all too solitary...
  Look out, we've company!

HUNTER: A strange fellow, coming downwards,
  a bit worn-out looking; hello there wanderer!

●

WANDERER: I've come from the tops of the Alps,
  I've bathed in the air, but I didn't stay in the bath;
  you get dressed and resume the journey,
  with company or without, but preferably with!
  What's that land in the distance called, Hermit?

HERMIT: It's called the Land of Wishes!

WANDERER: The Land of Pious Wishes?

HERMIT: Pious and impious
  according to...

WANDERER: ...to the desires!
  Well then! I'm to have company, I see!
  Whom do I have the honour of addressing?

HUNTER: I'm a soldier!

WANDERER: And I am a wanderer!
  Travelling incognito is best, believe me,
  one ought always to make acquaintances,
  but never get to know anyone,
  besides you never do anyway,
  you only think you do... And so:
  in company, without friendship, without enmity,
  leave a gap of two paces, not too close,
  and forward march! And downwards, then the level path!
  One upwards slope, one downwards!
  A tavern, a billet, a little glass,
  but keep a straight course for the south!

HUNTER: With the sun as our lighthouse, we won't go astray,
  it's never extinguished and the keeper never sleeps...
  I think he's left us, our Hermit?

WANDERER: Yes, let him go! He doesn't belong down there, where we shall take our path!

He has made his choice, and said his farewell to the world!

HUNTER: Maybe he is right to do so!

WANDERER: Don't look down!

'Society and frivolity' rhyme, like hither and thither, but we don't go hither, we go…thither!

Scene 2 – Beside the windmills

In the background, an overcast sky. At the two sides, the windmills, called Adam and Eve, one on each side, as well as an inn on the right.

The WANDERER and The HUNTER sit at a table with glasses.

WANDERER: It's peaceful down here in the valley.

HUNTER: A bit too peaceful, according to the miller,

WANDERER: who sleeps, no matter how much water runs;

HUNTER: since he runs after the weather and the wind…

WANDERER: futile tasks which give me a certain distaste for windmills.

HUNTER: Just as with the noble knight Don Quixote de La Mancha

WANDERER: who, nevertheless, never changed his course to suit the way the wind blew,

HUNTER: rather to the contrary;

WANDERER: which led him into certain difficulties. Are we playing beggar my neighbour?

HUNTER: Mr Incognito, why do you drink so much?

WANDERER: Because I am always on the operating table and so I always anaesthetise myself!

HUNTER: Then I shan't ask anymore!

WANDERER: Perhaps I have said too much!

HUNTER: Imagine! I still can't guess what you do!

WANDERER: Stop guessing, it's more fun that way.

HUNTER: I suppose so yes! – It's been cloudy all day today.

WANDERER: Let me drink up some of this, then you'll see things lighten up! (*Drinks.*) Do you know Greek? Do you know what *Oinos* means?

HUNTER: *Oinos* means wine.

WANDERER: Yes, wine! You have studied then?

HUNTER: *Noli me tangere!* Don't touch me! I bite!

WANDERER: Have you noticed that the grape is shaped like a wine bottle, and the vine stalk like a corkscrew? A distinct signature.

HUNTER: But the juice of the fruit of the vine has none of the characteristics of chloroform,

WANDERER: until the grape has been trampled underfoot and left to rot in the dregs and the draff,

HUNTER: so that the spirit of the wine is released from the squalid shroud of substance,

WANDERER: and rises up to the surface like the scum in the sea,

HUNTER: from which Aphrodite was born,

WANDERER: naked.

HUNTER: Without so much as a vine leaf to cover herself,

WANDERER: for clothes are only the consequence of the Fall, – Are you always this serious?

HUNTER: Are you always this jocular?

WANDERER: Who is the most curious minded of us two?

HUNTER: Now he's stretching out the snaring arms...

WANDERER: Subject to the general laws of attraction,

HUNTER: which is followed by mutual repulsion,

WANDERER: which is why it is best to keep two paces apart and march in open file...

HUNTER: as agreed, day and date as above! Full stop! Here come the actors!

●

WANDERER: May I borrow your glasses. I don't see very well.

What's that on the glass? It looks like hoar-frost,
crystallised water, or salt;
a tear, which has dried, hot at source,
it cooled so quickly and turned to rock salt;
the metal of the frames has rusted!
You cry often but in secret,
and the rivulets of your tears have etched their tracks

from each eye down to the corners of the mouth,
to extinguish the smile, before it turns to laughter.
You poor man!
Your half mask has worn away,
and when you show your teeth,
we don't know if it is to smile or bite!

HUNTER: Now the play begins! An idyll with windmills,
WANDERER: a pastorale in minor-major, look out now!

•

MILLER A: Well, neighbour, we're evens today. There's no wind at all; but apart from that I'm going to get your windmill moved, since you're damaging my livelihood.

MILLER E: You mean I take the east wind, but inasmuch as you take the west wind from me, I'd say we're quits.

MILLER A: But my windmill was here first, and yours was built out of pure spite. Since it's going badly for both of us, wouldn't it be better if it went well for one of us?

MILLER E: For you, you mean?

MILLER A: For you, you mean?

MILLER E: Yes, naturally!

MILLER A: But I meant for one of us, the most worthy, who has right on his side.

MILLER E: Who would that be?

MILLER A: Is it for us to judge in that matter?

MILLER E: I've got a better sieve than you, and my Eve, here, mills the grain quicker, turns easier, and has new sails.

MILLER A: But my Adam here, was built before yours, my mill screw is made of boxwood...

MILLER E: Hold on! We'll ask these men sitting here.

•

WANDERER: Here we go! Now we're going to get involved!

HUNTER: They want to hijack us as witnesses and maybe as judges, so that later they can sit in judgement over our judgement!

●

MILLER'S WIFE A: Come and eat your dinner now old man!

MILLER A: Wait a bit!

WIFE A: I can't wait!

MILLER A: You should learn never to be in a hurry!

WIFE A: Never?

MILLER A: Never, not so long as the world goes around, and words mean what they mean.

WIFE A: But then your cabbage will get cold!

MILLER A: Cabbage is it? Well, that's different! I'll come at once!

WIFE A: But the world will stop turning and words won't have any meaning anymore!

MILLER A: Did I say that? Then I take it back!

(*They go.*)

●

WANDERER: He sold his birthright,

HUNTER: for a bowl of cabbage,

WANDERER: and very tasty it was too.

HUNTER: But now we'll have Eve's miller upon us; see how he's lurking around, stalking us – he wants something from us, some information to enrich his knowledge; look at him staring at us…inspecting us with his eyes, examining our clothes, shoes, hair and beards; he's a thief!

●

MILLER E: Excuse me!

WANDERER: Now he wants to fool us into talking to him! – Don't answer!

MILLER E: Where are you gentlemen from?

WANDERER: That's none of your concern!

MILLER E: Strictly speaking, no it isn't!

WANDERER: We're going to be very strict, so, go your ways!

MILLER E: I'm not going to take anything…

WANDERER: You wouldn't find that very easy either…

MILLER E: I am, on the other hand, going to give something…

WANDERER: We don't need anything!

MILLER E: Well, I'll be! – Anyway, I thought I'd give you gentlemen something, and take nothing in return – a piece of information! A valuable piece of information! (*Pause.*) You see, they're going to blow up the hill behind here – (*Pause.*) – and, one, two, three, it will be raining stones down on our heads.

(*The HUNTER and the WANDERER stand up.*)

WANDERER: Why didn't you say so at once?

MILLER E: You didn't want to hear! But sit down, there's no rush, the engineers give a warning first!

WANDERER: Listen now, is this the road to the Promised Land?

MILLER E: It's the direct route…

WANDERER: Are we going to have fine weather this afternoon…?

MILLER E: We can expect more stormy showers; it's unsettled weather hereabouts.

WANDERER: Is it like that all year round?

MILLER E: Always unsettled, all year round, year in, year out.

WANDERER: And the next village is called?

MILLER E: That's none of your business! Admittedly it's more fun to give than to take, but it's no fun being robbed. Thief! – Do you have a passport?

WANDERER: What do I want with a passport?

MILLER E: Well, there are robbers in the woods, and anyone who doesn't want to say where they're from has to be searched.

●

HUNTER: There! Now we're involved!

WANDERER: In something that bears no resemblance to a windmill idyll.

MILLER E: I'm going to fetch my neighbour and his farm hands, so we can establish your alibis...

WANDERER: That's a strange way of...

MILLER E: Yes, because I'm the parish constable...and my neighbour is a juror... (*Goes.*)

WANDERER: And now they have become friends; Herod and Pilate!

HUNTER: In fact I came out here today, in order to save myself; but he who tries to save himself loses himself. So, let's cast ourselves back into the maelstrom again...

WANDERER: and risk sinking,

HUNTER: but not to the bottom,

WANDERER: thanks to a certain life-buoy which sensible folk keep about them! – Look, a woman!
(*The GIRL comes in.*)

HUNTER: Just what you might expect in the presence of Adam and Eve,

WANDERER: without expecting there to be any kind of Paradise.

HUNTER: Full stop! Now, let it begin!

●

WANDERER: I think attack is the most advantageous policy... What's your name, my child?

GIRL: Guess!

WANDERER: Let me see now! – Blond, miller's daughter, small build, round face, your name is Amalia!

GIRL: How do you know that?

WANDERER: I could tell!

GIRL: If I'd been dark, tall, oval faced, what would my name have been then; if I had been a blacksmith's daughter?

WANDERER: Jenny, of course!

GIRL: That's right!

WANDERER: Now I've taught you something, what will you give me in return?

GIRL: You shall have...to tell me where you find the wisdom to read people's faces?

WANDERER: Life, experience, certain books, an inborn superiority of understanding and a good portion of acquired clear-sightedness... Tell me; why don't you want to marry the other miller's son?

GIRL: You know that too!

WANDERER: But you should marry him, then you'd settle the windmill question without it having to go to court – you sell the one windmill and have it moved to the next parish, where it is needed.

GIRL: So clever, you're so clever...

WANDERER: But I can tell that you don't like the miller's boy, I suspect that you would really prefer one of the robbers in the woods, eh? The one with the black eyes and the big moustaches...

GIRL: Now you're scaring me... Are you a fortune-teller?

WANDERER: As you can hear; but I can only tell the fortunes of young people.

GIRL: Why's that?

WANDERER: Because old people are so cunning.

GIRL: (*To the HUNTER.*) Is that true?

WANDERER: Don't speak to him, he doesn't want to get involved! Talk to me! Give me something in return for all you've learnt in this short time, otherwise you'll be in my debt, and you don't want that!

GIRL: Yes, I'll give you something, so that you leave here fully recompensed, richer than when you arrived, loaded with learning which I take nothing in return for...

WANDERER: Well I never!

GIRL: For a start I'm not called Amalia –

WANDERER: No, Jenny; what did I tell you?

GIRL: No, not Jenny either! And next; there's no miller's boy. Third, the next parish owns four windmills, so the windmill question remains unsolved. And in addition I can give you a little piece of advice. Don't use the familiar term of address to a young girl you don't know, you never know who you might be talking to, however clear-sighted you may think you are. Furthermore, don't be disloyal to a friend, when a third person comes along, because when you are alone again and need him, maybe he won't be still to hand.

WANDERER: I haven't been disloyal!

GIRL: Yes you have; you were making fun of him just now
to try to impress me – that wasn't very nice. – Now
you're on the defensive – and if you asked me now what
my name is, I wouldn't answer in the way you did just
now to the miller, when he wanted to save you from the
robbers in the woods...

HUNTER: (*Gets up.*) Would you care to sit down, young
lady?

GIRL: That's right, I am a young lady, from the manor
house, and not the miller's daughter... (*To the
WANDERER.*) Go in to the miller and say hello from
me, then he'll give you the passport; go now, and say I
sent you...

WANDERER: But I have to know your name!

GIRL: (*Sits.*) I don't give out my name to strangers, and if
you had any manners you wouldn't ask for it! Off you go!
(*The WANDERER goes out.*)

●

GIRL: It's fine for you, free to roam,
meet lots of people, get to know them...

HUNTER: Get to know them?

GIRL: 　　　　　　　　　　　Yes! That's not true!
But you become acquainted...

HUNTER: 　　　　Hardly that even; but guessing at riddles
is also a pastime!

GIRL: 　　　　　　　　Because what people say
is not worth much!

HUNTER:
　　　Although; it can be translated;
for all languages can be called foreign,
and we are all strangers to each other, or become so.
We all travel incognito,

GIRL: 　　　　　　　　　　and incognito before ourselves!
You are in grief, but you're not dressed in mourning,

HUNTER: and you are dressed as a miller's daughter, but
　　　　　　　　　　　　　　　you are a lady!

GIRL: And your friend?

HUNTER: Only an acquaintance but unknown
                                        to me entirely.

GIRL: What do you think of that man?
HUNTER: Everything and nothing!
    But I haven't summed him up yet!
GIRL: What were you two doing up there?
HUNTER: Taking the air, and
                                        forgetting!

GIRL: But why forget? Without memories
    our lives are empty nothingness...
HUNTER: and with memories there's a cargo that sinks the
                                        ship!

GIRL: Unladen ships are the worst in a storm...
HUNTER: that's why one takes on ballast...
GIRL: And lowers the sail
HUNTER: like the windmill.
GIRL: Because otherwise the sails break...
HUNTER: But the sails turn best up on a hill...
GIRL: but best of all in the vales, on the plains...
HUNTER: where the air is so thick,
GIRL: ...that you can see the charcoal stacks,
    and count the parish churches with a naked eye,
    and all the night stars...
HUNTER: not on the horizon,
GIRL: but at the zenith,
    and the zenith is everywhere,
    when you've reached the horizon...
HUNTER: Tell me, when did I
                                        reach it?

GIRL: You are sitting there, at the point you strove for
    in the morning of the day! Isn't it sweet?
    To discover the new when you have attained the old?
HUNTER: But the country there in the distance?
GIRL: Go, and you shall reach it...
    But if you tire, then it will recede! –
    No mortal has the pole star in ascendant,
    but still they journey to it, turn again,
    and others follow the same route and are forced back.
    Do like them! But learn along the way.

HUNTER: One drags and dredges, nose down at the nadir...
GIRL: But with your eye now and again fixed upon the
zenith! –

(*A signal upon a horn.*)
HUNTER: (*Listens.*) Listen!
GIRL: I hear it but I don't understand!
HUNTER: I'll translate!
   You hear only sounds but I hear words!
GIRL: What does the brass say?
HUNTER: 'answer now, where are
you, where?'

(*The horn replies; 'here!'*)
GIRL: Someone is calling you!
   (*Another signal.*)
HUNTER: 'Follow me hither, follow me hither, follow me
hither! Hither!'
GIRL: I can hear you are a soldier, or see it rather!
   Someone is calling you; we part as suddenly as we met!
HUNTER: Not quite so suddenly, not quite so easily...
   Come along the road a bit with me
   to the next village!
GIRL: And your friend?
HUNTER: People like him you can find at the bar in any inn.
GIRL: How cruel you are!
HUNTER: I've been to war!
   There it's a matter of advancing! Not staying still!
GIRL: And that's why I'm going; otherwise I'd stay!
HUNTER: And if you go, you take something with you.
GIRL: And if I stay then you'll take something from me!
HUNTER: (*Looks outwards.*)
   Look there! They're arguing! Soon they'll be fighting –
   They are fighting! And I'll be called as a witness!
   You should go, don't get involved.
GIRL: You'll think of me then?
HUNTER: Of you, for you,
   with you, through you! Now, farewell!
   A flower, seen through the garden fence,
   giving a moment's joy to the traveller,
   unopened bud, the most beautiful,

exudes its perfume on the wind, one second, then it's all
over!

And so onwards!

GIRL: Farewell! Onwards! (*She goes.*)

●

HUNTER: Now I'm down! Tied up, ensnared
in the grinding mechanism of justice,
with a net of tangled emotions, on slender wings,
linked with a stranger, and involved
in an affair which doesn't concern me!

WANDERER: Are you still here? I thought you had gone,
but you must be a faithful soul.

HUNTER: Did you get involved in a fight?

WANDERER: I gave the miller a knuckle sandwich for
making fun of me. All that business about rock blasting
and robbers in the woods was lies. Anyway, we're
summoned to the autumn assizes, me for my part in the
fight, and you as a witness.

HUNTER: Did you give our names then?

WANDERER: No, I made up a couple of names on the
spot.

HUNTER: How could you dare to do that? We could be
prosecuted for falsification... Fancy getting mixed up in
something in this way! – What did you call me?

WANDERER: I said you were a traveller called Incognito!
And these peasants accepted it!

HUNTER: And now I'm to give evidence against you?

WANDERER: In three months' time, yes! Let's make use of
our freedom and journey onwards! – They say there's
going to be a party in the next village!

HUNTER: What party is that?

WANDERER: A kind of *jeux floraux*, or feast of fools, in
which the biggest blockhead in the village is crowned
with a golden crown, made of paper...

HUNTER: Priceless! What's the name of the village?

WANDERER: It's called Eselsdorf, but this one is called
Lügenwald, because only liars live here.

HUNTER: *Enthevten, exelavnein,* after which they departed, [2]
WANDERER: *parasangas treis,* three parasanger.[3]
HUNTER: and so they did!

Scene 3 – In Eselsdorf

Eselsdorf. To the left, a blacksmith's; to the right a bench where the HUNTER and the WANDERER sit to one side.

HUNTER: We've wandered about together quite a bit now,
WANDERER: and become no better acquainted; not even
    so that I might guess who you are.
HUNTER: I've told you, I'm a soldier; which means I'm
    always fighting, fighting to keep my personal
    independence…
WANDERER: But you don't always win.
HUNTER: One cannot expect to.
WANDERER: especially since defeats are the most
    instructive,
HUNTER: for the winner,
WANDERER: but the worst thing is, you can't always tell
    who has won; for in the last war the victor lost most.
HUNTER: Which war?
WANDERER: By the windmills!
HUNTER: May I borrow your penknife, I've lost mine up
    in the hills.
WANDERER: We mustn't be inquisitive! – If, for example,
    you were to look closely at this knife, it would tell you
    rather a lot. The large blade is almost unused – the
    owner is therefore not a professional; the small blade on
    the other hand, exhibits traces of lead and coloured
    crayons; he could be accordingly, an artist, but only
    need be an amateur; the corkscrew is rather worn out –

2 Greek – 'after which they departed', from Xenophon's *Anabasis,*
describing soldiers returning from a defeat at Kunaxa 401 BC.

3 Greek measurement of distance, three parasangas approximately
eighteen miles.

we can feel that, the bottle opener too! But then there is a drill and a saw! Yes, and a pick-lock – that's more eloquent, even though it's only included in the knife by chance. No information there then!

HUNTER: So!... This is Eselsdorf! And here comes the schoolmaster; we shall keep quiet this time, so we don't get involved.

WANDERER: We could try!

SCHOOLMASTER: (*Comes in.*) Abracadabra, abracadabra, abracadabra. (*Looks at the strangers.*) No! They didn't hear! – One more time! – Abracadabra, abracadabra, abracadabra! – No! They're gentlefolk, they've got self control! – My good sirs, he who says nothing is in agreement; my question, gentlemen, is would you like to receive a deputation of the village's foremost intellectuals who challenge you, sirs, to a debate. If I don't get an answer, I shall consider the offer to be accepted! One, two, three!

HUNTER/WANDERER: No!

SCHOOLMASTER: Splendid!

WANDERER: You are no fool, sir, considering you are from Eselsdorf.

SCHOOLMASTER: I am the only sane man in the village, and for that reason I must act the fool otherwise they'd lock me up! I have an academic education, I have written a tragedy in five acts, in verse, called *Potamogeton*, it's so damned foolish that I ought to have won the prize, but the village blacksmith out-flanked me and submitted a memorial to the Nation's Destroyer,[4] Karl XII, and so I was overlooked. You think, sirs, that I am subjective, because I talk about myself, but there are two reasons for this; in the first place I have to introduce myself, and in the second place, you wouldn't like it, would you sirs, if I talked about you! – Here comes the village blacksmith,

---

4 Karl XII, Swedish king at the height of Sweden's power. Strindberg in his *History of Sweden* held him personally responsible for, among other things, the disastrous defeat at Poltava, which led to Sweden's decline. See also *The Burned Site.*

I shall disguise myself, otherwise he might think I am
sane, and have me put away. (*He puts on his ass's ears.*)

BLACKSMITH: (*Comes in.*) Abracadabra, abracadabra!

SCHOOLMASTER: Poppycock!

BLACKSMITH: Is that remark directed at me?

SCHOOLMASTER: Life is a battle, and so are we!

BLACKSMITH: Do you mean the struggle for
emancipation, or free trade?

SCHOOLMASTER: Two times two equals four, add six,
makes eight. Do you follow?

BLACKSMITH: Arithmetic is my preserve, it is my main
subject...*quator species,* which means the four principles of
arithmetic, including fractions, excluding ordinary whole
fractions, and decimal fractions.

SCHOOLMASTER: Sometimes, even the great Homer
would fall asleep...

BLACKSMITH: But six and four make eleven, and if you
move the comma two steps to the left, then it is as level
as a nail. Not so, gentlemen, am I not right?

WANDERER: Quite right, six plus four makes eleven, and
not eight!

BLACKSMITH: We now pass to the easier components or
if I must so express it; topics of conversation. My good
sirs, a topic of conversation is not the snout growing
from out of my nose, if I may so express myself, even if
we suppose the topic of conversation to be an easy one.
An easy subject, falls, on closer inspection, into two
equal parts; first comes the subject, which is to be
the substance of all that follows, then comes the
conversation, as if by itself. The topics, there again,
could be as numerous as...as the days in the year, or
even more; let us say the drops in the ocean, or even
more; let us say the sand in the desert, not that I've been
in the desert, but I can imagine pretty well what it looks
like; on the other hand I have taken the steamer once, it
was expensive gentlemen, I am presuming you have
never made such a trip, but that wasn't what I wanted to
say!...

SCHOOLMASTER: The Guano Islands lie 56° north and 13° east by east, full south.

BLACKSMITH: Is that a dig at me? I don't like digs...

SCHOOLMASTER: But it was nothing compared to Karl the Great!

BLACKSMITH: No, but it's harder to shoe an ambling horse so that it doesn't get lopsided heels.

SCHOOLMASTER: Hafiz[5] says, quite rightly, in the third *Sura*, first folio, page seventy-eight onwards 'Eat man! you don't know when you'll next see bread again!'

BLACKSMITH: I just want to inform you that it is pronounced *foglio*, in the way of *embroglio, seraglio*. Or maybe it's called leaf?

SCHOOLMASTER: Yes, yes, yes!

BLACKSMITH: Fair's fair; that's what I always say. Do you know, schoolmaster, the year of Julius Caesar's birth? This will get him!

SCHOOLMASTER: Year 99, Before Christ!

BLACKSMITH: Before Christ! That's impossible; we start counting at year one, and you can't count backwards, can you?

SCHOOLMASTER: Can't you count backwards?

BLACKSMITH: Look out now! Don't start disputing, look out! He has such a feeble head, something may happen! – Can't you tell me, schoolmaster, what is the difference between rye and wheat?

SCHOOLMASTER: Julius Caesar was born 99 and died 31...

BLACKSMITH: Hear that? How's that? Live backwards, did he? – The difference between rye and wheat, that's, in the first place, the cereal price or the index of market rates, in the second place it's the free customs, because rye has a protective duty on it and wheat is excise-free! Nicely put, eh?

SCHOOLMASTER: Yes, yes, yes!

BLACKSMITH: But the money standard, that's another matter! I'm a silver man myself, I wont deny it, and the stock exchange, that's something else again, the official

5 Hafiz, Persian lyric poet 1320–1389.

stock quotation, that's also another thing, and *agio* is also another thing.

SCHOOLMASTER: What's that then?

BLACKSMITH: What is it? Do I really have to tell you that? Don't you think I've got anything else to do? Haven't I paid my dues, am I not married; I only ask! Only asking! If anyone has any objections I should like to have a word with him in private. Do you know what that is? Behind the stables. Don't say a word, I can't bear to be answered back. I must never be answered back. Do you consider all these questions to be resolved now, to my advantage, or shall we go behind the stables? I'm a very serious man, but I'm not to be toyed with! – Now, gentlemen, do you know what an ass you have before you, I don't mean me, I mean the schoolmaster, who believes one can be born before the beginning of time! Well, I'll tell you what kind of a fellow he is! Well, he's the stupidest wretch ever to don a pair of shoes; he's so stupid that he thinks there is such a place as the Guano Islands – there's no such thing of course! – (*Takes out a bottle and has a swig.*) He doesn't know the difference between rye and wheat – and he drinks as well – perhaps you think that I also drink, but I just pop off a few corks, you know, you can't call that drinking because that's something else. – To know something, my good sirs, that is a virtue, but the schoolmaster, he knows nothing, and this man is given the task of educating children; but he is a despot as well, a tyrant, a ruffian; so now you know who he is!

WANDERER: Wait a bit! I don't of course intend to answer you back, because then you will want to fight, nor do I propose to question you because then your knowledge would show itself to be wanting. Nor shall I invite you for a drink, because that isn't necessary, any more than I shall reason with you, because you would never understand what I meant, and you would never admit that I was right, but I should like very much to ask you something.

BLACKSMITH: Ask away, but ask nicely!

WANDERER: You are a character aren't you!

BLACKSMITH: Yes, a real character, in a word, a strong character.

WANDERER: And are you a silver man besides?

BLACKSMITH: I am proud to be a silver man.

WANDERER: You don't recognise the gold standard in the world markets?

BLACKSMITH: Not gold! No!

WANDERER: Not in private use either?

BLACKSMITH: Let me think for a moment! (*Aside.*) Is he trying to cheat me in some money changing? (*Aloud.*) I won't answer that! I don't want to answer, no-one can force me to answer – and although I have remarkable good sense, I don't understand what you are saying!

WANDERER: Don't you? Are you afraid that your strong character might give way in the attempt?

BLACKSMITH: Are you answering me back? Don't, because I am the absolute ruler in this village, I am a despot!

(*The WANDERER laughs.*)

Don't look at me, I am a terrible despot!

WANDERER: I am not looking at you, I just laughed.

BLACKSMITH: Don't laugh! I have six thousand votes in the local council; and that's nothing to laugh at! I have five children, all well brought up, all highly talented, especially in the way of brains, two of them I admit have gone to America! But these things happen, and one of them has taken a wrong turning...but he's paid for it, so it's nothing worth mentioning, nothing at all!

WANDERER: (*Aside.*) He is superb!

HUNTER: But it has to come to an end! I'm suffocating!

BLACKSMITH: I'll just go and fetch my manuscript, and the party can begin! But you mustn't go, gentlemen, I'm the mayor here and I hold sovereignty here; the schoolmaster will read from his tragedy *Potamogeton*, meanwhile. It's not so bad for the work of a dilettante, but many dogs attend the death of a hare, so to speak!

SCHOOLMASTER: And the verses trip along by
themselves, like great big goslings.

BLACKSMITH: Is that a dig at me?

SCHOOLMASTER: It can't very well be can it since you
are fully grown.

BLACKSMITH: Fully fledged, it's called, if you're talking
about the bird family; read nicely for the gentlemen, I'll
be back soon, but don't slander me in my absence.

SCHOOLMASTER: Well it's hardly possible in your
presence!

BLACKSMITH: That's true, and of the two evils, one
choses the best; therefore: slander me in my absence, but
not in my presence. (*Goes.*)

●

WANDERER: What kind of village is this, is it an
institution?

SCHOOLMASTER: Yes, they're so wicked that they have
gone mad.

WANDERER: Aren't you under supervision?

SCHOOLMASTER: I'm under observation, because I'm
suspected of being sane.

WANDERER: Come with us then, and we'll fly the field!

SCHOOLMASTER: Then we'll all be rounded up!

WANDERER: It's not just nonsense then?

SCHOOLMASTER: Wickedness is the mother of madness,
and its child at the same time.

WANDERER: Who is this blacksmith?

SCHOOLMASTER: One of the false idols Isaiah spoke of;
he is made of the wickedness of others, envy, hatred and
lies. The blacksmith became the mayor, because the
baker was the most worthy; after I had done twenty-five
years' faithful service, the day was celebrated with a
party for the blacksmith; in the last festival of the ass,
the blacksmith received the laurel wreath even though he
had written the worst verses.

HUNTER: Better to flee than to fight badly; we can't fight
here, so we flee.

WANDERER: It's really very dangerous here!

SCHOOLMASTER: But most dangerous of all is to flee.

WANDERER: Can't we trick them since they're all numbskulls?

SCHOOLMASTER: But they're cunning like all numbskulls –

WANDERER: We'll give it a try! – Blacksmith!
  (*The BLACKSMITH enters.*)
  Abracadabra, abracadabra!

BLACKSMITH: What can I do for you? Are you leaving, gentlemen? No, please don't leave!

WANDERER: We're only going to the next village to fetch the requisites for the festival.

BLACKSMITH: What did you say you were fetching?

WANDERER: Requisites.

BLACKSMITH: You shall requisition them I suppose? Requisites are always welcome; is it mainly stuff from the forge?

WANDERER: Yes, horseshoe nails, the bushes for carriage wheels, scythes and spades...

BLACKSMITH: Marvellous!

WANDERER: But we need the schoolmaster with us to help us carry it all...

BLACKSMITH: He's so weak, and so simple-minded!

WANDERER: But requisition orders are just pieces of paper, he can manage those!

BLACKSMITH: Very true, very true...but wheel bushes are heavy, he can't...

WANDERER: But a requisition order for a wheel bush is no heavier than a requisition order for a nail.

BLACKSMITH: Very true, very true... oh alright then, go! But come back!

WANDERER: Do you realise that if one goes one has to come back...

BLACKSMITH: But wait a bit: what is it that goes and goes but never comes back?

WANDERER: A clock, that would be, but we are no clocks, and therefore we will come back!

BLACKSMITH: That's logic, and I understand logic! But
  wait a bit; won't your clocks come back with you?
WANDERER: They aren't clocks, they are watches.
BLACKSMITH: Very true, clocks sit upon church steeples,
  whereas watches are something else entirely. But wait a
  bit! Alarm clocks, sometimes they don't go off! Ergo...
WANDERER: We're going, that's the main thing!
BLACKSMITH: Quite so; that's the main thing! And it's
  logical; I like logic in all of life's circumstances; and
  I can only follow a very strong logical argument...
WANDERER: Which is why you shan't try to follow us.
  We are not a logical argument.
BLACKSMITH: Quite so! And therefore I shall stay at my
  post, and you shall go. Off you go!
WANDERER: Sing the ass's praises O rhyme-smith!

Of all the beasts on earth you are the wisest,
and of them all your hearing is the finest,
your long upstanding ears like bones,
can hear the grasses growing under stones,
and you can see both east and west together:
on resolute stiff legs you brave the weather,
your strength of character straining at your tether
Your will is law unto your master,
he bids you stop, and you go all the faster;
he tells you run, you stay to eat the heather.

BLACKSMITH: That's very well said – for the mammal in
  question belongs to the world of the underrated, the
  camp of the mute, and deserves truly to be re-ha-bi –
WANDERER: – litated! But have you ever heard a mute ass?
BLACKSMITH: No, but I don't pay any attention to that;
  what I pay attention to is character, strength of character,
  and it is for that reason that I understand that
  misunderstood animal, I feel solidarity with it, yes I do.
WANDERER: You stand by that do you?
BLACKSMITH: I stand by that!
WANDERER: Then let's go!
BLACKSMITH: Wait a minute! I stand by, it but I don't
  stand alone, I have opinion and party behind me; all

right-thinking, enlightened, unprejudiced people, in a word; the nation is gathered around my standard; and when I remain standing, I want to show you that you are wrong, because what's right is right; is that logical?

SCHOOLMASTER: The highest right is the highest wrong!

BLACKSMITH: And the voice of the people is God's voice! Come in people, gather, o nation!

(*The PEOPLE enter, just a few individuals.*)

WANDERER: The nation is it? But they are so few!

BLACKSMITH: They are few, but you don't see the deep phalanxes behind them.

WANDERER: No, I can't see any!

BLACKSMITH: You don't see them, for the simple reason that they are invisible! That's logical. – People! These learned charlatans are suggesting, that there exist islands called Guano. There is no such thing is there?

PEOPLE: No!

BLACKSMITH: These gentlemen are therefore liars and dumb-heads! – Is there a punishment severe enough that can be dealt out to such rascals as spread about lies?

WANDERER: Yes, there is one cruder than all others: exile!

BLACKSMITH: Yes, that's not bad! But we shall have proofs first. – There is a fellow here suggests that Homer slept!

WANDERER: Occasionally!

BLACKSMITH: Occasionally or all the time, it's the same thing; it's just sophistry. Do the people believe that a bard can sleep, have you even heard anything so idiotic?

ONE OF THE PEOPLE: But he must have slept at night!

BLACKSMITH: At night? Is that an answer? Did I give permission to anyone to answer? Come behind the stables, and I'll give you an answer!

ONE OF THE PEOPLE: Is it a question of taking sides?

BLACKSMITH: Yes, a man should take sides, otherwise he becomes a characterless waverer.

●

SCHOOLMASTER: Won't you read from your Karl the Great, so we can get away from this gurgling, our strangers are in a hurry apparently.

(*Aside to the HUNTER and the WANDERER.*) He's not called Karl the Great, but we have to call him that otherwise we'll be locked up.

BLACKSMITH: I heard what he said! And I saw you grinning, and whoever grins is in collusion. – Take them in! You know what I mean. – Seize them! – He isn't called Karl the Great, but we call him that since he was quite simply Great! – Gag them, lock them up, until they can think better thoughts!

(*The HUNTER, WANDERER and SCHOOLMASTER are seized and are to be taken away.*)

HUNTER: But we are in exile, and we were going to town to make requisitions...

BLACKSMITH: That's quite correct, everything is correct. We shall let you go, but on your word of honour that you will come back again, and under a promise, that is you promise me, to be grateful, for an ungrateful person is the heaviest burden the world carries. I have a wife who holds soirées, well it sounds silly I expect, but they are soirées, and I await you there gentlemen, upon this summons!

WANDERER: So, free then! But at what price?

HUNTER: Is that what you call freedom, to be bound by the claims of a word of honour to a literary soirée?

BLACKSMITH: Be gone! But – the nation remains!

(*The HUNTER, WANDERER and SCHOOLMASTER go.*)

(*Curtain.*)

Scene 4 – A lane in the city

A city lane (arcade and shops) in Thofeth. In the first wing on the right a restaurant; in the other a photograph shop, in the third a shop selling shells; on the front to the left flowers and fruit, in the second wing a Japanese tea and perfume shop.

The HUNTER and the WANDERER sit outside the florist.

WANDERER: You are so melancholic.

HUNTER: We've come too far down!

WANDERER: Have you been here before, in Thofeth?

HUNTER: Yes, I've lived here.

WANDERER: I could tell.

HUNTER: We must have some chloroform – my wounds are beginning to ache!

WANDERER: *Vinum et circenes.* We'll have some free drama here; this is supposed to be the gutter of the town, everything drains into it! (*He waves into the restaurant; A WAITRESS brings wine.*) Won't people recognise you here?

HUNTER: Quite impossible, for I have allowed my beard to grow, cut my hair and washed my hands this very morning. In this village one is unrecognisable if one washes!

WANDERER: But the waitress is looking at you.

HUNTER: Perhaps I resemble one of her old friends.

WANDERER: Here comes a little diversion –

(*An ORGAN GRINDER with a monkey comes in.*)

Come here, organ grinder, spare our heads for a small sum.

ORGAN GRINDER: Heads?

WANDERER: Ears then! Here's a gold coin if you promise not to play!

ORGAN GRINDER: It's the monkey that's the main attraction!

WANDERER: Then we'll watch it, but without accompaniment.

ORGAN GRINDER: But there are words to it as well...

WANDERER: Is it true that you villagers are descended from a monkey?

ORGAN GRINDER: *Is* it true? You'd better watch it, mate!

WANDERER: When I look at you a little closer I think it must be true! – I'm sure of it, I'd swear to it! Let me see the words to the song! – Yes, but this creature by Jove looks more like an old goat.

ORGAN GRINDER: Yes it really does! Then it must be one, I suppose!

WANDERER: Do you really believe that this mammal in the red dresscoat shooting a pistol is the father of all mankind?

ORGAN GRINDER: If you are a free-thinker sir, then you'd better watch out... We are all orthodox here in this town and defenders of the faith.

WANDERER: Which faith?

ORGAN GRINDER: The only true faith: The Evolution of Species.

HUNTER: So now we might be charged with blasphemy! – Where did the schoolmaster get to?

WANDERER: He disappeared of course, as soon as he had made use of us.

HUNTER: Shall we go?

WANDERER: What's the use? Whether we fall into the hands of this lot or another lot, it's a matter of indifference.

HUNTER: Because people are lying in ambush like highwaymen, tricking each other. Look in through the restaurant window, where the girl is standing staring at you with hooded eyes as if she were asking you to receive her out of pity and mercy. She's beautiful, and can arouse feelings other than sympathy. Suppose you would want to save her from the heavy, rather humiliating work in there; supposing you would give her a home to protect her from the worst buffets of life, then she would, after a short time, have stolen your friends, separated you from your family, your boss and your benefactors – in a word, eaten you up.

WANDERER: and if I don't permit it, she'd sue me for cruelty,

HUNTER: and for ruining her youth...but the worst of all would be that you would enter in to a family you don't know,

WANDERER: but which I suspect... Imagine, she's standing in there tugging at me, sucking me in...stirring up a whirlpool; she's weaving a web which feels like warm air... Wait, I'll go in and pull it down,

HUNTER: or get caught in it.

(*The WANDERER goes into the restaurant.*)

●

HUNTER: (*Alone.*) Man overboard! –

●

PHOTOGRAPHER: (*Approaches with a camera.*) May I take your portrait, sir?

HUNTER: No!

PHOTOGRAPHER: Please do me the favour, sir, I'm so poor.

HUNTER: But you mustn't put me in the window, nor make cigarette cards out of me, nor soap wrappers; and if I come out looking like an aborigine or the latest multiple murderer, then you must destroy the plate!

PHOTOGRAPHER: You are suspicious, sir...

HUNTER: Not at all, but I am a little cautious!

(*The PHOTOGRAPHER waves towards his shop, from which his wife then appears.*)

●

PHOTOGRAPHER: May I introduce my wife, she usually helps with the developing and fixing, come, Eufrosyne; I have promised to oblige the gentleman with a photograph even though I am extremely busy – come Eufrosyne...do come and converse a little with the gentleman while I work!

EUFROSYNE: (*Sits down.*) You must be born lucky, my good sir, to happen to find such an artist as my husband... He is the most skilful I have ever seen, and if this picture isn't a good one, then you can say that I don't know art! You ought to appreciate the value of his work, and not pretend that you are doing us a service.

HUNTER: Wait a minute...

EUFROSYNE: Yes, you needn't look so self-important; when you ask a favour of someone, you should be grateful.

HUNTER: Now wait a minute...

PHOTOGRAPHER: (*Calls out.*) Gotthard! – Come here, you've put the plates in back to front...

GOTTHARD: (*Comes out.*) I haven't put any plates in at all...

EUFROSYNE: Do you answer back your father, your own father?

GOTTHARD: I didn't know anything about cameras... I deal with shells, I do...

PHOTOGRAPHER: You deal with them, yes; but do you sell any? Ask this gentleman if he needs any shells, I thought he said something just now concerning shells...

HUNTER: I haven't said anything about shells, I spoke of cigarette packets and soap...

EUFROSYNE: Gotthard, bring the cigarettes, don't you hear the gentleman wants cigarettes?

HUNTER: I wanted to avoid having my picture in a cigarette packet and wrapped around a bar of soap...

GOTTHARD: (*Sits down.*) You're a difficult man to deal with, sir, I can see that; but let's try to sort this out reasonably...

EUFROSYNE: You're right, Gotthard, we shall acquaint this gentleman with our circumstances, then he'll see; ask Klara to come out here.

GOTTHARD: (*Calls.*) Klara!

●

(*KLARA, the florist, comes out.*)

EUFROSYNE: Try to sell a flower to this gentleman, he's so frugal or rather, so mean, that he refuses to buy a shell, even though Gotthard has the most beautiful shells I've ever seen.

KLARA: (*Sits down.*) Perhaps he can be talked to, even though he looks so self-important. Is he a hunter?

EUFROSYNE: You can see that for yourself.

KLARA: He kills animals, he shouldn't do that anyway because it's a sin, but he looks cruel too; like all drunkards; the man who drinks in the morning, that man is a drunkard...

HUNTER: (*To KLARA.*) What have you done to your husband? (*KLARA looks horrified.*) It's a sin to kill people! – Don't you know that?

KLARA: You think so do you?

HUNTER: Yes I do!

KLARA: Do you hear, witnesses, hear what he's saying?

ALL: Yes, we heard!

HUNTER: May I just say a word! Just one?

GOTTHARD: No! Why should he be allowed?

HUNTER: I don't intend to say what you think, but rather something quite different.

EUFROSYNE: (*Curious.*) Go on then!

HUNTER: Has Möller been arrested yet?

(*They all stand up in horror.*)

●

WANDERER: (*Comes out from the café.*) What's going on now?

HUNTER: Has Möller been arrested yet?

(*They all disperse, but in a threatening manner.*)

For the third time! – Has Möller been arrested?

(*They all disappear.*)

●

WANDERER: What did that mean?

HUNTER: The village secret! They all know that Möller did the latest murder, but no-one dares give evidence because they lack proof. The consequence of my bombshell in the meantime, is that we had better get out of here. – Come!

WANDERER: I can't!

HUNTER: Stuck?

WANDERER: In an ale-house, dregs in the glasses, matchsticks and cigar ash, pawed by the young men, covered in smoke, underslept, and yet, despite it all, I am bound to her...

HUNTER: Fight loose!

WANDERER: I can't!

HUNTER: Then let's get away!

WANDERER: I can't!

HUNTER: Well, stay then!

WANDERER: I can't! – I can't do anything!

HUNTER: Then I bid you goodbye...

WANDERER: We'll meet again...
HUNTER: You always do, when once you've met.
WANDERER: Farewell then! (*Goes in to the café.*)

●

HUNTER: (*Alone, walks a little along the arcade, stops with no
pretended purpose outside the PHOTOGRAPHER's.*)
This was once mine...
long ago! My peregrinations
in the rainy season, under a glass ceiling;
when the yellow-grey daylight weighed upon the mind,
in here were always lighted candles,
flowers and fruits, delighted my eye;
and the shells whispering their tales of the sea;
here are some portraits of familiar faces
and unfamiliar faces,
they used to be my company in the loneliness!
A glance, an expression sufficed me
to feel kinship with mortals...
They sit here still... Here is my oldest friend,
grey-haired now for certain, but his image
like leaves in autumn!
has only yellowed –
Here are relatives, and former relatives –
a brother-in-law who is no longer my brother-in-law –
and here! – O Saviour of the World help me!
For I perish! – My child!
My child that is not mine,
was once, but is no longer!
Someone else's! And yet mine! – – –
And this was my café!
Our table! Very long ago –
all this stopped existing,
but yet remains – in the memory!
The fire that cannot be extinguished,
that burns but doesn't warm –
that burns but doesn't consume...

●

(The old JAPANESE man comes out from the tea shop. He looks like a dying man. The HUNTER goes to him and supports him.)

JAPANESE: A human being, at last! Where are you from? Where are you going?

WANDERER: From the great highway; how can I be of service?

JAPANESE: Help me to die.

WANDERER: There's time enough for that.

JAPANESE: Don't say so; I can't wait any longer; I have no one to turn to for the last services, for in this village of Thofeth there is no one...

HUNTER: What services do you mean?

JAPANESE: To hold my sword, while I...

HUNTER: I don't want to do that – why do you want to die?

JAPANESE: Because I can't live any longer.

HUNTER: Tell me the long story then; in a few short words.

JAPANESE: Yes! – Yes! –

I left my country – because I had made myself guilty of a bad deed – – – I came here determined to be a decent person by strict observance of the laws of honour and conscience – I sold decent goods at an honest price; but in this society people only want fake goods at a low price. So then I had to either find something, or go under. Instead of distilling perfumes from the essences of flowers, I gave them chemicals; and instead of the tea leaves, I gave them those of the sloe and the cherry-tree. My conscience said nothing to me at first – I had to live! – But one day, fifteen years ago I woke up: it seemed to me then as if everything I had experienced, and done was written in a book; and now the book was opened. Day and night, night and day, I read all the false entries in my account, all the irregularities; and I have struggled but in vain. Only death can release me, because most wickedness is in the flesh; the soul I have cleansed through suffering –

HUNTER: In what way can I help you?

JAPANESE: This: I take a sleeping draught, and will become like a dead man – you will have me put into a coffin which will be taken to the crematorium...

HUNTER: But what if you wake up – ?

JAPANESE: That is exactly what I'm counting on! In one moment I want to feel the cleansing atoning power of fire – suffer a short while – and to experience the blessedness of release –

HUNTER: And then?

JAPANESE: Then you will gather my ashes in my most precious vase...

HUNTER: And put your name on it... What are you called?

JAPANESE: Wait! – I have wandered, suffered and erred under the name Hiroshima[6], the name of the place of my birth! But in my country, when a person dies, he puts aside his old accused besmirched name, and receives a new one, which is called his eternal name. Only this name is set upon the gravestone, along with an apothegm, whilst an offering is made to the dead from a branch of the Sakaki tree.

HUNTER: Have you prepared all this?

JAPANESE: Yes I have! – Look, here!

HUNTER: What does this name mean?

JAPANESE: *Harahara to*; that is; 'rustling leaves, rustling silk' – but it also means 'falling tears'.

HUNTER: And this epitaph?

JAPANESE: *Churu hana wo –*
nanika uramin –
Yo no naka ni –
Waga ni tomo ni –
Aramu no kawa –

HUNTER: And that means?

JAPANESE: Distracted flowers – why am I enraged?

6 Not a translator's fantasy, Strindberg actually used this name in the original.

Even I myself – along with them –
Must perish by the will of the gods.

HUNTER: I shall carry out your last wish… But don't you
have any surviving relatives, next of kin?

JAPANESE: I had once! I had a daughter, who came here
three years ago when she thought I was dying. She came
to receive her inheritance. But when I didn't die she
became angry – couldn't hide her feelings – and went
away again. From then on she has been dead to me.

HUNTER: Where should this take place?

JAPANESE: Outside town – by the crematorium.

HUNTER: Should we go together or meet there?

JAPANESE: We can meet in the bower at the inn…in a
while. I shall just shave and have a bath…

HUNTER: Well then, we'll meet there!

JAPANESE: (*Goes into the shop, nods.*) Here comes the
murderer! – Watch out!

HUNTER: Is that him?

JAPANESE: Watch out! He's the most powerful man in this
town – (*Goes.*)

●

MÖLLER: (*The murderer comes in; still, self-important, with
hanging, somewhat awkward arms; he stares at the
HUTNER.*) It's not…?

HUNTER: No, it's not!

MÖLLER: I see, then it must be…

HUNTER: No; used to be… The one you mean, he's not
around any more…

MÖLLER: Then you're dead?

HUNTER: Yes! – Twelve years ago I committed hari-kari;
I executed my old self; and the one you see before you
now, you don't know, can never get to know!

MÖLLER: Yes, I remember, you were stupid enough to step
up to the pillory and publicly confess, on the blood-red
carpet, all your sins and weaknesses…

HUNTER: And the whole of society enjoyed it, they all felt
like better people, and felt themselves to be vindicated

by my civic death. They had neither sympathy nor a word of approval for me admitting my faults.

MÖLLER: Why should they have?

HUNTER: But when, after ten years of suffering, I had atoned and put everything to rights, it occurred to me that I ought to confess your sins too! Then it was quite another matter...

MÖLLER: Thank Christ for that!

HUNTER: You, for example, who have murdered...

MÖLLER: You say such things...when you don't have any proof...

HUNTER: I know you are the most powerful man in this community, that you tyrannise even the Duke himself, and that this is because of a gang of freemasons around here...

MÖLLER: What's that?

HUNTER: You know! – An alliance – not the holy alliance...

MÖLLER: And what about you then?

HUNTER: I have never belonged to it – but I recognise the signs...

MÖLLER: Look in the stationer's window there, you'll see who you are!

HUNTER: You mean that caricature? That's not me; it's you. That what you look like inside. It's your creation and welcome to it!

MÖLLER: You have a knack of shaking off your own vermin!

HUNTER: Do the same in the same way, but not onto me – Execute yourself, as I did, as I had to do, after you had made a scapegoat out of me, to bear the weight of your guilt!

MÖLLER: What do you want?

HUNTER: For instance there once was a little ape who wrote the following piece of nonsense; that if he stood alone on Gaurisanker[7], and the flood came and drowned humanity, then no harm would have occured so long as he survived. At the time of the next carnival the

7 A mountain-top in the Himalayas.

Gaurisanker was carried in procession, and on top of it
was I, not the little ape. What do you say to that? – And
on my birthday, he was celebrated, not I! When I
invented the new isolators, it was you who won the prize!
But when you had committed a murder, it was me they
accused! But all the same, when sugar prices rose on the
stock exchange, people blamed my isolators, even
though you had won the prize for inventing them. Can
you imagine anything so inverted, doubly inverted?
You'd have to stand on your head and turn everything
inside out.

MÖLLER: Have you any proof, since you dare to call me a
murderer?

HUNTER: Yes I have!

(*MOLLER is surprised.*)

But I don't dare to use it before a jury composed of your
friends, because you would deny the facts and have me
arrested. – Say now, who is the girl in there who
entrapped my friend?

MÖLLER: It was – your daughter!

HUNTER: (*Clutches at his chest, retches, and when he holds his
handerchief to his mouth it gets covered in blood.*) That child,
the one you brought up! – Now I shall go to the
crematorium. (*Out.*)

Scene 5 – In the park
beside the crematorium

*Outside a Columbarium; an avenue of cypresses stretches upstage. A
bench, a chair, a table.*

HUNTER: (*Comes in, alone.*) What do I see here? A collection
of urns;
but all alike?
A pharmacy, a museum? No!
A columbarium, a dove-cote;
but no doves, no olive leaves
only husks, the corn grows elsewhere;
in urns ashes, therefore all alike,

dust resembles dust –
these human fates –
now numbered and labelled –
'Here lies' – yes, I knew you,
but you never got to know yourself...
and you; you went around in disguise all your life,
your long burdensome life;
and when I took off your disguise, you died!
Idolater! That was your name,
your quality! We were forced to worship
your dismal life and your contemptible children,
but forced to for otherwise we'd be sacrificed
and every Saturday carved up with a blunt knife
and lynched in the Sunday papers –
robbed of bread and reputation!

MURDERER: (*Comes in, has been listening and still is.*)

HUNTER: Light of this nation Thofeth, you gathered the
nation around your funeral bier; though dead,
you still counted the wreaths,
and threatened revenge upon the missing names!

MURDERER: There's beauty at a graveside!

HUNTER: This is no grave, it's a jar with a bit of muck in
it! – No, a stone! He was slowly turned to stone...

MURDERER: You mean he died of calcification –

HUNTER: Turned to limestone, yes!

MURDERER: Tell me a little about yourself!

HUNTER: I did that thirteen years ago, until you were
tired of it. But here lie the ashes of a man I could have
spoken well of, except that he, because of that, was
murdered by you! Your victim never did wrong for the
sake of it, acted only in self-defence and when he didn't
want to be your accomplice, then he was killed, and
plundered.

MURDERER: You've been talking to that villanious
Japanese...

HUNTER: Do you intend clinging onto me now, like he
did, the great shining light?

MURDERER: Don't speak ill of the dead, say 'the poor man'.

HUNTER: That's what you always say about crooks who
get caught with their fingers in the till...but never about
your victims...get away from me now...quickly!

MURDERER: I'll go when I want to!

(*HUNTER picks up his bloody handkerchief and throws it.*)

I can't bear the sight of blood, it's a peculiarity of mine!

HUNTER: Since the fourth of April!

(*The MURDERER withdraws.*)

(*To the JAPANESE.*) Are you ready for the journey now?

JAPANESE: I am; but let us sit here
while the ovens are fired up!

HUNTER: With pleasure!

(*They sit down.*)

Well, tell me, now that life lays at your feet
like slaughtered game, hunted and conquered,
how does the journey seem to you?

JAPANESE: (*After a pause.*) A line with many loops in it,
like hand writing
as it appears on blotting paper – back to front –
first forwards, then backwards, upside down,
but you can read it in a mirror –

HUNTER: What was the hardest to endure?
of all the stones you hit your foot against?

JAPANESE: (*Thinks.*) I saved an enemy once –
and afterwards he hacked me down! –
You see, to be made to regret something good
you have done – that is sometimes the worst!

Another time I spoke up
for one oppressed! – He became my enemy –
he took everything from me
and I was left defenceless in an unequal combat;
for he had it down in writing from me
that he was a better man than I!

But all that is as nothing,
nothing counted against the fact of life –
the humiliation of wandering
a bare skeleton dressed in flesh,

and moved by sinews and strings,
a little motor in the machine room of the breast,
driven by the heat rising from the belly's coal-hole –
and the soul, the spirit, sits in the heart,
like a bird in the rib-cage,
a chicken coop or a net.

Little bird, soon I'll open the cage,
and you can fly – to your home,
the island of flowers and of the sun,
where once I was born,
but wasn't allowed to die!
Look here! My best vase, family heirlooms,
which shall now contain ashes from ashes –
whereas it once held flowers
set upon the table at parties,
where young eyes
and rosy cheeks were once reflected
in gold-rimmed wine glasses – – –
and a small hand dealt out food to the children
the best food of the table –

Then you became a flask for tears, dear vase!
For everything life granted us
is there for us to lament with tears.

I remember, it was around the New Year
when the children held their dolls' party –
in our house we keep all the dolls from generation to
                                        generation –
A child!
What is more perfect of its kind
than this little creature?
Neither man, nor woman,
but both of these and neither –
A person in miniature.

Tell me, wanderer, I forgot about you
for all my sorrows – say a word

about yourself! About your fate –
How do you see life, how did you see it?
What did you find to be the hardest, the bitterest?
HUNTER: More bitter than death – that was,
    to be constrained to take the great mockery seriously –
    to hold sacred what was so crude!

    If I smiled at the joke, I ended up in tears;
    and when in all the coarseness I became coarse myself,
    then I felt ashamed!

    And this!
    I was a preacher;
    I began speaking well of mankind,
    elicited all that was finest,
    had high hopes from life –
    what are known otherwise as ideals –
    the bright flags aloft –
    beckoning people to holidays and celebrations. –
    But now – how bitter – all my fine words
    and thoughts – I must take back!
    Beauty doesn't exist in life –
    it cannot be realised on earth –
    the ideal doesn't exist in practice!
JAPANESE: I know – but it is a memory,
    a hope, a beacon by which one sets one's sails –
    and so; they are praised high!
    Let the flags fly high
    All the better to be seen,
    and show the way – up to the sun!
HUNTER: The ovens are beginning to glow...
JAPANESE: And casting a red glow in the cypresses
    shining like a rosy dawn
    when the sun rises –
    Welcome, day! Farewell, night!
    With your heavy dreams!
    For the last time I shall get dressed
    and go to rest, fall asleep –

And when I awake – I shall be with my mother,
wife, children and friends!
Good night, poor creature. (*Goes.*)
(*The stage is lit and we can see up in the clouds the same
image as in the first act the land of wishes.*)

Scene 6 – At the final gate

*Upstage, two while gates which open onto a low-lying sandy beach
and the blue sea. To the left a red cottage, a hunter's house in a beech
wood; to the left a hornbeam hedge and an orchard. Outside the
house, to the left, a table set for namesday celebration. Above the
hedge we can see a shuttlecock flying up and down. A pram with a
blue hood pulled up is standing by the gate.*

HUNTER: (*Comes in, absorbed in thought.*)
Yes! – Alone! – It's the end,
when you want to hold on to your life
and not take it to market
to barter your way into a position –
not let yourself be stolen,
not let yourself be cowed...

When my thoughts cleared,
and I finally realised
that I was locked inside a madhouse,
a house of correction,
then I wished to lose my mind,
so that no-one would guess what I thought –
'*Telo, Telo, Mandriai*'
I want to be mad! I want to be!
And wine became my friend –
and I hid myself in a veil of intoxication,
in the cap and bells of drunkenness I was forgotten,
and no one guessed who I was –
Now it has changed its nature,
the drink of forgetfulness has become that of recollection –
and I remember everything, everything –
The seals are broken, the books are opened!

They read themselves out loud;
and when my ear tires, I see;
I see, see everything, everything, everything!
(*He comes to himself.*)
Where have I come to? The sea?
A beech wood, a hunter's cabin –
and there, a shuttlecock, rising and falling;
a little wicker pram, a new-born child,
the pram's hood like the blue cupola of the sky,
arching over the sleep of the innocent;
in the red house, behind green shutters,
a couple are hiding,
who have concealed their happiness!
For there is happiness, doubtless,
but it's brief like lightning,
like sunshine, like the convolvulus –
one flower and *one* day,
and then finished! – – –
The chimney smoke rises up from the kitchen,
with the well-stocked larder at the back,
a little cellar below,
a light filled veranda facing the woods –
I know how it should be –
how it once was!...
And here a table laid for a namesday
for the little one!
A little altar to childhood,
to hope, to the joy of innocence,
built on its own happiness,
and not at the expense of others –
and there is the beach
with white, clean, soft, warm sand –
with shells and shingles
and the blue water to paddle in
with bare feet...
I see its been decorated with leaves, and the paths have
been raked,
they're expecting guests – a children's party!
They've watered the flowers –

the flowers of my childhood.
The blue wolfsbane with two doves in it –
the imperial lily with its diadem,
the sceptre, the apple –
The passion flower of suffering
in white and amethyst, with the cross
and the lance, and the nails –
visited by busy bees, who from its cup
make honey
where we find only gall –
and there the most beautiful of trees
in the children's pleasure garden!
From the dark green leaves they are peeping
the pretty berries two-by-two –
the red and white cheeks of the heart cherry –
tiny children's faces – brother and sister!
playing, caressing each other in the wind...
Between branch and trunk, a songbird
has built its nest –
invisible singers, a song on the wing...
Hush! The gravel is crunching under a little foot,
here comes the little mistress!

●

CHILD: (*Comes in, takes the HUNTER by the hand and leads him to the pram.*) Walk quietly and I'll let you see the doll! – There's the doll! That's what we call her! – But you must walk on the path because its been raked – Ellen did it, because we're expecting visitors! – It's my namesday today –
Are you sad?
HUNTER: What's your name, my child?
CHILD: My name is Maria.
HUNTER: Who lives in this house?
CHILD: Mummy and Daddy.
HUNTER: May I see the namesday table?
CHILD: But we mustn't touch anything...
HUNTER: No, I shan't touch anything, dear child.
CHILD: Do you know what we're having for dinner today?

– We're having asparagus and strawberries! Why are you
sad? Have you lost your money? You can take one of the
crackers from the table but not the biggest one, because
Stella's going to have that one. Do you know, Stella got
crumbs in her bed last night, and she cried and then
there was a storm and we were afraid and Mama closed
the damper. Yes, she ate sandwiches in bed and the
sandwich broke because it was that brittle bread they buy
in the town – We're going to tell a story now, can you
tell stories? What's your name?

HUNTER: My name is... Karthafilos.

CHILD: No, you can't be called that...

HUNTER: Ahasverus then! Who wanders the earth...

CHILD: Let's talk about something else – do your eyes
hurt?

HUNTER: Yes, my child, they hurt ever so much –

CHILD: You shouldn't read by candlelight when you go to
bed! That gives you pains in your eyes.
(*A hunting horn is heard.*)
Here comes Daddy! (*Goes.*)

●

HUNTER: My child!
My child!
She didn't recognise me! What luck...what luck for us
both!

●

Farewell, lovely vision!
I don't want to stand in the way of the sun,
and cast a shadow on the little ones' flower beds –
I know the father here – and the mother too
you beautiful metaphor
lame maybe, but beautiful!
A memory perhaps; or more than that:
a hope a summer's day in the woods
by the sea – a namesday table, a cradle!
A sunbeam from a child's eyes,

a gift from a tiny hand –
and so onwards again, and out – into the darkness!

Scene 7 – The dark woods

In a dark wood.

HUNTER: Alone! – I've lost my way – In the dark.
'And Elijah sat beneath the juniper tree and he wished to
die, and he said: "It is enough! Take my life, Lord."'

VOICE: (*In the dark.*) He who wants to lose his life, shall
keep it.

HUNTER: Who is that speaking in the dark?

VOICE: Is it dark?

HUNTER: Is it dark?

●

WOMAN: (*Comes in.*) I ask, became I cannot see – I'm
blind!

HUNTER: Have you always been blind?

WOMAN: No. When the tears ran out, my eyes stopped
seeing!

HUNTER: It's good to be able to cry!

WOMAN: But I can hear instead, and I know your voice!...
I know who you are!
I believe in you, I do!

HUNTER: You oughtn't to believe in me, nor in any
human being; you should believe in God.

WOMAN: I do!

HUNTER: But only in God. The sons and daughters of
men are not to be believed in...

WOMAN: You were a barrister once?

HUNTER: I was the advocate of the One Truth against the
idolaters – you always wanted to idolise, yourselves,
your families, your friends – but you never wanted to
grant simple justice –

WOMAN: You sometimes abandoned your cause!

HUNTER: When I had been tricked into sympathy with the

unjust, under the false impression that he was a poor ill-
used wretch, then yes I abandoned the unjust cause.

WOMAN: You were an evangelist once too, but you tired
of it!

HUNTER: I didn't tire of it; but I found that I couldn't live
the life I preached, so I stopped preaching to avoid being
called a hypocrite! – And when I discovered that there
was no practical appreciation of the beautiful teachings,
then I banished their realisation to the land of wish
fulfilment!

WOMAN: And now you are dead?

HUNTER: Yes, civically, but not spiritually! I struggle,
therefore I am alive! I don't exist; my deeds alone live
on! Good and evil! The evil I have done I have
admitted, and suffered for, tried to make good by doing
good!

WOMAN: Do you still want to take up man's cause?

HUNTER: When they are in the right, not otherwise! – – –
I happened once to press a man's claim, confused in my
mind by the gratitude I owed him; but by this I ended
up doing grave wrong to an innocent man. – That's how
it is with our best feelings – They mislead us into bad
actions!

WOMAN: You accuse...prosecutor!

HUNTER: Who am I accusing?

WOMAN: The management!

HUNTER: Get behind me, Satan! Before you tempt me into
blasphemy!

WOMAN: Satan?

HUNTER: Yes, Satan!

WOMAN: No one was as black as you.

HUNTER: Because you blackened me, so that I would be
like you. – But explain this; when I confessed *my* sins,
you felt as if you were guiltless, and thanked God that
you weren't like me, even though you were at least as
shabby as I was.
I saw once an execution as a child – the crowd were a
sanctimonious mob; and on their way home they were
lamenting, and then went into the taverns and spoke ill

of the dead, by which means they managed to feel like better people... But then, some of them returned to the gallows hill, and took some of the dead man's blood – as a cure for epilepsy; they dipped their handkerchiefs in his blood – look at this one! – True, you are blind! – Hold it, your hands are your eyes. (*Hands her his bloody handkerchief.*)

WOMAN: It feels like red – but it's sticky – and it smells like – like the butcher's shop. – No, I know now. – A relative of mine died recently, he coughed up – first his lungs, then finally his heart itself.

HUNTER: He coughed up his heart?

WOMAN: Yes!

HUNTER: (*Looks at the handkerchief.*) I believe it!
  The goat, as we know, is not a clean animal, but on the Day of Atonement he had to carry all the sins of the world; and, thus equipped, he was driven out into the desert to be consumed by wild animals! That's the scapegoat!

WOMAN: Do you mean that you suffered for the wrongs of others?

HUNTER: For my own *and* those of others; that is for others as well!

WOMAN: Weren't you something else before you became a lawyer?

HUNTER: Yes, I was an architect! I built many houses, not all of them were any good, but when I built well they were angry with me because it was good! So they gave the work to others, who did worse than I! That was in the town of Thofeth, where I built the theatre.

WOMAN: People say it's beautiful!

HUNTER: Keep that is mind then, when I have ceased to be – and forget me!

WOMAN: 'I don't exist, the good I have done exists.' Why did you never have compassion for your fellow human beings?

HUNTER: The question is unjustly framed! Did you ever see anyone have compassion for me? No! – How could I then return feelings that were never granted to me? –

And besides, who was it who first said: 'Pity poor mankind.'[8]

(*The WOMAN disappears.*)

●

HUNTER: She's gone. That always happens when you try to defend yourself.

●

TEMPTER: (*Enters.*) We meet at last! Now, we can talk, but it's a bit dark here, so let's have a bit of light. There, lovely! – (*It gets lighter.*) – now we can see each other – it's so important to be able to see one another when you want to talk sensibly. A message from the Grand Duke, he sets a price upon your talents – and offers you a position as architect to the ducal court, with a pension of such and such an amount, living quarters, fuel, up-keep et cetera, you understand!

HUNTER: I don't want a position –

TEMPTER: Wait a bit, on condition that you, well – in a word that you conduct yourself like a human being, a normal human being.

HUNTER: Let's hear it; I should like to know how a normal human being conducts himself.

TEMPTER: Don't you know? – Why do you look so crazed?

HUNTER: That look I shall answer with two words; I look crazed, because I have gone crazy. That is, I have been the kind of person who believed what people say, straight away; therefore I have always been deceived. Everything I have believed has been lies; therefore my whole being has been falsified; I have drifted about with false opinions about people and about life, counted with false terms, circulated false coin without realising it; and so I am not what I am. I can't be amongst other people, cannot speak, cannot cite the words of another, cannot appeal to testimony for fear it should be false! In several instances I have been an accomplice in the anchor chain

8 A quote from *A Dream Play.*

we call society, but when I became the same as all the
others, then I went out and became a highwayman, a
man of the woods.

TEMPTER: That's all just talk – now, let's get back to the
Grand Duke who requires your services.

HUNTER: He doesn't require my services, he requires my
soul...

TEMPTER: He requires that you should take an interest in
his great enterprise...

HUNTER: I cannot... Go away now, I haven't long left to
live and I want to be alone to settle my accounts...

TEMPTER: Ha ha! The day of reckoning is here,
then I shall present my invoices –
bills and suits –

HUNTER: Yes come on! Bring on your despair,
Tempter; you want to fool me
into a cowardly denial of the good God!

From the pure air of the Alps, I stepped down here
to wander yet a while amongst the children of men –
to take part in their small concerns;
but it was no open road,
just a track through the undergrowth –
I was caught in the bushes –
shreds of my clothes caught in the thorns;
people gave so they could take back with interest,
offered gifts that could be later called debts –
men served so that they could later rule,
set you free so to later bind –
I lost my companion along the way –
one trap followed another –
and I was pulled into a millwheel –
and came out the other side –
Saw a ray of light from a child's eyes
which led me – out here in the darkness.
Now you come along with the bills –
what? Now he's disappeared too!

So I am alone!
In the night and the darkness!
Where the trees sleep and the grass weeps

from the cold, with the going-down of the sun,
but the animals keep watch, though not all,
the bat is spinning his intrigues,
and the snake slithers beneath the poisonous mushrooms –
and the light-shy badger stirs abroad
after sleeping all the day –
Alone! – Why? – – –
A traveller in another land
is always a stranger, alone.
He trudges through villages and towns,
stops, pays his bill, passes on –
until the journey reaches its end – and he is home!
But it's not finished...
I can still hear...a dried branch
snapping – a heel-iron on a rock's ledge –
it's that fearsome blacksmith,
the idolater with his flint knife –
he's looking for me –
and the miller with his mill wheel
that pulls you in –
where I nearly got stuck –
the people in the arcade, the arcade,
a net that's easy to fall into
and difficult to get out of. –
And the murderer, Möller –
with his bills and suits –
his alibis and libels –
the man without honour!
What do I hear now? – Music!
I recognise your tones, and your little hand!
I don't long to meet –
for the fire that warms at a comfortable distance,
burns when you come too close! –
and now; a child's voice in the dark!
You dear child, my last bright memory,
following me in the forest of the night!
On the final journey to the distant land –
the land of fulfilled wishes,
a mirage looming up over the Alpine tops

invisible from the valleys – obscured
by dust from the highway, and smoke from the chimneys!
Where have you gone to, o fair vision,
land of longing, land of dreams?

If only a vision I want to see you again
from a snow-white summit, in crystal clear air –
from the hermit's cave; where I shall remain,
waiting to be released!
He'll find me a hollow there I'm sure,
under the cold white blanket:
and write in the snow a fleeting epitaph:
Here lies Ismael[9], Hagar's son,
once called Israel,
because he fought with God
and never gave up the struggle until conquered,
by the Almighty's goodness.
O eternal one! I won't let go your hand,
your hard hand, until you have blessed me!

Bless me, your humanity,
that suffers, suffers from your gift of life!
Me first of all, who has suffered most the pain
of never being who I hoped to be!

The End.

9 The son of a servant woman, as Strindberg describes himself in his
autobiography's title.

Strindberg: The Plays

Translated by Gregory Motton

Volume One

The Father
Miss Julie
The Comrades
Creditors

ISBN: 1 84002 062 8

Volume Three

The Dream Play
The Dance of Death I &II
Easter
Advent
Crimes and Crimes
Swan White

ISBN: 1 84002 089 X

Volume Four

The Bond
Before Death
The First Warning
Mother Love
Playing with Fire
To Damascus

ISBN: 1 84002 090 3